The Occupy
Movement Explained

IDEAS EXPLAINED™

The Occupy Movement Explained

From Corporate Control to Democracy

NICHOLAS SMALIGO

OPEN COURT
Chicago

Volume 13 in the Ideas Explained™ Series

To order books from Open Court, call toll-free 1-800-815-2280, or visit our website at www.opencourtbooks.com.

Open Court Publishing Company is a division of Carus Publishing Company, dba Cricket Media.

First printing 2014

Printed and bound in the United States of America.

ISBN: 978-0-8126-9855-8

Library of Congress Control Number: 2014942377

Contents

Preface

In the Fall of 2011, Occupy Wall Street and the wider Occupy movement burst unexpectedly into the awareness of people around the world. In the United States, the movement forced into public attention the related issues of widening economic inequality, the suppression of First Amendment rights, and political corruption of a government run by and for corporate power. Today the Occupy movement is often praised for having "changed the conversation" about inequality in the United States. Inequality and its social and political effects are now common knowledge, regularly discussed in the mainstream media, and we have the Occupy movement to thank for having put the glaring issue on the table. But the legacy of Occupy is too often reduced to this single contribution. Even if we count this as the sole "success" of the Occupy movement (as many do), by reducing the movement to having simply changed the conversation, we miss out on *how* Occupy succeeded in doing so.

If Occupiers changed the way people in the United States see their society and government, they accomplished this in a way that broke with standard conceptions of how to influence public discussion. They did not simply come up with a catchy slogan about the ninety-nine percent, they did not *simply* take to the streets, and they certainly did not operate through any official political channels. Occupy succeeded in changing the mainstream conversation by creating spaces in which participants could practice anti-authoritarian politics and non-capitalist forms of labor and mutual aid. It was this feature of the Occupy movement—a feature that was never really understood by the mainstream media—that created an eruption of popular energy that managed to shift the mainstream dialogue. Before Occupy could "change the conversation," it first succeeded in transforming the lives of its participants.

It's on this aspect of the Occupy movement, more than any other, that this book focuses. The Occupy movement succeeded in transforming the lives and perspectives of so many people by bringing them into contact with a radical tradition of anti-capitalist and anti-authoritarian practice, which has been nurtured beneath the surface in recent decades, during which public life and discussion has been almost entirely swallowed by economic values.

For those whose lives were transformed through participation in Occupy, the movement succeeded in changing the way we think about and imagine political and social life. More than merely shifting the discourse or adding a few new terms like "the ninety-nine percent" and "inequality" to the contemporary political lexicon, Occupy introduced what was for many a new *ideal* of politics—a guiding vision that can inspire hope. The ideal introduced by Occupy not only points us in a direction for personal and collective action, but can also give us the courage to criticize the existing society. Without hope, criticism just feels like kicking someone while they are down. It's only when we have a sense that a better world can be built that criticism becomes not only sensible, but our responsibility. Participants in Occupy are the inheritors of a world of technological wizardry where everything seems possible *except* political hope. Through Occupy, participants learned that through collective action, we can not only break the rules, but develop a different set of rules altogether.

The ideal that Occupy rekindled is hardly new. It's one that erupts from time to time, and is buried beneath the surface at others. It is a dangerous ideal, one which threatens not only some one group of individuals who hold enormous power over others, but the very foundations on which such power rests. Long ago, this ideal was called "democracy"—the rule of the common people. More recently, since the word "democracy" has come to mean "rule by (wealthy) representative, vetted by corporate power," this ideal has been called "direct democracy" or, at times and in some variations, "participatory democracy." In some circles, the same ideal has been called "anarchy" by both its friends and its foes. The meanings of each of these terms overlap at some points and diverge at others but the point is not the label. The point is that Occupy delivered a glimpse of a different world: a world of free people, working together in voluntary, mutual co-operation for the common good. It was only a glimpse, but it was enough to shift the terrain of what many of us thought possible. It was not perfect, but it was enough to convince us that there is much more to be gained by walking and growing in the direction it opened up than by turning back to the dead values that currently serve as norms for mainstream life in the United States: the endless growth of the economy for its own sake; the apathy-inducing, conversation-narrowing, cynical maneuvering of party politics; the hostility of interpersonal competition fostered by a society in which the highest aspiration on offer is career success; and, perhaps summing it all up, a world in which the destruction of the ecosystems on which life depends appears as the inevitable cost of "progress"—a term which has lost all moral significance. Occupy asserted a space in which these fundamental problems of our social life—and others—could be honestly examined, because it refuted their inevitability.

But it is an ideal that's dangerous for those with power, and the people with a vested interest in the current economic and governmental systems fought back against its proponents. They fought back with evictions that exposed a militarized police force and an integrated national surveillance apparatus, mobilizing the anti-terrorism "Fusion Centers" constructed in the wake of 9/11. This massive network of policing, whose overreaching power was justified by the fear of mass murder of innocents, was mobilized for the purpose of spying on and suppressing the terrifying crime wave of people camping together in parks. Of all the documents that have been released so far about government and corporate surveillance of the Occupy movement—and we should assume those that have been released are only the tip of the iceberg—one stands out as particularly frightening. In 2012, a Freedom of Information Act Request by the Partnership for Civil Justice Fund revealed that the FBI knew about—and perhaps was even involved in planning—an assassination attempt on organizers involved with Occupy Houston. In a heavily redacted document, the FBI makes reference to planned "sniper attacks" against Occupiers:

> The identified [redacted] as of October planned to engage in sniper attacks against protestors [sic] in Houston, Texas, if deemed necessary. . . . [Redacted] planned to gather intelligence against the leaders of the protest groups and obtain photographs, then formulate a plan to kill the leadership through suppressed sniper rifles. (Barna 2014)

The phrase "if deemed necessary" is particularly discomforting, suggesting that this was not an FBI investigation of some lone individual planning an attack, but rather a report on someone who was taking orders from above, a bureaucrat with a sniper rifle. As of June 2014, the FBI was under a court order to explain why it continued to withhold more information on this matter. Whether the plot was the construction of the FBI itself or some other group, the fact that they failed to warn the activists who were its potential targets speaks volumes about the FBI's concerns for the lives of demonstrators. There's no question that if the FBI had evidence that anyone "planned to engage in sniper attacks" against a banker, CEO, or politician, this information would lead to some warning for the target. In this case of Occupy Houston, no such warning came.

Occupy touched a nerve within the dominant power structures. In hundreds of locations across the country, it fostered spaces in which people were gaining hope in a better world and the courage to refuse the rules of this one. The energy generated in such spaces was contagious, and emanated outward, inspiring new movements of protest and resistance and breathing new life into existing activist networks. After two months of public encampments, the state decided the party was over, and cracked down hard, often at night and under the cloak of a media blackout. But images escaped, and the state gave us all a glimpse of the other world that it has been building: a police state, ready to reveal itself "if deemed necessary."

In discussing the Occupy movement with many people for whom it is already a distant memory, we sometimes hear that it simply "fizzled out." In light of the police repression that those of us who participated in it encountered, many images of which were broadcast on national television, it is both curious and, frankly, infuriating, to hear people refer to it as having "fizzled," as if we had all just naturally run out of steam. Certainly, there was burnout. Certainly there were interpersonal and organizational challenges, fractures, and brick walls. Certainly, there were internal critiques and breakaway groups and high emotions. Certainly there were also police infiltrators, stoking the flames of division. But none of these things explains the disappearance of Occupy from public spaces in the United States like the criminalization of public protest which occurred in the late Fall of 2011 through the spring of 2012. There were plans for reoccupations around the country, and those plans were crushed by the police—which is to say, by batons on heads. Occupy had opened up a space for the injection of a radical politics into the mainstream of US political awareness, and those in power, at local and federal levels, decided that such a space should not exist.

What is perhaps even more disconcerting than the idea that Occupy "fizzled" is the peculiar way that I observed many who participated in Occupy respond to the evictions and successful efforts on the part of police around the country to prevent re-occupations in the spring of 2012. Within a few months, I noticed that many of the people who I had worked alongside at Occupy sites seemed embarrassed to bring the whole experience up. It was as if we had met in a dream, and now were unsure whether we had really seen each other. In a journal entry from mid-2012, I wrote, "How can you tell the difference between a moment of hope and a collective delusion?" During Occupy, we experienced something that felt more real than the everyday world, a space in which we were fully ourselves, our actions and our thoughts and our criticisms mattered because we were numerous and we were bold. After, a sense of shame set in. We were embarrassed for having hoped. It occurred to me that perhaps this was the more insidious and ultimately, more effective way that social control is maintained today: those in power convince us we are crazy for imagining things can be different.

Ultimately, the shame at having hoped is a sham. It's the way we finish off, in our hearts, the work the police started with their tear gas. Occupy, far from being a collective delusion, was a collective burst of sanity in an insane world. This book is an attempt to provide a snapshot of that moment. Though it probably doesn't read like one, it is, more than anything, a love letter. Because even though it can seem like delusion afterward, it is when we're in love that we are closest to the really existing richness of the world. I try to capture and, in some way, understand, a moment that changed me and others. I grasp that it is not the whole of the movement—that much is left out, underanalyzed, not followed through with. But I hope that it succeeds in communicating for those who were not there something of what was so powerful about the practice of the occupation of public parks in the fall of 2011, and provides a resource for understanding both why this was going on and why it mattered. Also, I hope it serves as some preparation for understanding the next eruption of radical practices in the United States—whenever and wherever that may occur.

I was an active participant in both Occupy St. Louis and Occupy Carbondale—two blips on the Occupy map that hardly had impacts outside of their local areas. The intensity of my own experience with the Occupy movement, far outside of its center of gravity in New York City, speaks for how influential it was. There are a number of excellent books that have come out detailing the experiences and lessons of those closer to the epicenter of the movement, including David Graeber's *The Democracy Project: A History, A Crisis, A Movement*; Nathan Schneider's *Thank You, Anarchy: Notes from the Occupy Apocalypse*; Mark Bray's *Translating Anarchy: The Anarchism of Occupy Wall Street*; and others. There are also a number of edited volumes that compile the reflections of many different participants, including *We Are Many: Reflections on Movement Strategy from Occupation to Liberation*, edited by Kate Khatib, Margaret Killjoy, and Mike McGuire and *Dreaming in Public: Building the Occupy Movement*, edited by Amy Shrager Land and Daniel Land/Levitsky. I have made use of all of these works and more.

The Occupy Movement Explained is an effort to communicate some core features of the experience that many Occupy participants gained and introduce the reader to some of the debates and questions raised by the movement. I offer it in a spirit of hope, based on the conviction that whatever next Big Event occurs in the ongoing struggle to challenge both capitalism and the power of corporations hold over contemporary life, the Occupy movement will be a constant reference point. The more people understand the practices it employed, the histories it drew on, and the challenges it faced, the better chance we'll all have at getting free—together.

A Note on the Title

As a participant in the Occupy movement, I would probably myself have been somewhat disconcerted if I had encountered a two-hundred page book claiming to "explain" this complex movement. This book is the thirteenth volume in Open Court's *Ideas Explained* series, which provides accessible introductions to complex ideas and, more recently, social movements. The opportunity for me to write the book was conditional on accepting this series-related title. The idea that the Occupy movement could be "explained"—let alone by *me*—may strike some people as having a ring of presumption that conflicts with the very spirit of the movement, but that is far removed from my intention in writing the book. Occupy Wall Street's *Statement of Autonomy* implores others: SPEAK WITH US, NOT FOR US. This book is intended as an act of *speaking with*, and not *speaking for*. There is nothing "definitive" or "official" about the account I present here. I have done my best to contribute to a task which I believe urgently needs to be done: to clear away misconceptions about the movement and convey an accurate sense of what it is and what it means.

"Explaining" has a deservedly bad rap in activist circles, because it usually (not always) involves one person arrogating to themselves the responsibility of speaking on behalf of those who speak or think differently. This process always involves interpretation, and something is usually left out, changed, or explained away. Explaining what others are saying, especially with their actions, tends to blunt the edge, change the content, subtract the energy of the expression, all in the name of translating it into "respectable" terms. Further, the explainer usually has interests and a position of his own—and it is usually a 'he'. In Occupy camps, there was a tendency toward "man-'splaining," in which usually educated, white, men attempted to "explain-it-all" to those whose discontent they perceive to be less sophisticated. Inevitably, I may have fallen into this trap in these pages.

Nevertheless, some will be attracted to the straightforward title. If you are, this book is written primarily for you, with the hope that the title will be read as *an* explanation, as one voice among many. Certainly, given the opportunity, others would emphasize different parts of the movement. My choices as to what to emphasize are based on the many conversations I've had with people who were curious or intrigued about Occupy, but were confused by the images they saw in the mainstream media. The book is an attempt to give those who missed the exuberant moment of Occupy some understanding of what went on, and what might go on in the future.

Readers will note that I focus on the United States and do not explore the fact that Occupy was, in fact, a global movement. There are two main reasons for this: first, the limits to my own knowledge and time, and, second, my perception that radical politics are uniquely absent on the US scene compared with other countries where Occupy encampments were set up. Despite the rich living tradition beneath the surface, in the mainstream US discourse, anti-capitalist and anti-authoritarian movements are completely off the radar and the memory of past radical struggles is all but crushed. People in the US were therefore uniquely unprepared to make sense out of a movement inspired by anarchist practices, offering a radical critique of both the economy and the power of corporations over politics.

The Occupy Movement Explained, then, is not a full history of the movement, nor an exhaustive account of the major actions or their consequences. It is an introduction to a moment, an attempt to walk the reader through some of the experiences that participants in Occupy went through, and an attempt to think about some of the broader questions about our shared political and economic life that the movement raised.

Acknowledgments

My first thanks go to Leslie Brown, the best boss anyone could ask for during a moment of social eruption. Without Leslie, this book would not have been possible. Thanks to my helpful and patient editor, David Ramsay Steele, who convinced me at a few critical points that the project was worth completing. I think he was right. Thanks to all the St. Louis Rebels from 2011. Thanks to Sarah Toten and Kiddo; Joe Hassert, Kyle Cheesewright, Matthew Williams, Katy Wyant, Nora Klein, Nichole Nicholson, Kara Nichols, Adam Turl, Treesong, Maggie, David Hanley-Tajeda and all the participants in Occupy Carbondale; Marisa Holmes for reading and providing feedback on Chapter 1. Thanks to participants in two group interviews at 16 Beaver St., including Rebecca Manski, Matt Tinker, Nathan Schneider, Drew Hornbein, Manissa McCleave Marawahal, Charles Lenchner, Claiborne McDonald, Ilona Bito, Scott Berzofsky, Roland, and Charlie. Thanks to Rachel Schragis and Thiago de Mello Bueno. Thanks to Sarah Ross, Ben Almassi, and Claire Pentacost with the Prison + Neighborhood Arts Project, and to the students at Stateville Correctional Facility. Special thanks to Cody, Kim, and Bo; April Rohman, Pip Freeman; Soraya King; and Koz Collective for making my stay in NYC possible and excellent. Thanks to participants in a public reading at Gaia House, including Honna Veerkamp and Wago Kreider. The following friends, comrades, teachers, and groups have helped me to produce what is good in this book: Sarah Lewison, Clare O'Connor, Ken Stikkers, Sara Beardsworth, Steven Miller, Elissa Johnson, Randall Auxier, Compass Collective in the Midwest Radical Culture Corridor, A.K. Thompson, Crispin Sartwell, Amy Partridge, Matthias Regan, Brian Holmes, Robbie Lieberman, Phillip Brewer, Sarah Baumgarten, James Anderson, Steve Onderick, Maggie Miller, Nathan Staley, and many others. Finally, my deepest thanks go to my brother, my father, my mother and my sister. This book is dedicated, with love, to Linda and Paige.

1

Wake-Up Call

Bowling Green Plaza is a small, oblong park in lower Manhattan, the northern edge of which is home to the famous *Charging Bull* statue. The statue is a celebration of the—supposedly—primal "animal spirits" of aggression that are—supposedly—channeled through the stock-market, thus—supposedly—resulting in their use for the public good. It is September 17th 2011 and today there are around two thousand people gathered in Bowling Green who beg to differ on each of these suppositions and a good many more. After three years of the Great Recession and its "jobless recovery," after millions of people were kicked out of their homes so the banks could stay profitable, after ten years of wars that Wall Street continues to benefit from, these protestors have an increasingly long list of evidence suggesting a conflict of interest between "the market" and the public good.

To anyone who has been to a protest on the Left, it is familiar. A couple of hundred people gather with signs and chants. The police decide this gathering should stay away from the *Bull*. They push the crowd to the southern end of the park, a cobblestone plaza below the steps of the Roman-pillared Alexander Hamilton US Custom House, now the home of a Bankruptcy Court and the Museum of the American Indian. This building stands on the site of the earliest Dutch colony on *Mannahata*, the "island of many hills" in the language of the Lenape people. The wall from which Wall Street gets its name was built to keep the Lenape out after the Dutch massacred over a hundred of them for refusing to pay tribute to the Dutch West India Company.[1]

---

[1] Kraft 1986, pp. 223–24.

This history is alive in the minds of some present there today, but hidden from most. At the moment, there are organizers trying to figure out what the group's next move should be, there are people chanting in hopes that their enthusiasm will be contagious, there is some disappointment at the relatively small turnout, no doubt giving rise to a few cynical comments here or there. And amidst the hubbub and uncertainty, a blond-pompadoured man in a white suit with a priest's collar calling himself Reverend Billy ascends the steps of the museum, holding a large plastic cone to amplify his voice. "They must be wondering,"[2] he shouts,

> *When will the progressive American conscience wake up?!*
> The sleeping giant of progressive Americans is up on one elbow now, a little bit hungover from decades of consumerism and militarism, but . . . when we wake up, we're sixty times the size, a hundred times the energy of the Tea Party!
> They hope that they can keep us in their demonstration pens. They hope that we won't notice that they're taking away our right to peaceably gather, our rights of speech and press, our right to be here; they'll shut down public space as much as they can.
> But they don't know, they don't know, what shape our Tahrir Square will take! They don't know what shape our Madison Rotunda will take. They don't know what shape our Puerta del Sol will take. Even the stock-traders, even the police themselves, they know the rich are taking everything that isn't nailed down!

Reverend Billy and his Stop-Shopping Choir have been a staple at protests and progressive rallies for almost two decades. Clearly a satire of televangelists, Reverend Billy can at times move beyond irony and tap into the honest tradition of liberation preaching. This tradition gives voice to suffering borne from injustice and stirs courage in people to challenge the authority of Pharaohs, past and present. In denouncing the power of Wall Street today, Reverend Billy denounces the power of men in suits who sit in front of screens and steer massive flows of capital from one set of hard-drives into another; he denounces their indifference to the lives

---

[2] Reverend Billy's speech from the steps of the Museum of the American Indian: <www.youtube.com/watch?v=AP_nDOBSiIg>. The transcript is my own. I encourage readers to simply read my transcript out loud in their best televangelist voice.

destabilized and threatened in the wake of their unrelenting trades; he denounces the power of their money over a political process that has become dominated by a form of legalized bribery called "lobbying."

The crowd marches on the sidewalk in a slow procession up Broadway, two-by-two to avoid the charge of obstructing pedestrian traffic, and soon spills into Zuccotti Park, a granite city-block nestled between skyscrapers. At this point, most people seem to expect a march on Wall Street, a series of chants and fliers and perhaps even some confrontations with the police. The police themselves likely expect a similar set of skirmishes. They have already blocked off 1 Chase Plaza, headquarters of J.P. Morgan Chase and the initial location the protestors had planned to assemble.

What's so peculiar about Occupy Wall Street, what has made it both a unique and uniquely misunderstood event, is that those involved declined to follow the expected formula. Instead, members of a group called the New York City General Assembly invited the massive crowd to form discussion circles and ask one another why they had come down to Wall Street that day and what they wanted out of this gathering. "Many had shown up to what they thought was a protest, but what they got was a giant meeting."[3]

This was an unexpected shift, one that flew in the face of the recent history of protests in the United States. But whatever activists had been doing, it wasn't working. And the time was ripe for something a bit different.

From Bush to Obama

In the winter of 2003, I participated in a collective experiment with about thirty-six million people around the world. We were in some of the darkest political hours we could imagine at the time: a traumatized population, still reeling from the psychic devastation of a terrorist attack, was being manipulated to support the invasion of a country that had nothing to do with the terrifying event. The media and the political establishment was in lockstep support for an invasion based on lies and constantly repeated propaganda. It was in this context, with the aim of averting an unnecessary and unjustified war, that over the course of the winter of 2003, around

---

[3] Schneider 2012, p. 25.

thirty-six million people the world over took to the streets in the largest protests ever to avert a war that had not yet begun.[4] For myself and those I went with, it ended up being a kind of experiment testing the effectiveness of protest in our time. And for many it yielded a very clear lesson: not effective.

On the weekend of Martin Luther King Jr.'s birthday, a carful of friends and I travelled to Washington DC from our college campus in Connecticut. I had been to a few large protests before, but this was the first one I felt really passionate about. We were suspicious about whether marching in the streets would have any effect at all on the course of events we saw unfolding on television—public opinion polls showed overwhelming support for an invasion and almost no articulate dissent was happening on the screens. Still, we figured that if anything could make a difference, it would be people flooding the streets in protest.

And there were a lot of people there. Estimates after the fact put the number of protestors in DC at "several hundred thousand."[5] My friends and I walked the streets amidst the crowd, steered this way and that by its flow. I'm not sure what I was expecting from the protest itself. Did I expect it to be exhilarating? Liberating? Thinking back, I saw the protest as a means to an end. I was operating with the not-quite-articulated assumption that if we go into the streets, then those in power will "hear our voices" and perhaps reconsider their course. From this perspective, the protest was simply a tool, one which employed all of our bodies in a way that was supposed to somehow alter the decisions of those in power.

And from where I stood, it seemed like those in charge of the day's events viewed the protest that way as well. Thousands of us were herded into a park to listen to one speaker after another talk about the crimes and lies of the Bush administration. We assented in various ways: nodding, cheering, chanting. As the speeches went on, my friends and I grew increasingly bored. The cold grew less tolerable. As the later speakers began focusing not on the impending war, but on things like reparations for slavery, I lost interest entirely. I'm ashamed to say that, at the time, the connection between slavery and the war I was opposing seemed only tenuous.

---

[4] This number comes from the French political scientist Dominique Reynié.
[5] Ruane 2007.

I had not yet learned how to see these events as so many poor people and people of color around the world do, as two processes in the long European and American tradition of seizing control over the land, resources, and labor of those with less power, while justifying the process through sometimes overt, sometimes concealed, racism and religious bigotry. My privileged upbringing had allowed me to remain astonishingly ignorant of how persistent this pattern is in American history, and the past seemed like the past.[6] Still, this protest was not the place where I was likely to really understand those connections. They were being preached as if they were obvious truths. For many, they *were* obvious truths. But, at the time, not for me.

Standing amidst the crowd and in the shadow of signs denouncing the invasion, I remember feeling both disengaged and even a little creeped-out. In hindsight, what stands out so clearly for me about the Iraq War protest is that as a "participant," absolutely nothing of consequence was asked of me. I was expected to simply stand there, to repeat chants, maybe to hold a sign. Since the protest was all about "sending a message to those in power," the only role for any of us in the crowd to play was to be a body grouped into a mass. One more head in the head-count in a protest that would be ignored by the mainstream media anyway.

At the end of the day my friends and I felt dispirited and cold. In spite of that, we also felt like we could pat ourselves on the back: we "took to the streets," didn't we? We did what citizens are supposed to do when they feel like their concerns are being ignored, right? Still, it felt pointless, even absurd. A whole bunch of people who more or less agree with one another getting together on a street and shouting, in the hopes that the people we all believed to be either stupid, crazy, evil, or some combination of the three, would suddenly have a change of heart. It was as if we all knew in our guts it was futile, but had to give it a shot anyway. The results of our experiment: the protest was widely ignored in the media, the drumbeat to war only picked up steam, and on March 19th the United States began its "Shock and Awe" campaign on the people of Baghdad, without a shred of evidence that a single person subjected to this barrage of weapons had anything to do with the September 11th attacks.

---

[6] For the relation between colonialism and racism, see Mills 1999. For one excellent illustration of how "the past is not the past," see Alexander 2012.

Political hope, the sense that we can together create a better world, was in short supply until Barack Obama stepped onto the world stage. Though I'm often embarrassed to admit it now, I was an enthusiastic supporter of Obama's ascent to the Presidency in 2008. I was among those who claimed the symbolic power of an African-American man in such a position was something worth supporting. But apart from that, Obama both effectively wielded the rhetoric of social movements and, importantly, *asked us for something more than just money.* The enthusiasm Obama sparked has to be seen in light of the wider context of the cynicism and dis-empowerment of the Bush administration. This cynicism, however, was not yet complete: it had not fully given up on the current political and economic structures.

The excitement of Obama's campaign came from the sense that there was a kind of grassroots political action that could engage with existing political institutions in some way other than yelling or chanting or marching in the street. Obama and his hope-centered campaign was widely effective in rekindling the political energies that had been smoldered, suppressed, and diverted in the first decade of the twenty-first century through experiences like my own. These political energies that Obama tapped into sought action on the grand issues that we all were concerned about but didn't have political space to move on. The idea that Obama would push aggressive action on climate change and the various fronts of ecological devastation that we face was a central motivating factor for me, because these dangers seem to require a complete revision of how we think about labor and economics. They imply a vision of social progress that is not captured by the words "jobs" or "growth" or "development"— indeed, these words are seen as invitations to continue on the same path of a "progress" that is destroying the ecologies on which we all depend.

Obama's rise was not about the actual policy proposals he put forward, but rather by the sense of collective power his campaign unleashed. He was carried into the Presidency on a wave of political energy that was "utopian"—by which I mean it pointed to a world that does not yet exist, to a need for structural change in the institutions and practices of our everyday lives. In other words: no matter how he acted when he was in office, Obama was going to be a disappointment.

But few could have predicted just how disappointing he would be. The most important aspect of this is not his failure to perform the miracles people expected of him. Rather, it is that he did perform the one miracle none of his supporters expected: in the face of universal condemnation of Wall Street, in the wake of high-level admissions of fundamental mistakes in the free-market ideology that says the answer to every social question is to deregulate markets,[7] Obama managed to oversee not just the continuation, but the expansion of Wall Street's power! Everyone thought that the financial crisis of 2008 was something that would change the world. "Surely we can't continue to let Wall Street retain its power over the lives of millions?" to which Obama replied, "Yes we can!"

I've thought about this course of events from time to time and it has continually occurred to me that I learned a lesson from it all: true or not, I walked away from the Iraq war protests with the understanding that protests are stupid, ineffective, and creepy, while electoral politics stimulates our hope for a better world only to steer it into the existing structures of power. But, I now realize that other, bolder peers of mine did not succumb to defeat so easily. Rather, they dove deeper into organizing, into struggle, into the radical reality that would burst into daylight with Occupy Wall Street.

All Roads Lead to Wall Street

"Wall Street" is more than just a street in lower Manhattan. It refers to a whole sector of the economy that deals with investing large amounts of money for the sake of gaining more money. Since the 1970s, these profits have increasingly come from "financial services"— fees and interest collected on debt. In other words, most of what is registered as "profits" is not tied to production of consumer goods at all, but rather to extracting interest and penalties from working people, students, and sick people. The short street that runs east-west on the southern tip of Manhattan Island and the blocks around it are home to a number (but certainly not all) of the investment banks and hedge-funds that the term "Wall Street" points toward. The financial crisis of 2008 and the ensuing Great Recession have brought near-universal criticism of how those working in the financial sector behaved in the preceding

---

[7] Knowlton and Grynbaum 2008.

years. Since 2007, ten million people in the United States have been evicted from their homes as a result of the housing bubble.[8] That kind of displacement is usually associated with wars. Here it resulted from a conflict of interest: poor people's need for houses to live in and Wall Street's need for endless growth in profits. When push came to shove, the United States government and its law-enforcement agencies were far more interested in protecting the bankers from lost profits than in protecting millions of people from eviction.

Though everyone shouts publicly about how Wall Street messed up big time, and many seem to be confident they will do it again, not everyone is convinced there is something fundamentally wrong with what the people at Wall Street firms do for a living. John Cassidy summarizes the justification for Wall Street in this way:

> When the banking system behaves the way it is supposed to . . . it is akin to a power utility, distributing money (power) to where it is needed and keeping an account of how it is used. Just like power utilities, the big banks have a commanding position in the market, which they can use for the benefit of their customers and the economy at large. (Cassidy 2012, p. 57)

According to this view, what happened in 2008 was either a perversion or a horrible accident, in which banks sought "to exploit their position and make a quick killing." Wall Street lost sight of its supposed true purpose and its firms started making bets that were in their own short-term interest, disregarding the interest of both "their customers and the economy at large."

Not everyone is convinced that Wall Street strayed from its proper task. For many, Wall Street epitomizes a fundamentally undemocratic system of power that has no legitimate role to play in a free society. Indeed, they might push further and argue that Wall Street was and is successfully executing its real task of keeping power concentrated in the hands of the wealthy. One way to present this perspective might be to elaborate on Cassidy's metaphor that imagines Wall Street as a "power utility" distributing "money (power)" rather than electricity.

---

[8] Gottesdiener 2013.

It's worth pointing out that the power of money, unlike electricity, derives solely from a social context developed throughout a few centuries, one which was consciously desired by a few people and forcefully imposed upon many others. This fact does not make it into mainstream political or economic discussion. But it is true, and is central to a number of the critiques of Wall Street and capitalism that influenced many Occupiers. George Caffentzis, a philosopher and a contributor to *Tidal*, the Occupy Theory/Occupy Strategy working group's journal, illustrates succinctly this point about how money has come to appear as that which makes the world go 'round:

> Most people can find in their genealogy or in their own lives some point when their ancestors or they themselves were forced from lands and social relations that provided subsistence without having to sell either one's products or oneself, i.e., they suffered Enclosure. Without these moments of force, money would have remained a marginal aspect of human history. These moments were mostly of brutal violence, sometimes quick (with bombs, cannon, musket, or whip), sometimes slower (with famine, deepening penury, plague), which led to the terrorized flight from the land, from the burnt-out village, from the street full of starving or plague-ridden bodies, to slave ships, to reservations, to factories, to plantations. This flight ended with 'producers becoming more dependent on exchange' since they had no other way to survive but by either selling their products or selling themselves or being sold. (Caffentzis 2013, p. 238)

Enclosures displace people from their means of subsistence or assert property rights over land or resources like water, firewood, music, ideas (such as patents), and pretty much anything that can be bought and sold—"commodified." As nature and human products are enclosed upon, money becomes increasingly the only available means for people to obtain what they need and desire to live healthy and meaningful lives. In order to get this money, they now have to do the bidding of those who have it. The "power" that is "distributed" by Wall Street is actually the power to *control* human beings who are dependent on money, the power to direct the labor of those who depend upon wages for access to their livelihoods. In light of this fact, the meaning of a "job" can be more precisely defined. This is what it means to have a "job": to have a set of actions you can perform throughout the day that are more or less reliably exchanged for money.

Once you have money, its value consists in its ability to get other people to perform actions in exchange for it. Think about it: all money ever does is get someone else or a whole series of people to perform a set of actions, to either do something for you or give you something. Those who have the power to direct large amounts of money have power over the actions of people on their jobs. Indeed, many people's jobs are simply to control and limit the actions of others. Money lays channels through which human activity is directed in a society where people are dependent upon wages. There are limits to this power, but on the whole it is reliable. As long as people have no other way to sustain themselves, they will, in general, take orders.

In light of this broad consideration, it becomes a bit easier to see why not everyone thinks it is a fundamentally good idea to allow traders on Wall Street to have that kind of power over the activity of others. Among those who dissent are those who have resisted and challenged capitalism since its creation: socialists and anarchists of all stripes, as well as indigenous and peasant communities, on whom the wage-system was and is still often imposed with violent force. Each of these are long and deep traditions of anti-capitalist organizing, thought, and action, and each were present and influential in Occupy.

But most people in the contemporary United States have no knowledge of this radical history or the various political philosophies that take this insight into the power of money as foundational, including various socialisms and anarchisms, as well as the beliefs and practices of colonized people the world over. These perspectives cut beneath most political and economic debates and get to the root of the power of Wall Street: it is a system of control, in which a few people exercise power over the lives of many. To think radically means to get to the root, and to begin from insights like this. To use Cassidy's metaphor, the task for radicals is not merely to let Wall Street distribute power, but to raise fundamental questions about how power is generated and distributed in society, while imagining and experimenting with the construction of alternative forms of power creation and distribution. Such a project is born from the basic truth, obscured by a metaphor like Cassidy's: it is always we—the vast majority of people—who generate the power that Wall Street and other hierarchical institutions accumulate.

Politicians and the corporate media typically pretend that such radical critiques of Wall Street either do not exist at all or are only put forward by a few crazy people. In fact, people who held such ideas have been important forces in shaping history, and the complete disappearance of anti-capitalist perspectives from public debate is actually a rather new phenomenon. In the wake of the crisis of 2008, such ideas began to seem a lot more plausible to many who would have otherwise dismissed them. Why weren't people flooding the streets in outrage at the widespread unemployment and evictions as the wealthiest remained insulated from the effects of the crash by huge government bailouts? Obama's miracle was to perpetuate hope in a system that appeared hopeless. But by the summer of 2011, the magic had worn off and a new symbol of hope had appeared amidst the disappointment: masses of people in the streets throughout the Middle East, Spain, and even in Madison, Wisconsin.

Whereas Obama had been a symbol of the ability of an individual from an oppressed class to rise to high office, Egypt's Tahrir Square became a symbol of everyday people themselves taking to the streets against the concentrations of power that dominated their lives. What would an American "Tahrir moment" look like? How could a movement challenge a power that is not symbolized by one dictator, but by a whole system of money-power that spreads its tentacles throughout the social world, structuring the everyday lives of millions? The Spanish *indignado* movement offered the most hopeful example. The *indignados* flooded public squares like Madrid's Puerta del Sol with large-scale experiments in direct democracy, calling into question the very idea that politicians could "represent" their interests. These protests, however, were nowhere near as highly visible in the American media as the Arab Spring. In early 2011, there were rumblings of a democratic awakening around the United States as well, the most significant of which was the capitol building occupation in response to Wisconsin governor Scott Walker's assault on collective bargaining rights. Something was in the air; power and authority were being challenged the world over and, in America, that means the power and authority of Wall Street over both our economic and political life.

Born on the Internet . . .

The name "Occupy Wall Street" was coined by Micah White, senior editor for the Canada-based anti-consumerist magazine

Adbusters. Known for their beautifully crafted, culture-jamming counter-advertisements, *Adbusters* sent out a "tactical briefing" to their ninety-thousand-person email list on July 13th 2011. The briefing included the photoshopped image of the ballerina on the *Bull.*

The ballerina's costume evokes the 1920s, an era when Wall Street's ravenous accumulation set the stage for the Great Depression. However it was interpreted, this image of the ballerina and the *Bull* played a role in getting all these people down here. So the sculpture, once itself locked away by the cops for having been installed without permission, is surrounded by fences on September 17th. Those fences are surrounded by rows of New York City police officers—presumably there to protect the statue from anyone who might be planning to perform ballet on its head. In the cloudy background are shadowy figures in gas masks. Below the image was the following message:

#OCCUPYWALLSTREET
Are you ready for a Tahrir moment?
On Sept 17, flood into lower Manhattan, set up tents,
kitchens, peaceful barricades and occupy Wall Street.

This striking image and its mysterious instructions were a follow-up to an earlier briefing, in which *Adbusters* claimed the Arab Spring and a spate of people's assemblies in public squares that had been organized in Greece and Spain marked "a worldwide shift in revolutionary tactics." The email was exactly what many around the country were waiting for: an opportunity to bring home the radical aspirations and actions that were igniting the world.

Founded in 1989 by documentary filmmakers Kalle Lasn and Bill Schmalz, *Adbusters: Journal of the Mental Environment* is an advertising-free journal that publishes articles and images aimed at critiquing and undermining consumerism. By "consumerism," they mean how the capitalist economy's demand for "growth" in terms of money ultimately amounts to a demand for people to buy more and more. The capitalist economy is actually not interested in whether you "consume" what you buy—only that you buy it. It is the point of exchange that matters from the perspective of those who are only interested in accumulating money.[9]

The task of the marketing industry is to ensure this ever expanding increase in buying through advertisements that encourage us to associate our self-worth, beauty, social ideals, and personal love-ability with commodities. *Adbusters* is like an anti-marketing firm, composed of creative people trying to use their powers of image-making and persuasion against the economy of perpetual growth. According to Lasn, "what we're trying to do is pioneer a new form of social activism using all the power of the mass media to sell ideas, rather than products.[10]

Shortly before he founded *Adbusters* in Vancouver, Lasn had become convinced that America was no longer a country in any traditional sense of the term.[11] Rather, it functioned more as a

---

[9] For a critical discussion of the concept of "consumption," see "The Very Idea of Consumption" in Graeber 2007.
[10] Motavelli 1996, p. 41.
[11] Lasn 1999.

brand, strategically deployed by the world's most powerful corporations whose ravenous lust for profit was rapidly destroying the
ecological basis of human life on the planet. America, for Lasn, is
a carefully managed imperial symbol used primarily as a front for
corporate powers. The uses to which it is put bear little connection
to the political aspirations or principles that the country claims as
its own. Some have suggested that since *Adbusters* is a Canadian-
based magazine, it is somehow out of place to criticize Wall Street
and its influence on American politics. Such criticisms are mis-
placed. Since corporations traded on Wall Street and supported by
the American brand have economic and ecological effects capable
of harming everyone, everyone around the globe is a legitimate
critic of that system.

In 2011, Micah White was senior editor of *Adbusters* living in
Berkeley, California. White became inspired by the tactic of occupation back in 2009 when thousands of students, teachers, and
parents organized mass protests against budget cuts and tuition
hikes in the University of California system. Amidst protests and
walk-outs, some students took control over buildings at campuses
around the state.

One of the more radical pamphlets produced during this student uprising is entitled "Communiqué from an Absent Future."
The pamphlet is a devastating critique of the role of the university
in sustaining the capitalist economy, giving voice to a generation
whose future has been captured in a vicious circle of debt: "we
work and borrow in order to work and borrow." But the text isn't
only critical. The authors discuss the importance of the tactic of
occupation—the act of taking over a space such as a school building or square and using that space for experimenting with a different kind of power, with "the creation of a momentary opening in
capitalist time and space, a re-arrangement that sketched the con-
tours of a new society."[12] However briefly they last, occupations
hold the promise of puncturing and transforming the everyday
flows of money-power that are taken for granted.

In a letter to the student movement, White had invited the students to get involved in a long-term struggle to "build a mental
environment movement capable of smashing corporations, down-

---

[12] Research and Destroy 2009, p. 19.

Student occupation of Kerr Hall at University of California, Santa Cruz, 2009.

sizing consumer spending and building egalitarian communities." This kind of long-term project can only be sustained by a radical hope that another, better and more just world is possible. Such a hope depends upon some experience, however fleeting, that convinces us to broaden our imagination and therefore our sense of what is possible. Radical politics is always a battle over the imagination. Perhaps occupations could be a vehicle for this kind of hope? Perhaps the experience of occupation, through creating an "opening in capitalist time and space," is uniquely suited to expanding the imagination? Soon after his experience at the university occupations at which the slogan "OCCUPY EVERYTHING" had been scrawled onto walls and banners, White dreamt up a phrase: *Occupy Wall Street*.

In 2011, as protests and occupations were kicking off all around the globe, White shared his nascent meme with Lasn, and the two began planning to launch it. According to Lasn, the date of September 17th (soon to be known as S17) was selected for partly strategic, partly personal reasons: it gave some time to plan and spread the word, but it is also Lasn's mother's birthday. They didn't seem to factor in that S17 is also the anniversary of the signing of the U.S. Constitution.

On July 13th, *Adbusters* hit send on a tactical briefing addressed to ninety thousand "redeemers, rebels, and radicals out there." Referring to a combination of the Egyptians' refusal to move from Tahrir Square and the Spanish indignados' direct-democratic assemblies, they wrote:

> The time has come to deploy this emerging stratagem against the greatest corrupter of our democracy: **Wall Street, the financial Gomorrah of America.**
>
> On September 17, we want to see 20,000 people flood into lower Manhattan, set up tents, kitchens, peaceful barricades and occupy Wall Street for a few months. Once there, we shall incessantly repeat one simple demand in a plurality of voices. <www.adbusters .org/blogs/adbusters-blog/occupywallstreet.html>

And with that, the spell was cast. The call-out was posted on Reddit, "the front page of the Internet," where users post articles and vote to move them up or down the page. Within a day, the site OccupyWallSt.org (soon to be dubbed "storg" to distinguish it from the various similar websites) was registered by a group of trans-gender anarchist cyber-activists. The homepage was adorned with the phrase "The Only Solution Is World Revolution!"

. . . Raised on Face-to-Face Communication

But big talk on the Internet is no indication of how a protest or demonstration will actually go. S17, the day when Occupy Wall Street began, was different because of a combination of luck and the preparatory work done by a group called the New York City General Assembly (NYCGA). And most of this work was done not on the Internet, but in weekly assemblies of their real bodies in Manhattan's Tompkins Square Park. It was in these assemblies that decisions were made that resulted in a different kind of "protest" than many in America had experienced: a protest that used organizational tools that inspired rather than alienated. It would change the whole conception of what "protest" could be for many of us made cynical by past Leftist events, including the anti-Iraq war protests.

But it almost didn't happen that way. The first meeting to organize for Occupy Wall Street in NYC was at Bowling Green on August 2nd, and from the reports of those whose ideas and actions would heavily influence Occupy, this meeting was standard fare: a group of people on a microphone shouting slogans with pre-printed placards and demands. The kind of gathering that asks nothing from its participants except for shouting and marching.

Among those in the crowd was David Graeber, an anthropologist and anarchist. Much of Graeber's scholarly work and activism centers on what is called "prefigurative politics," protests and social movements that attempt to "prefigure" in their organization the kind of world they are trying to create. From this perspective, a rally run by a small group of people making decisions about what is going to get said and done is actually the worst kind of political protest. Because it does not offer any agency to most of the participants, it simply reinforces a power hierarchy in which a few make the decisions and everyone else has to go along with them. Such protests tend to lead to either thoughtless leader-following or a sense of alienation from the event—just like in mainstream politics. Graeber, on the other hand, is a student of the Global Justice movement, and has learned that effective demonstrations and actions employ organizational tools that get as many people involved as possible. They foster a "horizontal" shared power grown from relationships between equals, rather than "vertical" relationships of power flowing from an elite downward. This approach to organizing encourages spontaneity, listening, relationship building, independent action—and the opportunity for catching those in power off-guard.

Graeber and some others had come down to Bowling Green because the event had been billed as a "General Assembly"—a people's meeting in which individuals are given the space to speak and organize for themselves, without representatives or a hierarchical structure. General Assemblies had been happening in recent years in Argentina, Greece, and Spain in response to financial crises and government-imposed austerity measures. Those who came to the Bowling Green rally with the hopes of engaging in such direct democracy were sorely disappointed. They found a socialist political party, the Workers World Party, had organized the event with pre-printed signs, demands, and slogans. Upon realizing that a General Assembly was not going to happen unless they created one themselves, Graeber and a few others started to form a break-away meeting. After some back and forth, a Greek activist named Georgia Sangri got on the microphone and shouted: *"This is not a General Assembly! This is a rally put on by a political party! It has absolutely nothing to do with the global*

General Assembly movement!" This outburst and the confusion it helped generate was effective in creating a separate meeting conducted on horizontal principles.[13]

To the surprise of many present, no one from *Adbusters* was there. Apparently, *Adbusters* had come up with the idea and produced some images, and left the rest of the organizing to the whims of people on the ground. Those in the break-away meeting didn't know what else was planned or who else was involved, but they decided to organize for S17 anyway. They broke up into small working groups to generate proposals. Graeber joined the Process group, which, he reports,

> was primarily composed of anarchists, determined to ensure that the group became a model. We quickly decided that the group would operate by consensus, with an option to fall back on a two-thirds vote if there was a deadlock, and that there would be two facilitators, one male, one female, one to keep the meeting running, the other to "take stack" (that is, the list of people who've asked to speak). We discussed hand signals and nonbinding straw polls, or "temperature checks." (p. 33)

And so this "process," a set of organizational tools meant to encourage the direct participation of everyone present at the meeting, became the model for the NYCGA.

Throughout the month of August, in Tompkins Square Park and around the city, you might have found the following message on a quarter-sheet flyer:

GENERAL ASSEMBLY

We are the **General Assembly of NYC**—We are building a horizontal collective **open to anyone,** we are recovering the political dimension of our lives ("politics" in the sense of organizing our lives with others), which has been kidnapped by the elites in power—We are part of global network of Assemblies functioning in the same way. The **General Assembly of NYC** is here to stay, its life will go beyond a particular action.

However, we are strategically supporting a **call for action on Sept. 17 in Wall St.,** because it's already out there attracting people,

---

[13] Graeber 2013, pp. 30–31.

it will be worth it for our global movement to have a protest in such a hugely symbolic place.

OCCUPYWALLST.ORG—TAKETHESQUARE.NET—
USDAYOFRAGE.ORG
SAT, AUGUST 20 @ 5pm
TOMPKINS SQUARE PARK

The NYCGA was more than just a series of planning sessions for the occupation of Wall Street. It was a political project of its own, one aimed at "recovering the political dimension of our lives." The assembly recognized this as a long-term process of building relationships of mutual aid and shared power. In that process, mass actions and demonstrations have a role to play, but they are less important than the day-to-day work of reorganizing our lives into strong communities, creating processes for material support, decision-making, and taking action that are independent of and a challenge to the existing power structures.

With this long-term vision in mind, some of the more experienced assembly members did not have very high hopes for the events of S17. After all, the financial district in lower Manhattan is one of the most heavily policed and surveilled areas in the world. It seemed highly unlikely that anything like an "occupation" would be allowed to occur. Many of those drawn to the NYCGA—particularly those who were relatively new to horizontal organizing—were there because of the Internet hype surrounding S17 and Occupy Wall Street. But something strange was happening: they found themselves increasingly committed to the organizational tools being used in the assembly. Nathan Schneider recounts one participant's experience with the assembly process:

> It pushes you to be more respectful of the people there. Even after General Assembly ends I find myself being very attentive in situations where I'm normally not so attentive. So if I go get some food after General Assembly, I find myself being very polite to the person I'm ordering from, and listening if they talk back to me. (Schneider 2013, p. 20)

A successful assembly creates a space for people to listen to one another, to learn from one another, and to gain a very different perspective on the rest of their social relationships. As a result, tiny experiences like the one described above emanate outward from

General Assemblies. They are experiences in which the social world lights up, and we recognize that so much of our lives and interactions are impersonal or on auto-pilot. These experiences are, admittedly, a *very* small step toward the NYCGA's goal of "recovering the political dimension of our lives," of re-envisioning how we make decisions and organize our social lives together. But they are a necessary step. They helped foster a mood of emotional openness, of strong bonds, and of trust among people who sometimes just met. It may sound ridiculous, but experiences like this are as fundamental to what the Occupy movement would become as any statistic about the wealth of the one percent.

We! Should Become! The Ninety-Nine Percent!

But we can't forget the wealth of the one percent! And it wasn't only relationships that were being generated in the Tompkins Square Park meetings of the NYCGA. Apart from experimenting with horizontal organizing, the NYCGA was also cooking up ideas that would become hallmarks of the Occupy movement: the slogan "We are the Ninety-Nine Percent!," the Tumblr page of the same name, and the working groups that would form the basis for the interlinking, decentralized forms of organizing that Occupy relied upon.

People involved in the Occupy movement were by no means the first to discuss inequality by highlighting the immense power of the wealthiest one percent in the country. This statistical breakdown has been a staple of people writing for economic justice for decades. In May of 2011, before *Adbusters* had sent out the call to Occupy Wall Street, Nobel Prize–winning economist Joseph Stiglitz made use of the idea in a *Vanity Fair* article entitled "Of the 1%, by the 1%, and for the 1%." As the title suggests, Stiglitz argued that America was now effectively a plutocracy—a government by and for the wealthy. Stiglitz put the bad news this way:

> It's no use pretending that what has obviously happened has not in fact happened. The upper 1 percent of Americans are now taking in nearly a quarter of the nation's income every year. In terms of wealth rather than income, the top 1 percent control 40 percent. (Stiglitz 2011)

Levels of inequality have been on the rise since the 1970s. While for most workers, real wages have stagnated over the same period, the after-tax income of the one percent has increased by 275 percent. At the same time, household debt has increased dramatically. The rich have been getting richer while most other people have had to go into debt to make ends meet.

According to mainstream American political discourse, there is no *class divide*, let alone *class struggle*. The Right likes to speak of "class warfare" whenever people organize from below, but ignores the fact that "class struggle" is going on whenever tax-cuts for the rich are enacted or cuts to entitlements are pushed through.[14]

Throughout the Cold War, anyone who pointed out that the interests of the super-rich were actually counter to the interests of the vast majority of people in the United States risked being associated with the Soviet Union. This was certainly career suicide for politicians, but also for the many anti-capitalists who saw the USSR as a nightmare that bore no resemblance to their vision of a free and just society. While radicals were critical of the United States and the capitalist "West," they were equally unwilling to give support to the Soviet Union. As a result of the legacy of the Cold War, many people in the United States are either repelled or even confused by talk of "class struggle." But that doesn't mean it isn't going on. Indeed, as the statistics about the gains of the one percent show, over the last thirty years class struggle has been in high gear. As Warren Buffett so clearly put it, "there's class warfare going on alright, but it's my class, the rich class, that's making war, and we're winning."[15]

Those organizing for S17 in the NYCGA were well aware of the American aversion to openly discussing economic class. Still, in 2011 there was outrage at the paralyzed political system, lingering resentment over the TARP bailout, and we were in the midst of something called a "jobless recovery"—in other words, it counts as a "recovery" as long as the rich are getting richer, even if poor folks still can't find work. These and many other factors made the time ripe for a novel attempt to reintroduce class into American political discourse. Writing to fellow members of the NYCGA on their email list, Graeber apparently took his inspiration from Stiglitz and proposed the following slogan for the movement they were trying to create:

---

[14] For a nice discussion of the various uses to which the German word *Klassenkampf* (class struggle) has been put, see Nunberg 2011.

[15] Stein 2006.

What about the "99% movement"?

> Both parties govern in the name of the 1% of Americans who have received pretty much all the proceeds of economic growth, who are the only people completely recovered from the 2008 recession, who control almost all financial wealth.
>
> So if both parties represent the 1%, we represent the 99% whose lives are essentially left out of the equation. (Graeber 2013, p. 40)

This proved to be an important innovation. It both named the one percent as a group with disproportionate power over both political parties *and* attempted to conjure into existence some new entity: the ninety-nine percent.

If there is a one percent, then there must be a ninety-nine percent. But just because the ninety-nine percent exist as a group of people who share something in common (namely, not being among the one percent), it doesn't mean that the ninety-nine percent actually *know* and *feel* themselves to share anything in common. Nor does it mean they should. Indeed, as we will see, to refer to ourselves as the ninety-nine percent is to seriously blur many of the actual operations of class, race, and gender oppression in the United States. The slogan can best be read as an invitation to create the sense of a common experience across huge differences within American society against the plutocratic rule of the one percent. But how could such a sense of unity be constructed in a society where people are isolated from and even afraid of one another?

It would turn out that one of the most effective tools for creating such a sense of shared experience was a Tumblr page set up by Chris, an activist involved in the NYCGA. Thinking about how he could help promote both the S17 occupation and the "We are the Ninety-Nine Percent" slogan, Chris describes having "just one of those random thoughts you get throughout your day that make you go 'Huh, I should write this down', before going on to do whatever it is you're doing. Except in this case I actually wrote it down." The thought was this: start a Tumblr page and "get a bunch of people to submit their pictures with a handwritten sign explaining how these harsh financial times have been affecting them, identify themselves as the '99 percent', and then write 'OccupyWallSt.org' at the end."[16]

---

[16] Weinstein 2011.

This pattern would end up being one of the major ways the movement spread through social media, connecting the stories of people from around the country and around the world and revealing an often hidden world of fears, anxiety, and suffering from debt, joblessness, lack of access to medical care, and the threat of evictions. Within a few weeks, the posts on this Tumblr page would ricochet around various social media sites on the internet. People in front of computer screens everywhere were able to see their own daily struggles and fears mirrored in the struggles and fears of others. What they may have been taught to think of as their own personal failings suddenly started to appear as something that was being imposed on wide segments of the population. Such connections would begin to construct a shared sense of struggle, and with it a sense of belonging to a new group called "the ninety-nine percent."

The NYCGA was creating slogans and websites for the upcoming S17, but they were also organizing themselves into working groups to prepare for who-knew-how-many people to descend upon the financial district. Working groups were in charge of food, training for nonviolent direct action, selecting various potential sites to form encampments, and providing legal observers to protect protestors from police brutality. On September 1st, some members of the NYCGA who had been involved in an earlier encampment against city-wide budget cuts called "Bloombergville" decided to do an experiment to prepare for the planned occupation of Wall Street. They wanted to test whether they could sleep outdoors in the financial district by appealing to a federal law that allowed sleeping on public sidewalks, as long as pedestrian passage was not blocked.

A curious passerby told the proto-Occupiers that the bankers and traders on Wall Street were not going to be convinced of anything by some young people sleeping on the street. They should get into politics. They should play by the rules—that's how to get the attention of the powerful. He was met with a reply that would be reiterated time and again in the coming months: it's not about talking to the one percent; it's about talking to everyone else. "Say we do this September 17th action," one participant explained while gesturing to the financial district. "I know we're not gonna reach *these* guys. But we're trying to get the people in New York City. We're trying to get the teachers unions, we're trying to get the average people walking around." Wall Street is an important symbolic site, but the hearts and minds the Occupiers were after don't work there.

Some of the rhetoric that night grew lofty. Jez Bold declared that we were witnessing the beginning

> of a Second American Revolution. True emancipation can never happen through the present dominant institutions, because they are the very ones that generate or replicate the hierarchies of injustice. We have, yes, a one-line emancipation cry: *Wall Street Is All Streets.*
>
> [*everyone chants*] *Wall Street Is All Streets!* (Atchu and Jez3Prez 2011)

When the police arrived, the protestors tried out their argument that it was within their right to sleep on the sidewalk as long as they did not obstruct pedestrian traffic. The police weren't buying it and arrested nine of them anyway, shutting down the night's events. A later court ruling upheld the protestors' claim that they were not breaking the law and the charges were dropped. Still, notice how the police successfully ended the demonstration by overstepping their boundaries without regard for the actual law. This would soon be recognized as something of a pattern.

After this experimental occupation, those skeptical that S17 would live up to *Adbusters'* rhetoric had even more reason to lower their expectations. According to anyone who knew, anyone reasonable, anyone with experience, those coming into lower Manhattan on S17 to Occupy Wall Street were going to be attacked by the police and either arrested or dispersed—and probably very quickly. And it might have gone that way, if it weren't for this peculiar moment when two thousand people walked into Zuccotti Park and did the last thing anyone expected: sat down and talked.

The Process Is the Message

Activist and filmmaker Astra Taylor was there on S17, and recorded her surprise about the course taken:

> The first day I arrived and surveyed the scene, I was totally dispirited: same old, same old, and not very substantial. Since the authorities had locked down the area in anticipation of the day's events, demonstrators were dispersed and outnumbered by police. But then I followed the impromptu procession into the park where they are now

encamped. I hooked up with a group of friends and we had an "assembly" with a bunch of strangers and talked economics for two or three hours. It was kind of nice to be at a protest and, instead of marching and shouting, to be talking about ideas. It felt like the script had changed. (Schmitt et al. 2011, p. 3)

Some of these small groups compiled lists of possible demands and grievances. Some groups also discussed the question of demands in a way that would become one of the hallmarks of Occupy, reflecting on "why it was problematic to make a demand, how in order for a demand to be meaningful, one must have some power to leverage."[17]

The NYCGA, for its part, had already decided to forgo making demands on the grounds that it legitimized the authority of the current power structures. Their project of recovering their political lives implied making demands of themselves and one another, of developing as far as possible relationships that could meet their needs directly, without seeking permission or approval from those in power.[18] This would come to define a dominant ethos of the Occupiers, as well as one of the most contentious debates within the movement.

Still, though none would be officially endorsed by the General Assembly, demands were listed by various groups. Here are the demands that came out of one group's discussion on Day 1:

- **To repeal the *Citizens United* Supreme Court decision (through a Constitutional amendment)**

- **To remove the bull sculpture from Wall Street (as suggested to us by a man who walked by dressed as a banker but wearing a noose instead of a tie)**

- **Some form of debt cancellation (either for everyone or just for students)**

- **Pay-as-you-go military intervention (so that wars could not be waged without Congress agreeing to finance each step immediately)**

- **Taxes on small financial transactions (one version of this is known as the Tobin tax)**

---

[17] Eli Schmitt in Blumenkranz et al. 2011, p. 5.
[18] Sitrin 2011.

- Full employment

- A social wage or guaranteed income (also described as a nega-
tive income tax)

- Universal care centers (for children and the elderly)

- To reinstate the Glass-Steagall Act (a banking reform passed
in 1933 and partially repealed in 1980)

- Paid sick leave for all working Americans

- Greater political transparency in general. (pp. 4–5)

Occupy Wall Street did not refrain from making demands for lack
of ideas—all these and more were present and articulated time and
again in the coming months. But none was to be held aloft as *the*
demand.

The "demand for demands," foisted upon the movement by the
mainstream media and traditional Leftist groups alike, missed the
importance of what was going on in the encampments. In the
Occupy encampments, we saw the widespread resurrection of a
political ideal that had been buried by the Bush administration,
evoked and manipulated by the Obama administration, and dismissed as impossible by the prevailing common sense of capitalist
America: the ideal of *participatory democracy,* the more *direct* the
better. And this ideal was evoked through the use of a set of organizational tools developed in activist circles since the 1970s, but really
honed in the Global Justice movement of the 1990s and early
2000s. These tools were dubbed "the process," and, among many
Occupiers, this process was itself the message of the movement.

The consensus process is a set of tools for facilitating a discussion and decision-making among large groups, with the goal of
reaching consensus. The aim of the consensus process is not to get
everyone to side either for or against a given proposal. Rather, the
aim is to draw out all of the group's concerns about the proposal
in order to shape and modify it into a collective product to which
as many people as possible have contributed. The aim is not to
"win" people over to one side, so much as to transform both the
proposal and the "sides" of the group themselves through con-
structive and creative discussion. The process itself becomes a site
of transformation and community building, in which people learn
to see proposals from the perspectives of others and thus learn to
appreciate and consider those perspectives in the future.

It should be obvious that this is easier said than done. The point, however, is that this is a very different political ideal than the one implied by the structure of party politics. The activity of party politics implies the ideal of triumphing over the other side and treating disagreements as grounds for competition; the activity of consensus politics implies the ideal of constructing a world in which our interests are not in conflict, and of treating disagreements as grounds for attentive listening and mutual understanding. In a world like ours, one in which people's thoughts and concerns are consistently marginalized by the powerful, be it a politician sending people to a needless war or a boss ordering people around on the job, introducing such a political ideal is a powerful—and surprising—accomplishment. And yet, for thousands around the country, General Assemblies succeeded in convincing them that, while difficult and unlikely, the consensus process pointed in the direction of a world worth striving for.

On the afternoon of September 17th, the first General Assembly in Zuccotti Park got started, and two thousand people were suddenly exposed to the consensus process that the NYCGA had been using for weeks. There were a number of logistical issues that needed to be sorted out, chief among them was the problem of how to actually hear one another. Enter the People's Microphone. The idea is simple: one person speaks in slow, short phrases, and everyone within earshot repeats what they say, amplifying their voice so those out of earshot can now hear. In a particularly large group, the original speaker's voice might move through two or three waves of repetition.

The use of the People's Mic had a few important consequences. By requiring the speaker to choose their words carefully and fit them into short phrases, it discourages long speeches and encourages plain, direct language. It also encourages actual listening, since you have to repeat what is being said. On top of these obvious benefits, there is a more unexpected and somewhat incalculable one: when it is working well, when people are energized by the proceedings, the People's Mic forges the sense of a collective body through merging voices together in shared space. It moves beyond being an effective tool for amplification and becomes a community building experience in itself.

Many people were convinced the People's Mic was invented on the spot in response to the NYPD's ban on electronic amplification (like megaphones). While they did ban the use of megaphones, the People's Mic has a longer—perhaps *much longer*—history. According to Graeber,

> No one was quite sure where the People's Mic had originally come from. It was already a familiar tool to many California activists by the time of the WTO actions in Seattle in November 1999. In a way, it's kind of remarkable that it hasn't been attested long before—it's a perfect solution to an obvious problem that people in large assemblies must have faced time and time again for thousands of years. Perhaps it was widely used in earlier period of human history but was simply never remarked on because its use was considered self-evident. (Graeber 2013, p. 50)

Among the early problems to be solved on the People's Mic was the question of just what this massive group of people assembled in Zuccotti Park was going to do with themselves. Some wanted to stay and occupy the park—others wanted to march on Wall Street and attempt to set up an encampment there. Mike Butler, an activist who had been involved with the Global Justice movement, proposed the following solution over the People's Mic:

> There seem to be two positions. . . . Either we stay in the park, or march on Wall Street. . . . We don't know if they'll let us stay here overnight. . . . Clearly the thing the police want least is for us to march on Wall Street. . . . So I propose the following. . . . We make it known that we are going to occupy the square. . . . And if the police try to drive us out, that we will immediately march on Wall Street. (p. 53)

This proposal carried the day into the night, when two hundred or so people stepped together into unknown and unexpected territory. They carried with them the hopes of riling up the hearts and dreams of people around the United States, of waking up the progressive conscience that Reverend Billy had called out to just a few hours earlier. The standard protest script had been flipped. They were engaged in an experiment that was much broader in scope than marching and the chanting could capture. They were invited to listen to one another, to collaborate, to share their experiences and assessments of the problems facing the economy and the culture; to take control and responsibility over a small space and mobilize all their energies toward transforming it into portal to another world, a momentary opening in the time and space dominated by the power of money and the authority structures that pass for politics. Contrary to almost everyone's expectations, all this proved to be contagious.

2

The Ones We've Been Waiting For

It's early October 2011 and I'm packed into the basement of Gaia House Interfaith Center in Carbondale, Illinois. I'm here with nearly a hundred people, some of whom I know, most of whom I've seen around town but never actually spoken with. Nicole has a flow chart we copied from the Facilitation Team at Occupy St. Louis, and she is walking the group through the consensus process, explaining the steps and trying to communicate something of the spirit in which the General Assembly should be conducted.

She is explaining the hand signals. If you want to show approval for something, rather than clapping, simply hold your hands up and twinkle your fingers. If you want to show disapproval, rather than booing, point your hands downward and twinkle. If you think the assembly is not following its own process or people are speaking out of turn and cutting people off, signal a "point of process" by making a triangle with your two hands. If you have a point of information, some fact that is relevant to the discussion at hand, raise one finger in the air. If you have an ethical or safety concern with the plan of action being discussed, one that's so serious you feel the group may be betraying the spirit of the movement, then make your arms into an X to block the proposal. We will form breakout groups to discuss your concern and try to find a workable solution.

She is explaining the role of "Facilitator." The facilitator walks the group through the process, tries to keep things fun, eases the tension, and makes sure we are staying on task. The facilitator is someone in a temporary position of responsibility—not a "leader." The facilitator should not participate in the substantive discussions of the meeting, surrendering their voice and trusting the intelligence of the group and the process. Anyone can be trained in the techniques of facilitation.

She is explaining the meaning of the "progressive stack." The "stack" taker is the person who you signal if you want to speak. They keep a list of who has already spoken, and decide who will speak next. The stack taker will try to get a variety of voices from people of different races, genders, ages, and abilities. Those from groups that have been socially and historically marginalized will be privileged in the order of speaking.

The room is tense with excitement and everyone uses the hand signals like they're kids who have just found new toys—people wiggle their fingers to show approval, and the wiggling itself creates a slight buss in the mood. Our fingers are tiny conductors, channeling some newly discovered kind of electricity from New York, from St. Louis, from Chicago, from all the occupations that have sprouted like mushrooms, seemingly from nowhere, over the past few weeks. And here we all are, residents of a tiny college town and its surrounding rural areas in southern Illinois, brought together for a common cause. Which is . . . what, exactly?

Red Ink

For Drew Hornbein, everything seemed to be going great career-wise in August of 2011. After reading about Occupy Wall Street on Reddit, he started participating in the New York City General Assembly during the planning sessions for S17:

> I was doing freelance graphic design and web design. I had gotten involved in August with the General Assemblies leading up to it. Something about the format of the consensus decision-making General Assembly drew me in. . . . As September was coming around, I was finalizing this big contract with a client to a get a regular salaried position to do freelance for them, and you know I was looking at a pretty decent yearly income, and I had a number of steady clients, everything was really in place, and then the 17th happened. And it became very clear to me: this is what I need to do. I emailed my client and said "This is what I'm doing, I'm not going to be working anymore. I'm going to help you transition off of me, but I'm going down to Wall Street and I'm going to do this full time."

Reflecting on this somewhat rash decision, Drew said:

> I was getting my whole shit in order right before I dropped everything. There I am, "succeeding" on all fronts, but there's this pit of emptiness. And when I dropped everything, I was thinking, "You know, if this doesn't work out, I could be fucked. I could be throwing away the years of work I put in." But Occupy fulfilled that in a huge way. . . . It was the most fulfilling work that I've ever done, and I've never been in a situation where I felt more at ease, at home, connected with people, connected to the world and proud of the work I was doing. It felt like meaningful work. (Personal interview, August 2013)

The "pit of emptiness" Drew describes resonates for many people in his position: a feeling of meaninglessness, a feeling that even though everything is going "right" for them, it doesn't really matter because everything else is going to hell. Yes, it's nice to have a good gig and some financial security, but how does taking care of yourself help the wider problems of the world if the wealth to which you have gained access isn't available for everyone?

Whether through direct experiences of oppression or through education about the power dynamics of our world, many young people today are equipped with criticisms of our social and economic life that cannot be translated into meaningful action within the mainstream of US society. These criticisms are of many aspects of our lives: consumerism, ecological destruction, exploitation of people in other lands who make the products we purchase, the understanding that racism persists in US society and corporations are making profits off of imprisoning people, and so on.

The awareness of ongoing injustice makes any individual success bittersweet. They know their "success" within this society comes at a cost to those who are less privileged. This awareness leaves a shadow over every achievement that isn't direct opposition to that injustice. But for many of us, no real opposition appears available—we feel powerless in the face of injustice. We cope with this sense of powerlessness in various ways: perhaps we tell ourselves that things *cannot* change and that all one can expect from life is a little individual success. When we become convinced of this, the possibility of politics is over. This powerlessness grows into a "pit of emptiness," and is often interpreted as some fundamental existential condition—human life is thought of as absurd, without purpose, or even fundamentally destructive. That pit of emptiness can express itself in depression or anxiety, it can be filled with drugs and booze or other forms of "compensatory consumption" (say, becoming a shop-a-work-a-exercise-aholic). What is actually a condition of unfreedom—of the inability to transform the world in light of what we know to be true—is interpreted as a personal flaw, as if there is something wrong with you because you can't be happy benefiting from injustices.

In the early weeks of Occupy Wall Street, the Slovenian philosopher Slavoj Žižek paid a visit to Zuccotti Park. Žižek has done what many people think is impossible: as a philosopher and cultural critic, he has also managed to turn himself in to a world-famous celebrity, deftly toying with the media and finding ways to translate his radical analyses of contemporary society into movie reviews and jokes. At Occupy Wall Street, Žižek spoke on the People's Mic and, in his own style, theorized the significance of the occupation:

> Let me tell you a wonderful old joke from Communist times. A guy was sent from East Germany to work in Siberia. He knew his mail would be read by censors, so he told his friends: "Let's establish a code. If a letter you get from me is written in blue ink, it is true what I say. If it is written in red ink, it is false." After a month, his friends get the first letter. Everything is in blue. It says, this letter: "Everything is wonderful here. Stores are full of good food. Movie theaters show good films from the West. Apartments are large and luxurious. The only thing you cannot buy is red ink." This is how we live. We have all the freedoms we want. But what we are missing is red ink: the language to articulate our non-freedom. The way we are taught to speak about freedom—war and terror and so on—falsifies freedom. And this is what you are doing here. You are giving all of us red ink. (Žižek 2011, pp. 67–68)

What was going on in Zuccotti Park in late September of 2011, and what was soon to be going on around the country, defied the contemporary political landscape. Occupiers were tapping into a human experience that was more fundamental than could be expressed in the political language of the contemporary United States—something beyond Democrat versus Republican, Liberal versus Conservative, beyond "jobs" and "economic growth." Žižek's joke expresses this nicely: most people are going through their days without "red ink," without the language to express how wrong things seem, without the concepts to articulate how different the world should be. Occupy was a spring of red ink, of experiences that pointed in a new direction, of material out of which people could build up a vision for a different world.

But the source of this spring was not any phrase or slogan or meme. It was not any carefully constructed image, nor was it simply a matter of numbers of bodies in the street. Rather, the source of this "red ink" was the activities people were engaged in—ways of relating that answered to the "pit of emptiness" because they were intrinsically opposed to the ways current power structures function. The General Assembly, the Working Groups, and the encouragement of autonomous initiatives pointed toward a world that could, in principle, overcome and respond to the deep problems of this one. A world of a different kind of politics altogether.

All Day, All Week

Zuccotti Park was now "Liberty Square." During the first week, Occupy Wall Street was "charged with a secret extremity and transcendence—secret, because the rest of the world hadn't yet become aware of what was happening down in Liberty Square."[1] The various activities—marches, sit-ins, working groups, assemblies, and the creation of a village infrastructure in the park—were playing off one another, sustaining each other and overlapping. All this demanded effort, organization, communication, and to sum up: hard work. But this was work performed not for a wage, but out of a sense of justice and a desire for a better world. To the chorus of right-wing critics who would yell that the Occupiers should "get a job," a sign appeared during the early days that would remain the perfect response: "Lost my job, found an occupation."

S17 was on a Saturday, so for the first two days of OWS, there were few if any actual Wall Street traders in the area. That all changed Monday morning, as the minions of New York's financial district began to make their way to their desks, their screens, their daily cycles of buying and selling. At 7 a.m., a General Assembly began. The group was informed that marches to Wall Street were planned for 9 a.m., 11:30 a.m., and 3:30 p.m.

---

[1] Schneider 2013, p. 31.

But then somebody came to the front of the assembly and announced through the people's mic that he was going to march right then. Wall Street bankers were walking to work, and we were just sitting there. The commuters would already be at their desks by nine. He ran off and, promptly, more than a hundred others followed. They marched around the plaza first, chanting "All Day! All Week! Occupy Wall Street!" and then set off heading south on Broadway. The occupation was starting the workweek early. (p. 30)

These marches were both non-violent and yet filled with a rebellious energy that broke with the dullness of many protests. They stopped up foot traffic by flooding the sidewalks; there was swarming and break-away groups, there were no permits and no planned routes; people marched and chanted in different directions, groups used hand signals to communicate their movements in the moment. These were marches infused with improvisation, the spirit of the park extending itself to the doors of the Stock Exchange, where they chanted "Banks Got Bailed Out, We Got Sold Out!"

Occupiers also sought out ongoing labor struggles to which they could lend their energy and their numbers. One of these early support actions was a protest against Sotheby's art auction house on behalf of the IBT 184 Art Handlers' Union. In 2010, Sotheby's made $680 million and their CEO Bill Rupprecht gave himself a 125 percent raise. Things were going so well that Sotheby's decided it was time to go after their unionized workers. Management demanded over one hundred concessions from their contract and locked them out of work until they accepted those concessions, as well as the boss's demands that all new workers be hired without collective bargaining rights.[2]

On September 23rd, less than a week into the occupation, activists from OWS interrupted a Sotheby's art auction. "The activists staggered their entrances and planted themselves in the crowd of businessmen and women, all gathered to witness the sale of artwork, with prices ranging from the average salary of a working American to the average cost of an American home." One by one, occupiers raised their voices in the auction and were escorted out by security. Their message was that "the Sotheby's auction epitomized the disconnect between the extremely wealthy and the

---

[2] Flank 2011, p. 37.

rest of us." And there was something particularly offensive about such massive amounts of money being exchanged for art. As one occupier put it: "This is disgusting! Art is about truth."[3]

Solidarity actions were not just in support of organized labor. During the first week of OWS, the state of Georgia executed Troy Davis, a black man convicted of killing a police officer. Davis had spent twenty years in prison and maintained his innocence up to his death. On September 21st, Davis was killed by a state-administered, privately supplied, lethal injection cocktail. Occupiers held vigils and marches in his honor. In the writeup afterward, they reported:

> Tonight we were joined by a protest against the for-profit legal lynching of Troy Davis. We are all Troy Davis. If Troy Davis had been a member of the 1% he would still be alive. Together we numbered nearly a thousand strong and marched on Wall Street. The police arrested six of us and attempted to incite violence by splitting the march and boxing in protestors, in spite of this, we remained true to our principles of nonviolence. (p. 36)

The execution of Troy Davis highlighted how the power of the one percent, the tyranny of Wall Street, is felt very differently across the ninety-nine percent. What for a white man with a high paying job might be felt as a "pit of emptiness" attending his career success, for another person—particularly a black man in in the US—the economic and social realities of this society mean he has a 1 in 3 chance of going to prison in his lifetime.[4]

Each of these marches and solidarity actions were sites of learning for many Occupiers. For those that were not already aware of them, connections were being made between the power of corporations, extreme inequality, and the everyday workings of the criminal justice system. In the mainstream media, of course, an execution—if presented at all—is usually presented as an isolated incident or, at best, part of some trend. Occupiers, however, were actively connecting Davis's execution with the legacy of racism and the corporate power of today; they were connecting a lockout of

---

[3] Flank 2011, p. 37–38.

[4] Knafo 2013. For a study of America's racial caste system through the contemporary prison system, see Alexander 2012.

art handlers with the financial elite whose money makes the art world turn, and even with the meaning of art itself; and, of course, they were swarming Wall Street, making it clear that the problem was business as usual, not a few greedy bad apples. And for Occupiers, business as usual was no longer acceptable.

Marches and solidarity actions were going on every day extending the awareness, spirit, and messages of the occupation throughout the city. But the heart of OWS during these early weeks was the General Assembly, which formed itself twice a day. It took shape in the park like a living organism, as hundreds sat in rows facing the steps on the east side of the park, with the words of whomever was addressing the GA reveberating through the People's Mic. People from around the world showed up to get a taste of one of human culture's most prized and delicate fruits: direct democracy, people organizing their co-existence and making decisions for themselves without representatives, politicians, the threat of force, or the power of money. Free people, pursuing their common life together. It just happened to be in a small park surrounded by skyscrapers and hundreds of cops.

It doesn't quite work to call a General Assembly a "governing body." It's a structured meeting that strives to create a space of equal power among participants. In the early days and weeks, it was a place for decisions that affected the whole group, announcements, reports from various working groups, invitations to marches, solidarity actions, and drafting public statements that were explicitly attempting to speak on behalf of everyone. The everyday life of the park was organizing itself outside of the GA through the self-directed actions of individuals, groups of friends, or more official working groups. This has to be remembered, because otherwise the General Assembly is misinterpreted as just another strange organization you have to go through in order to get permission to do things. Though it is sometimes treated this way, this is not the intention.

Early on it became clear that OWS needed some sort of public statement drafted by the General Assembly. While some thought this should be a list of demands, eventually they decided a "statement of principles" would be more appropriate. Demands say what we want; principle say what we stand for. On September 19th, just two days into OWS, the General Assembly began work on their "Principles of Solidarity." They broke into small groups for thirty-five minutes and made lists of various principles that these smaller groups endorsed, then a working group was formed to compile and edit them into six clear statements. This process took place over the course of four days. On September 23rd the principles were offered up to the group as a "living document," something that would necessarily morph and develop with time. Here's a selection from the transcript of that GA:

7.3.2.3. There was a move for consensus but there were four blocks:

7.3.2.3.1. The first block, regarding the use of the phrase 'redistribution of wealth' and how it sounded dangerously similar to theft, explained their position. After it was decided, via consensus, that that particular item would be removed before positing online, the block was removed.

7.3.2.3.2. A second block was made regarding the importance of ensuring this document was 'open source'. After the sentiment was echoed by the group it was explained that document would 'open source' to as full an extent as possible. The block was then removed.

7.3.2.3.3. A third block was presented but then removed due to a misunderstanding.

7.3.2.3.4. A fourth block was presented pointing out that the media would misinterpret or not understand the document in its current form. The individual blocking proposed that the document not be put online until a finalized list of demands could be made. After much negotiation and discussion, the importance and urgency of getting something to the public was stressed and eventually the block was removed.

7.3.2.4. The GA then moved again for consensus and everyone was thrilled that consensus had been reached, the document would be posted online, in one of the most beautiful examples of a true democracy that I, personally, have ever seen. (Minutes of the NYCGA 9/23/11 <http://www.nycga.net/2001/09/general-assembly-minutes-7pm-92311>)

The last line perhaps gives a sense of how elevated the mood was in the park at that moment. And the mood was of concern for the process. Throughout the GA there were regular "vibe checks." Facilitators would ask, "How's everybody feeling? Feeling good?" The process thrives on good will, on comradery. And it matters if people are bored.

I asked one Occupier named Roland when it was that the GA "clicked" for him, when did he get the feeling that there was something special and important about this way of collective self-organizing. His example was surprising to me, because it seemed to be one of the trivial debates that tend to bog down GAs:

> It didn't make sense at first. But I think there was one GA where everybody was trying to come to consensus about this proposal about whether there should be tea. And I was like "why is all this time going to deciding whether there should be tea?" But then I realized it was actually a really comforting, reassuring thing, to have a cup of tea in the morning. It clicked that it is actually worth going through a meeting about whether there should be tea. It was about bringing people together. I liked that people would spend their time thinking about how to care for one another. (Personal interview, August 2013)

Little "Aha!" moments like this pile upon one another and help build a different perspective, a vision of a different kind of politics, a different use of our time, our labor. What if we spent our energy trying to figure out the best way to directly care for one another, without having to insert the need to make a profit in the process?

One of the most amazing media creations of the early days of Occupy was a video entitled *Consensus*. For would-be Occupiers around the country, this video was a glimpse of the impossible. The eight-minute mini-documentary takes us on a tour through the consensus model, highlighting the philosophical principle undergirding it all: "In our movement, it's really important to have our *means* reflect the *ends* we are trying to create."[5]

We're all familiar with the question about whether the "ends" justify the "means," whether it is permissible to use deceptive or immoral tactics in order to achieve noble ends. If you accept that the ends justify the means, then you might be tempted toward a political perspective that looks for a benevolent dictator—whatever gets things done. If you disagree and think that the ends do not justify the means, then you might be tempted toward idealistic

---

5 Meerkat Media Collective 2011.

inactivity, detachment from political life altogether. The General Assembly, and Occupy as a whole, followed a path through this dilemma. The consensus process was a set of tools, of "means," to achieve an egalitarian meeting. These means were directed toward the creation of a much more ambitious "end," that of a more egalitarian society. But this grander end was itself reflected in the GA. When one experiences a few hundred near-strangers in a park making decisions collectively and taking care of one another without hierarchical leadership, it is easy to ask yourself, "What if more things were like this?"

This integration of means and ends is one of the most powerful antidotes to the pit of emptiness, which thrives in a world of means without ends. When we work in order to earn money in order to pay our bills in order to stay in our apartment in order to keep our job—when we are caught in a cycle of means, without time or energy to use our capacities in labor that responds to our knowledge or our desires—then the pit of emptiness grows. When we challenge that cycle, individually or collectively, and begin to ask how we can start creating the kind of world we want in the here and now, we light up. The GA was lighting people up.

It wasn't only in the GA, but in the everyday life of the occupation that people were experimenting with making their means reflect their ends. Occupiers were forming new relationships and performing labor that pointed them toward a different and more satisfying kind of social power. On her first day, one Occupier, Allison Nevit, wrote:

> I was impressed by the organization and thoughtfulness. The protest community has established working groups on everything from sanitation to food to media to security. . . . People are busy! It takes a lot of time and energy to coordinate feeding people, keeping things clean, attending to medical needs, managing a media center, determining land use . . . addressing community concerns, etc. The people here are taking these things seriously and with a fantastic sense of community responsibility.

Nevit added an important caveat on the difference between how it looked from the outside and how it was on the inside: "One can't

---

[6] Flank 2011, p. 46.

really feel connected to it all unless one volunteers to help out with something. As with anything, it's in the working together that you become a part of the community and get to know people and feel like a contributing member."[6]

There were attempts to make the park "sustainable," both in terms of sustaining the occupations and reducing its ecological impact. They built a grey water system to filter dishwater and bicycle powered energy generators eventually ran the media equipment. They even removed the manicured flower beds and planted edible foods. Amidst the constant activity of organizing, marching, discussing, and debating, there was also a tremendous amount of attention given to the infrastructure of the occupation so that it too could begin to reflect the kind of world occupiers wanted.

Occupy unleashed a life-altering energy for so many because occupiers actually seized space and encouraged people to live an altered life: one where they could oppose the power structures of our current political and economic regime, connect their struggle with those of others around the country and the world, experiment with organizational tools that pointed in a new direction, and labor in ways that directly responded to their needs and the needs of others. Create a situation like that, and the pit of emptiness floods with red ink.

Inside and Outside

But it looks really weird from the outside. Some people who stepped into Zuccotti Park understood and embraced this self-organizing complexity immediately. Others, not so much. One of the earliest mainstream media reports of Occupy Wall Street came from *New York Times* columnist Ginia Bellafante. It ran on the fifth day of the occupation, and was entitled "Gunning for Wall Street, With Faulty Aim." Having spent a day wandering around the park trying to figure out why they were assembled and what they hoped to accomplish, Bellafante was not impressed with what she found. She describes a completely disorganized, carnival atmosphere full of people who were too scattered to know what they were protesting about—a perception that would become the standard right-wing line to dismiss the protests in subsequent weeks. But Bellafante was not a right-wing commentator. She makes it clear in her article that she things there are serious problems with wealth inequality in America, only that the folks in the park are going about addressing them all wrong:

> The group's lack of cohesion and its apparent wish to pantomime progressivism rather than practice it knowledgeably is unsettling in the face of the challenges so many of its generation face—finding work, repaying student loans, figuring out ways to finish college when money has run out. But what were the chances that its members were going to receive the attention they so richly deserve carrying signs like "Even if the World Were to End tomorrow I'd Still Plant a Tree Today?" (Bellafante 2011a)

Perhaps it's understandable that Bellafante thought the issues involved were so serious as to deserve a more organized and disciplined mode of expression. Perhaps the few people she spoke with were not very articulate or specific about what brought them down there. But there were a lot of other signs she could have chosen, which would have evoked a different sentiment and a different understanding of the occupation: "Democracy Not Corporatocracy" would have been a good one. It is as if a cartoon image of "hippies" was the only cultural reference point Bellafante could use to understand a protest that focused on something other than polishing itself for the mainstream media. As a result, Occupy first showed up in the *New York Times* as something of a joke.

On television, however, things were a bit different. Keith Olbermann was the first national news host to cover the OWS, and his sympathies for what he took to be its central concerns were apparent from the start. Olbermann took his fellow journalists to task with barely contained outrage:

> This rhetorical question is perhaps self-answering: a protest called "Occupy Wall Street," trying to underscore and gum up the financial industry's influence on who's rich and who's not—*why wouldn't that get extensive news coverage?* . . . After five straight days of sit-ins, shouting, and even some arrests, actual North American newspaper coverage of this event, even by those who have thought it farce or failure, has been limited to one blurb in a free newspaper in Manhattan and a column in the *Toronto Star.* (Olbermann 2011)

Olbermann implied that the mainstream media itself had an interest in ignoring or downplaying the significance of a protest movement that was directly criticizing the power of corporations and financial institutions over peoples' lives. He decided to make OWS and the issue of corporate power and wealth inequality a central focus of his show, giving the occupation a national television audience. These were the two basic options mainstream journalists would choose from in covering Occupy during the coming months. Bellafante recognized the importance of the issues being raised by Occupiers, but decided to mock them for the way they raised them. Olbermann, on the other hand, recognized that those issues were his issues as well and decided he was going to promote them, essentially coming to see himself as a part of the movement, using his platform to promote the messages of the movement.

Meanwhile, Occupiers were trying to get better at relating to the press and communicating their various messages and the diversity of the participants. In an early General Assembly, the Press Relations Working Group announced:

> 10.2.2. Ten people were interviewed for news coverage. Only one of them was a woman. The 99% are not 90% men. Today at 4 p.m. there will be a media training for women or people who are not male identified. If that describes you, and you have ever felt that you had to say something to the press, but that "it's not that important," "it's probably been said," "it can wait," or "someone else can probably say it better than me"—please come to this training! (Minutes of the NYCGA 9/26/11<http:www.nycga.net/2011/09/general-assembly-minutes-926-2pm>)

Still, even with diverse voices saying why they were down there occupying Wall Street, much of what was going on simply *couldn't* be communicated or understood in sound bites or by anyone who wasn't themselves engaging with it all. Both friendly and unfriendly media kept trying to fit OWS into a conceptual box they already possessed. But something different was going on.

Some controversy was stirred by a women who stood topless in the park, but her sign captured an important message for the media that was trying to simply get a quick understanding of what was up: "*I didn't say look, I said listen.*"

Communiqués and the Principles of Solidarity

Despite her plea, and the pleas of many others, mainstream media groups did very little listening to the daily communiqués that were being issued, as well as to the first collectively authored official statement of OWS: the "Principles of Solidarity." When you read the communiqués, it's easy to understand why they weren't considered helpful to the mainstream media. The communiqués summed up the major events of the day and made some broad statements about what Occupy Wall Street was doing. On day 3, for example, one communiqué opened: "We're still here. We intend to stay until we see movements toward real change in our country and the world. This is the third communique from the 99 percent."[7] While this may have made sense to those already hoping for "real change," the mainstream media doesn't typically have a framework for dealing with this kind of vague statement.

But just as OWS wasn't about communicating its message to bankers, these communiqués were not really intended for the press—they were intended for *us*, the blossoming ninety-nine percent, the people with whom Occupiers thought their actions would resonate. On day 5, they wrote:

> You have fought all the wars, you have worked for all the bosses. You have wandered over all the countries. Have you harvested the fruits of your labors, the price of your victories? Does the past comfort you? Does the present smile on you? Does the future promise you anything? Have you found a piece of land where you can live like a human being and die like a human being? On these questions, on this argument, and on this theme, the struggle for existence, the people will speak. Join us. (p. 33)

There was even poetic toying with the media in the early communiqués, particularly around the constant media demand for a single demand. Here are selections from the fifth communiqué:

> This is the fifth communique from the 99 percent. We are occupying Wall Street.
> On September 21st, 2011, Troy Davis, an innocent man, was murdered by the State of Georgia. Troy Davis was one of the 99 percent. *Ending capital punishment is our one demand.*
> On September 21st, 2011, the richest 400 Americans owned more wealth than half of the country's population. *Ending wealth inequality is our one demand.*

---

[7] Flank 2011, p. 26.

On September 21st, 2011, four of our members were arrested on baseless charges. *Ending police intimidation is our one demand*.

On September 21st, 2011, we determined that Yahoo lied about occupywallst.org being in spam filters.[9] *Ending corporate censorship is our one demand*.

On September 21st, 2011, roughly eighty percent of Americans thought the country was on the wrong track. *Ending the modern gilded age is our one demand*.

On September 21st, 2011, roughly 15% of Americans approved of the job Congress was doing. *Ending political corruption is our one demand*.

On September 21st, 2011, roughly one sixth of Americans did not have work. *Ending joblessness is our one demand*.

On September 21st, 2011, roughly one sixth of America lived in poverty. *Ending poverty is our one demand*.

On September 21st, 2011, roughly fifty million Americans were without health insurance. *Ending health-profiteering is our one demand*.

On September 21st, 2011, America had military bases in and around one hundred and thirty out of one hundred and sixty-five countries. *Ending American imperialism is our one demand*.

On September 21st, 2011, America was at war with the world. *Ending war is our one demand*. (Flank 2011)

Corporate media outlets likely didn't know what to do with something like this. This communiquée was the first public expression of a theme that would be eventually articulated in the *Declaration of the Occupation of New York City*: we refuse to select one single problem from the whole complex of problems we perceive. But again, it's understandable that media outlets didn't know what to do with something like this. In general, they are numb to poetry.

However, once the Principles of Solidarity were ratified by consensus in the General Assembly, there existed a clear explanation of what was happening in Zuccotti. The statement articulated not only *why* they were gathered and *how* they were organizing themselves, but also why they thought it was so important to gather and organize themselves in precisely this way. Here it is in full:

On September 17th, 2011, people from all across the United States of America and the world came to protest the blatant injustices of our

---

[8] During the first week of OWS, emails sent through Yahoo mail that mentioned "occupy wall street" were not reaching their destinations.

times perpetuated by the economic and political elites. On the 17th we as individuals rose up against political disenfranchisement and social and economic injustice. We spoke out, resisted, and successfully occupied Wall Street. Today, we proudly remain in Liberty Square constituting ourselves as autonomous political beings engaged in non-violent civil-disobedience and building solidarity based on mutual respect, acceptance, and love. It is from these reclaimed grounds that we say to all Americans and to the world, Enough! How many crises does it take? **We are the 99%** and we have moved to reclaim our mortgaged future. Through a direct democratic process, we have come together as individuals and crafted these principles of solidarity, which are points of unity that include but are not limited to:

- Engaging in direct and transparent participatory democracy;
- Exercising personal and collective responsibility;
- Recognizing individuals' inherent privilege and the influence it has on all interactions;
- Redefining how labor is valued;
- The belief that education is a human right;
- Making technologies, knowledge, and culture open to all to freely access, create, modify, and distribute.[9]

We are daring to imagine a new social-political and economic alternative that offers greater possibility of equality. We are consolidating the other proposed principles of solidarity, after which demands will follow. (NYCGA 2011a)

While some of this language might be unfamiliar, the Principles of Solidarity made explicit statements about what was going on and why. At that point, it should have been the task of those in the media to understand and interpret what, for example, Occupiers meant by "redefining how labor is valued." Instead, almost every aspect of this statement was marginalized, dismissed or simply ignored by media coverage. News outlets insisted continually that they were confused or, eventually, that the protests were simply about "inequality" or "jobs." In fact, as is clearly stated, Occupiers were "daring to imagine a new social-political and economic alternative that offers greater possibility of equality." Yes, inequality was a problem: but they weren't asking the politicians to solve it for them.

For the NYCGA, and for the hundreds of the most active participants in the Occupy movement, the whole point was this "daring

---

[9] This last principle was added a few months later.

to imagine" a world built on a different set of principles—and this "imagining" was not just in their heads, but in their bodies, in their collective action. Zuccotti Park was occupied, and the people in it were bustling to create something utterly unexpected by the world: a small-scale vision of what they wanted to see in every neighborhood. They were not organizing themselves against *specific* problems with the government or the economy: they were fed up with the whole process and convinced another world is possible.

And their message was spreading. After a week, occupations in Boston, Washington DC, Chicago, and other cities were in the works. And this proliferation of occupations was getting help from an unlikely, well-funded, and highly secretive organization: the New York City Police Department.

NYPD as Public Relations Firm

It's tempting to credit the NYPD for really thrusting OWS into the media spotlight and generating massive waves of sympathy for the protestors. Perhaps Occupy would still have grown into a major event if the police had been more restrained in their actions, but as it happened, they were not.

If you were in any way exposed to television or social media during the last week of September in 2011, you probably saw images of a group of young women screaming and crying while corralled in orange netting set up by the NYPD. There had been a number of images of police abuses—hair pulling, seemingly random arrests, groping of women by cops, even straight punches thrown at peaceful protestors—but something about this scene on September 26th was unique. Anthony Bologna (soon to be known as "Tony Bologna"), a white-shirted and thus high ranking officer with the NYPD, approached the women with a face full of malice. He reached past the lower ranking, blue-shirted officers and pepper sprayed a group of women directly in their faces. They were clearly not a threat to him or anyone else, and his actions were inexplicably horrendous. Temporarily blinded and falling on the ground, the women screamed in pain, and these cries and images were circulated around the Internet and shown on nightly-news programs around the country and the world.[10]

---

[10] Mackey and McVeigh 2011.

OWS moved into the mainstream spotlight on the back of images like this, which raised the question for viewers at home: why are police in New York City beating up peaceful protestors? Why are they pepper spraying young women? From a public relations perspective, this is probably not a bad way for a social movement to debut. Hits to the OWS website skyrocketed after the images were released. More people came down to Liberty Square. And more cities around the country started planning occupations of their own.

And a week after having dismissed the Occupiers as ridiculous utopians, Bellafante wrote in the *New York Times* that the NYPD was serving as the "unintended public relations arm" of Occupy Wall Street. After a discussion of police brutality, she concluded with a complete reversal of her forecast for the occupation. Whereas earlier she had claimed it was dwindling daily, she now predicted that "the encampment in Zuccotti Park is likely to remain indefinitely." The NYPD was creating media-miracles for the Occupiers, and "at this point, any attempt on the part of the police to close things down could only result in the resurrection of Emma Goldman."[11]

On October 1st, lightning struck again, as the NYPD arrested seven hundred people on the Brooklyn Bridge. The march had been organized in part as a response to the police brutality of the previous week. There was no clear plan in advance to stop traffic on the bridge, and many that marched on it actually thought the police were leading the march into the road. Those in front, however, knew they were engaging in civil disobedience and thought they were staring down the cops with thousands of people behind them. By the time the front of the march reached the center of the bridge, the police had blocked their path both in front and behind—the march was "kettled," in protest parlance. Marc Bray was standing on the bridge's pedestrian walkway, observing the march on the street portion of the bridge below:

> . . . what really grabbed my attention was the response of the group on the roadway to police encirclement. Instead of widespread panic, someone shouted "Mic-check! Mic-check!" . . . After many sat [in response to the call], there was an attempt to hold essentially an

---

[11] Bellafante 2011b.

impromptu GA right there in the middle to calm the situation and act as a group. It didn't last long as people stood up with the start of the arrests, but that moment of group solidarity and collective action in a moment of chaos really spoke to me. It seemed to say that this wasn't just another march ending in arrests, and this wasn't just another group of protestors. In retrospect, I realized that it poked a small hole in the layers of frustration that had been gradually obscuring my optimism over the years. (Bray 2013, p. 120)

Bray would go on to become an integral part of the OWS Press Team for months after this event. What he describes here happened over and over around the country. In the midst of intense confrontations with police, Occupiers used their own forms of self-organization to maintain calm and attempt to make decisions in line with the principles they were espousing. Naturally, this aspect of the Brooklyn Bridge arrests didn't get any mainstream attention. All people heard was that seven hundred people were arrested on the bridge. But that was enough to elevate the movement into the national spotlight and introduce the world to the Occupiers and their simple, radical message: *we, you and me, who appear to be different in so many ways, we actually have something very important in common. We are the ninety-nine percent. We are being exploited, we are being manipulated, we are losing hope, and it is time for us to act.*

The Occupy Movement or a Movement of Occupations?

The sudden media focus introduced a strange tension into the budding movement. Though *Adbusters* had begun with the phrase #OccupyWallStreet as a meme, as something that was meant to spread through the networks, the phrase had been given meaning by a group of people organizing face to face, reclaiming common space to experiment with recovering the political dimension of their lives. Now it was quickly becoming a brand called "Occupy"—and it seemed like everyone was doing it or trying to figure it out. What were they saying? What did they want? Who was behind it? The media wanted answers and everyone seemed to have the same questions: "Is this a Leftist version of the Tea Party?," "How is it going to influence the

Democrats?" "Why are they talking in unison and doing those weird twinkly things?"

This conception of the Occupy movement as a potential force in mainstream politics was at odds with the prefigurative, community-based kind of organizing being practiced. From this perspective, "the Occupy movement" as a brand was covering over what was going on: a movement of occupations. People assembling in public, claiming space for a different kind of political power. They were promoting, networking, sharing experiences, and strategizing through the Internet, but there was no unified organization or thing called "Occupy."

There was no central committee, and even if there had been it would have been impossible for such a group to steer the actions of people on the ground. The people who were participating in occupations and practicing direct democracy were stubbornly attached to a process in which each of their collective decisions were painstakingly debated. There was no unified strategy that had been agreed upon, but there was a shared commitment to a process, to which many people were being newly exposed and by which they were developing a new sense of what is possible. While many were interested in finding ways to frame their message or the occupation's practices in ways the media could comprehend, many others devoted themselves to the daily operations of dealing face-to-face with others, no media necessary.

With the construction of the brand "Occupy," it became possible to "occupy" without actually participating in an occupation. But there was an upside to this: it gave people an opportunity to participate who otherwise couldn't. One of the most remarkable sites of such participation was the "We Are the 99 Percent" Tumblr page, set up by one of the members of the NYCGA. Suddenly there were hundreds of posts on it every day. The posts were heartbreaking because they provided a glimpse into the private struggles and fears of Americans burdened by debt, low-wages, and a sense of complete isolation. At the same time, the Tumblr page was deeply inspiring, because one could see people connecting their struggles up with others, realizing that their financial problems are not actually so private and personal, but are shared problems that demand collective action in response. To read through the pages is to lose your illusions about "boot-strapping" your way to the top. Over and over, we see people who played by the rules, yet still are being crushed by the system. One commentator called them "Letters of Resignation from the American Dream."[12]

One post stands out for me as expressing the kind of sentiment that moved people out of their homes and into encampments:

> I can't find my future.
>
> I looked in college. I found debt.
>
> I looked to my parents. I found debt and heartbreak.
>
> I looked to my friends. I found grief and sorrow.
>
> I looked at the land. I found MY COMMONS DESTROYED, MY LAKES AND RIVERS AND SOIL AND TREES AND BEES AND WORMS DESTROYED.
>
> I looked at my fellow humans. I found disease, debt, sorrow, dissonance, hate, greed, misery, AND NO ONE CARES ANYMORE.
>
> Well. I care. An awful lot. I'M TAKING MY FUTURE BACK (IT'S MINE)
>
> I AM THE 99% (http://wearethe99percent.tumblr.com/archive)

The confluence of debt, ecological devastation, and a sense that hope for a better future is fading fast was a prevalent combination of concerns among young people driven to the occupations—people who see the need for a complete rethinking of economic and social life. It's important to recognize that this desire to "take back the future" cannot be thought of solely in "economic" terms. It's not about "getting the economy back on track" or "increasing growth." There are other values at stake—values that don't translate into dollars or stocks. The statistical fact that the top one percent control almost forty percent of the nation's wealth is just one really effective and important illustration of how out of control inequality has become. But economic inequality is a problem not simply because of some ideological conviction that everyone should be "equal." Rather, it's a problem because such massive concentrations of wealth provide rich people with *power over the lives of others:* power to direct their labor, power to influence the opinions of those in politics, power to influence public thought and conversation through the media. In short, power to control

---

[12] Roth 2011.

discussions and decisions about the future, and thus to construct and constrain the future itself. In the political spaces of the encampments, the power to imagine and produce a different kind of future was being reclaimed.

Another World Is Happening

By the end of October, there was an Occupy group of some sort in every major city in the United States, and hundreds of smaller cities and towns. More than just a new name for old activism, what was spreading was a set of tools for organizing and tactics for protest to which most people had never been exposed. The magic of Zuccotti Park was being transported to parks and squares everywhere. Something no one thought was possible was suddenly happening: not only were people suddenly talking about inequality and corporate power, they were protesting in the streets and engaging in civil disobedience. They were trying to disrupt the smooth flow of daily life that relies upon and reproduces structural injustices like economic inequality. They were coming together and listening to one another, changing their politics, their relationships, and their worlds.

On my first night in Kiener Plaza, the encampment site of Occupy St. Louis, I had this strange feeling that I couldn't recognize. I could only describe it like this: it was as if a dormant organ had been awakened, some internal piece of my body that had never been given a chance to function properly, to secrete its juices. The feeling I was flooded with was a different kind of hope than I had ever known: a hope in our collective power, a hope in our capacity to awaken, to learn, to grow, and to act; to build a world that actually responds to our needs and our knowledge and our best desires.

After a General Assembly, I took a walk around the plaza to try to calm the exhilaration I was feeling. I walked past a pile of signs that had spent their day receiving supportive honks from passing drivers, and one caught my eye. It was a line from June Jordan's "Poem for South African Women," a line that had been picked up by Obama in his 2008 campaign and was now back with a new meaning, written on a cardboard sign at an occupation: "We are the ones we've been waiting for."

3

"It Just Came Out of Nowhere"

For many of us, the Occupy movement seemed to come out of nowhere. Around the country, those newly exposed to consensus process and to the idea of occupations thought what they were witnessing and doing was completely novel and totally spontaneous, as if all this was being improvised on the spot.

While spontaneity was certainly involved, the organizational practices and tactics of Occupy fall into a long history. It just happens to be a history most of us don't know. In large part, this is because many young people in the United States have grown up in a political context where this history is considered irrelevant. Most of us have never been a part of a public discussion in which fundamental questions about the meaning of politics and the possibilities for human society have been raised as pressing questions. Perhaps people have been exposed to such discussions in the context of a classroom or in conversation with friends, but it's safe to say that few people have had these deep political conversations in a moment when they felt like they actually matter.

Another way to put this is to say that most people in the United States see themselves as living at "the end of history"—a time when all the big questions about social, economic, and political life have been asked and answered. Though few people would actually describe things in these terms, in practice most people in the US tacitly accept this strange view. The basic structures of representative government combined with a capitalist economy (where "growth" in the economy is an unqualified good) are accepted as unquestionable premises. The only role of politics, from this perspective, is to work out the details of how best to use the representative system to make the economy grow, while coping with the problems that pop up along the way.

This wasn't always the case. For much of the twentieth century, the Soviet Union existed in the public's mind as an alternative to these assumptions about the purpose of politics and economy. This alternative was, of course, widely perceived as a nightmare: an inefficient economy backed by the strong arm of an authoritarian state that criminalized dissent and spied on its own people. Once the Soviet Union collapsed, the US-style system seemed to have no competitors. It seemed to many as if a great battle of ideas that had been driving world history—the various answers to the question of how best to organize society—had been resolved. The combination of representative government and capitalist economics would now spread around the globe without any opposition worth taking seriously. Any opposition would be conceived as either a relic from the past or as irrational terrorism. For many, there is no conceivable opposition to the status quo that is worth dignifying with a response.

But not everyone has been living at the end of history. Throughout the twentieth century, plenty of people were opposed to the forms of politics practiced by *both* the US *and* the USSR. This opposition has a whole history of experimentation, of intervention, and of opposition that is more or less absent from mainstream memory. The mainstream US media and discourse are completely ignorant of their own radical tradition. "Radical" here means any thought and action that attempts to go to the *root* of things, to raise basic questions about social, political, and economic life. The organizational forms that came to the surface in Occupy Wall Street were the fruits of this long legacy of thought and experimentation.

The idea of "the end of history" relies upon the assumption that there is *a* history—one grand story of the human race that can be brought to its natural conclusion. This idea of history has been particularly well suited for colonial powers, which dismiss those they conquer as 'backward' and often frame their invasions as efforts to bring historical 'progress' to those left out of the grand narrative. In fact, there are many *histories*—different stories that sometimes interweave and intersect. For this reason, I use a metaphor in this chapter of "historical threads" to offer a tour through some of the most important histories that the Occupy movement wove together in public. I focus on the following "threads":

1. **Participatory Democracy,**

2. **Direct Action,**

3. **Prefigurative Politics,** and

4. **Formal Consensus Process.**

In the common spaces reclaimed by occupations, each of these often overlapping histories were brought together through collective action. Those who have refused to live at the end of history have been hard at work creating new possible futures. Before we start tracing these threads, however, we need to look at an idea most of us think we understand: democracy.

The Embattled Meaning of "Democracy"

. . . democracy is everywhere approved, though its true meaning is almost nowhere understood.

—RUSSELL L. HANSON

The word "democracy" comes from the Greek *demokratia,* which is usually translated as "rule by the people." But in Greek, the word *demos* referred not merely to "the people," but "quite specifically to 'common people' with little or no economic independence."[1] In the ancient city of Athens, democracy meant rule by the everyday people, by those men who were not from aristocratic backgrounds. Further, it meant these people ruled by popular assembly, by directly speaking about and voting on the decisions of government, without electing representatives to stand in their place. Today, the organizational structure that most of us associate with democracy is one in which elected representatives create laws, which are then enforced by a network of police and courts. Many people are surprised to learn that this association of democracy with "elected representatives" is both a recent historical development, and one that is in exact opposition to the classical meaning of democracy.

It's important not to idealize Athens: women, slaves, and foreigners were excluded from citizenship, and thus not allowed to

---

[1] Hanson 1989, p. 71.

participate. Because of this, it might serve us well to call ancient Athens not a 'democracy'—since many of the everyday, common people had no say—but a *nativist patriarchy,* a rule by native-born men. Nevertheless, Athens illustrates a conception of governance that does not rely upon elected representatives or individual rulers, but is founded on the principle that all citizens have the right to direct participation in the decisions that govern their lives. The principle was democratic, even though they had a narrow concept of who counted as a "citizen" which led to an undemocratic practice, one based on nativism and patriarchy.

When the term "democracy" was rediscovered by those in what we now call Europe in the sixteenth century C.E., it was similarly used to describe direct governance by popular assembly, "the rule of the commonaltie." During the upheavals of that period—the Protestant Reformation and the Peasant Wars, in which commoners, those who worked the land, rebelled against the Church, Lords, and Monarchies—the idea of rule by the common people was deeply appealing to many. Some of these common people fled the power structures of Europe and, when they arrived in a New Land, they created a "democracie." Thus the first modern constitution to use the term was that of the colony of Rhode Island in 1641:

> It is ordered and unanimously agreed upon, that the Government which this Bodie Politick doth attend unto in this Island, and the Jurisdiction thereof, in favour of our Prince is a DEMOCRACIE, or Popular Government; that is to say, *It is in the Powre of the Body of Freemen orderly assembled, or the major part of them, to make or constitute Just Lawes,* by which they will be regulated, and to depute from among themselves such Ministers as shall see them faithfully executed between Man and Man. (<http://avalon.law.yale.edu/17th_century/ri02.asp> italics added)

The term "democracy" was here consistent with its Greek use: an assembly of the majority of free men. It similarly excluded women and the people whose lands the colonizers had usurped. Still, it was called a "democracy" because a collective assembly was considered to be the only source of "Just Laws."

If democracy had always meant government by direct participation of all or most citizens, and was explicitly opposed to government by elected representatives, how did "democracy" come to be associated with "representation"? Like every story in the history of ideas, this is a complex one. But one core consideration is this: when a group of people who have been trapped by debt and rent, made to work for others their whole lives get together and start making decisions about how society should be organized, one of the first things to come into question is how wealth is distributed. Why do some people own the land, while others have to work it? Why do some people own the houses, while others pay them to live there? The question of why property is unequally distributed quickly arises.

For the architects of the US Constitution, this was unacceptable. James Madison, one of the authors of the influential *Federalist Papers,* the problem with democracy was that assemblies broke down due to "factions," and "the most common and durable source of factions" is the "various and unequal distribution of property." According to Madison, "those who hold and those who are without property have ever formed distinct interests in society." He asserts that these disparities in wealth and property "cannot be removed," since such divisions are "sown into the nature of man."

This is, of course, untrue. There have been myriad human societies that hold social wealth in common. Madison himself likely knew this, since he was probably familiar with the customs of Native American societies, but he ignored their forms of social organization because of the racist belief that these people were "savages" who had nothing important to contribute to the discussion about social and political life. Similarly, anything that disrupted or altered the laws of private property was perceived as savage, chaotic, or disorderly. For those who designed the representative system, this "disorder" was the main risk of democracy. Thus, for Madison, "the regulation of these interfering interests — the conflict between haves and have-nots—forms the principle task of modern legislation." In other words, rather than address the source of factions in assemblies by redistributing property, the aim of "modern legislation" is to maintain the unequal distribution of wealth and manage the consequences of those conflicting interests. Madison and his fellow authors of the *Federalist Papers* were explicit that this was an anti-democratic position.

So if the framers of the US Constitution were anti-democratic, in favor of a government by elected representatives which they *con-trasted* with democracy, how did the US come to be called a "democracy"? While there was on occasion expressed the idea that the representative system was a way of organizing a democracy that remained "stable" (which is to say, that kept the relations of property unchanged), the word did not come to be used as identical with electoral process until about fifty years after the US Constitution. According to Graeber:

> It was between 1830 and 1850 that politicians in the United States and France began to identify themselves as democrats and to use *democracy* to designate the electoral regime, even though no constitutional change or transformation of the decision-making process warranted this change in name. The shift in meaning first occurred in the United States. Andrew Jackson was the first presidential candidate to present himself as a democrat, a label by which he meant he would defend the interests of the little people. (Graeber 2013, pp. 169–170)

As political scientist Francis Dupuis-Deris puts it, "Jackson and his allies were well aware that their use of *democracy* was akin to what would today be called political marketing." Graeber puts it more bluntly: "it was basically a cynical ploy, but it was wildly successful—so much so that within ten years' time all candidates of all political parties were referring to themselves as 'democrats'" (p. 170).

Basically, this was a public relations scheme. Calvin Colton was one conservative author who promoted this scheme. For Colton, "the great struggle in America, and that on which the fate of the Republic is suspended, is between the Constitution and Democracy." He argued that the Constitution "was framed by men who foresaw the tendency of the public mind towards democracy, and who purposely constructed this instrument to arrest the downward progress." In 1839, Colton published an anonymous essay called *A Voice from America to England,* "in which he cynically argued that any American party, regardless of whether its principles were radical or conservative, was well advised to use the rhetoric of democracy to sell its cause to voters."[2]

This rhetoric caught on and has persisted to this day. In fact, the term has become so closely associated with the procedure of electing representatives that whenever popular assemblies turn up—as they do from time to time, for example, in radical social movements—these expressions of the democracy are often

---

[2] Hanson 1989, p. 79.

referred to as *anarchy*. The technical term used to describe government by assembly is "direct democracy," and this conception of democracy is generally promoted by anarchists. Many anarchists do not like to use the word "democracy" because of its close association with electoral politics. Historically and conceptually, though, there is a close association between anarchists and those who are in favor of government by popular assembly in which all are able to participate.

Thread #1: Participatory Democracy

Throughout the twentieth century, there is a strand of politics in which the idea of democracy is not considered identical with the representative system: that of participatory democracy. This tradition has been developed largely in and through grassroots social movements. Recall that in Occupy Wall Street's "Principles of Solidarity," the New York group stated a commitment to "direct and transparent participatory democracy." This signaled that the Occupiers were inheritors of this tradition.

The term "participatory democracy" was coined by the philosopher Arthur Saul Kaufmann back in the 1960s. Kaufmann was a scholar of the thought of American philosopher John Dewey, who understood democracy as a way of life, and not as not a particular system of electoral government. For Dewey, democracy is a set of cultural habits that presume individuals and communities capable of collectively inquiring into and solving their own problems. Indeed, Dewey was convinced that promoting democracy and promoting popular education were one and the same project, since free inquiry and the intelligent change of collective life demanded a democratic faith and freedom to experiment, both individually and collectively. For Dewey:

> Democracy is a way of life controlled by a working faith in the possibilities of human nature. Belief in the Common Man is a familiar article in the democratic creed. That belief is without basis and significance save as it means faith in the potentialities of human nature as that nature is exhibited in every human being irrespective of race, color, sex, birth and family, of material or cultural wealth. (Dewey 1939)

In the early 1960s, Kaufmann was teaching at the University of Michigan. A number of his students, influenced both by his

Deweyan conception of participatory democracy and by their participation in the Civil Rights movement, came to author one of the most influential radical political pamphlets in American history: *The Port Huron Statement* of Students for a Democratic Society (SDS).[3]

This statement by SDS launched the student movements of the Sixties, which helped in the desegregation of blacks and whites, organized against the Vietnam War, fought for women's liberation, and had an immeasurable impact in shaping the cultural climate of subsequent generations. The *Port Huron Statement*, advocates the following:

> We would replace power rooted in possession, privilege, or circumstance by power and uniqueness rooted in love, reflectiveness, reason, and creativity. As a social system, we seek the establishment of a democracy of individual participation, governed by two central aims: that the individual share in those social decisions determining the quality and direction of his life; that society be organized to encourage independence in men and provide the media for their common participation. ("Values," in Students for a Democratic Society 1962)

These aims required a reconsideration of the nature of politics. Today, our representative politics is predominantly *adversarial*. In America, there are two parties vying for power, which can only be achieved when there is relative cohesion within the party around a particular platform. These decisions are made in Washington DC, or in state capitols around the country, and they are hashed out for the most part by elected representatives and the various lobbyists the representatives must constantly turn to for financial support. In contrast to this system, SDS suggested the following principles to serve as the basis of political life:

- **that decision-making of basic social consequence be carried on by public groupings;**

- **that politics be seen . . . as the art of collectively creating an acceptable pattern of social relations;**

- **that politics has the function of bringing people out of isolation and into community, thus being a necessary, though not sufficient, means of finding meaning in personal life;**

---

[3] Hayden 2012.

- that the political order should serve to clarify problems in a way instrumental to their solution; it should provide outlets for the expression of personal grievance and aspiration; opposing views should be organized so as to illuminate choices and facilitate the attainment of goals; channels should be commonly available to related men to knowledge and to power so that private problems—from bad recreation facilities to personal alienation—are formulated as general issues.

Put simply, for SDS, politics was not reserved for politicians. The concept of participatory democracy was a call for people to make political engagement an active and meaningful part of their own lives. It was a place to be drawn out of our own private concerns and find strength and affinity with others sharing similar conditions, and to work together to alter those conditions.

The concept of participatory democracy can be seen as the recovery of the historical meaning of democracy in a new context. Though there was not the specific emphasis on the assembly form, there was the insistence that "rule by the people" did not simply mean the rule of elected representatives.

But the SDSers were predominantly white, predominantly middle-class college students. While no doubt Kaufmann was a good professor and expositor of the idea of participatory democracy, that can't possibly account for the tremendous appeal and influence it had. It was more likely their experience as allies in the Civil Rights movement that lent practical credibility to the idea of participatory democracy.

Many SDSers were influenced by the struggles to desegregate the Southern states, participating in "Freedom Rides," sit-ins, and other de-segregation efforts organized by the Student Non-violent Coordinating Committee (or SNCC, pronounced "snick"). While there were many different forms of organization involved in the Civil Rights struggle, mainstream historical memory tends to emphasize the charismatic leadership of figures such as Martin Luther King, Jr. and, less often, Malcom X. As different as these two leaders were, they both shared in common the reliance on structures of disciplined, top-down authority. But there were very important trends within the Civil Rights movement that were critical of this kind of leadership. Looking back at that movement with an interest in understanding the kind of participatory democracy emphasized by Occupiers, another figure stands out as more influential: Ella Baker.

Trained as a labor movement activist at the Highlander Folk School, Baker described her background role in the movement in this way: "You didn't see me on television, you didn't see news stories about me. The kind of role I tried to play was to pick up pieces or put together pieces out of which I hoped organization might come. My theory is, strong people don't need strong leaders."[4] This conviction was integral to understanding the participatory democracy that informed Baker's life of activism, and which deeply influenced a whole generation of black and white activists. There were three primary and interrelated directives for her activism that came out of the commitment to participatory democracy: *grassroots organizing*, a *minimization of hierarchy*, and *direct action*.

Grassroots is a word that is a bit over-used today. Because of the strong appeal it has had in previous social movements, many mainstream, hierarchical political organizations use it as a public relations gesture. For Ella Baker, grassroots organizing came out of a conviction that "in the long run [the people] themselves are the only protection they have against violence or injustice. . . . People have to be made to understand they cannot look for salvation anywhere but to themselves." Building grassroots networks meant building communities of mutual support that allowed people to rely on local relationships to address local problems, and to build reliable networks of activists to challenge larger scale problems.

Baker's emphasis on minimizing hierarchy in organizing was not a simple dismissal of leadership, but rather a rethinking of it. If standard models of leadership create a leader-centered group, a group of people that look to one in a privileged position for direction in thinking and, ultimately, permission to act, Baker aimed to build organizations that practiced "group centered leadership." As would be seen decades later in Occupy Wall Street, Baker "emphasized the role of the leader as facilitator, as someone who brings out the potential in others, rather than a person who commands respect and a following as a result of charisma or status." Even in Baker's day, she could observe the media's tendency to elevate a social movement leader into a celebrity and the pitfalls that came with such a process:

---

[4] Quoted in Mueller 1993, p. 51.

I have always felt it a handicap for oppressed peoples to depend too largely upon a leader, because unfortunately in our culture, the charismatic leader usually becomes a leader because he has found a spot in the public limelight. It usually means he has been touted through the public media, which means that the media made him, and the media may undo him.

And beyond this vulnerability to the establishment media, whose interests are ultimately not consonant with the movements they portray, there is the classic problem of leadership "going to one's head":

There is also the danger in our culture that . . . such a person gets to the point of believing that he *is* the movement. Such people get so involved with playing the game of being important that they exhaust themselves and their time, and they don't do the work of actually organizing people. (p. 64)

The emphasis on participatory democracy in organizing by activists like Ella Baker and others is largely absent from mainstream accounts of the Civil Rights struggle. Such a gap in the story is not only unfortunate because it neglects the kind of slow, patient, on-the-ground work that built the communities behind that movement, it is also dangerous. If we accept the mainstream version of the Civil Rights struggle as initiated and carried through by charismatic leaders, then we will be more likely to simply wait for a charismatic leader to bring about change in our own day. In short, we will be mistakenly led to believe that strong leaders are the only way change happens. If we are unfamiliar with the role participatory democracy has played in past social movements, we will be more likely to dismiss the Occupy movement, and to assume that people are going about changing the world all wrong. This widespread impression is largely born from an ignorance of how the world has actually been changed in the past.

Historical Thread #2: Direct Action

Participants in the Occupy Movement saw the tactic of occupation as a form of 'direct action'. The broadest way to define "direct action" can be found in Voltairine de Cleyre's famous essay on the subject.[5]

---

[5] Voltairine de Cleyre (1866–1912) was an American anarchist and feminist who wrote a number of influential essays and poems.

For de Cleyre, a person or group engages in direct action every time one attempts to solve a problem in voluntary co-operation with others and without seeking permission from an authority:

> Every person who ever thought he had a right to assert, and went boldly and asserted it, himself, or jointly with others that shared his conviction, was a direct actionist. . . . Every person who ever had a plan to do anything, and went and did it, or who laid his plan before others, and won their cooperation to do it with him, without going to external authorities to please do the thing for them, was a direct actionist. All co-operative experiments are essentially direct action. (de Cleyre 1912)

In this very broad sense, pretty much anything can count as direct action *except* passing the ability to solve problems off to others, for example elected representatives.

De Cleyre is writing in 1912, at a time when the term has become associated in the popular mind with "forcible attacks on life and property." This definition was being used to turn public sentiment against the labor movement, particularly the International Workers of the World (IWW), also known as the the Wobblies. The Wobblies were famous, among other things, for their slogan that "direct action gets the goods"—that it was only through workers directly stopping or taking control over their workplaces, and not through electing candidates to office, that their material conditions (the goods they have access to) would improve. This was naturally a threat to those in power, and they fought back by attempting to paint the Wobblies and those who espoused direct action as unpatriotic and criminal. De Cleyre wanted to show, first, that this kind of behavior—the attempt to directly confront those who have power over you—is the most normal thing in the world, and second, that patriotic Americans sing the praises of direct actionists of the past (for example, those who participated in what we now call the "Boston Tea Party," a riot that destroyed private property).

When activists today use the term "direct action," they are generally not using it in the broad sense defined by de Cleyre. A more specific meaning of the term was well defined by Dr. Martin Luther King Jr. in his "Letter from a Birmingham City Jail." Discussing the nonviolent direct action of Gandhi, King argues that when we engage in direct action to resist injustice, we "present our very bodies as a means of laying our case before the conscience of the community." Where words and negotiation fail, according to King, nonviolent direct action becomes necessary.

It is important to understand what King thinks such direct action has the power to do: it aims to "create such a crisis and foster such a tension that a community which has constantly refused to negotiate is forced to confront the issue. It seeks so to dramatize the issue that it can no longer be ignored." In the South prior to the Civil Rights movement, segregation was a part of everyday life—it was not up for discussion, and, in most cases, it was simply taken for granted as "the way things are." The acts of direct action that sparked this movement, from the lunch-counter sit-ins to Rosa Parks's refusal to give up her seat on a Birmingham bus, were attempts to disrupt the everyday reality of life in America, because the orderly functioning of that everyday reality was itself unjust. This was perceived by many white people as extremely threatening, creating, as King hoped it would, a crisis that required the injustice of segregation to be examined. Direct action, in this context, is an attempt to *foster a crisis of conscience within an unjust society* through the interruption of the everyday social order that those engaging in the action have judged to be unjust.

There is another way to describe direct action, which may be helpful in order to hold both the definition from de Cleyre and from King together in our minds at once. This comes from David Graeber: "in its essence direct action is the insistence, when faced with structures of unjust authority, on acting as if one is already free."[6] For Graeber, we engage in direct action when we ask ourselves what the best way to live would be, and then proceed to live that way, regardless of what side of the law that puts us on. This may lead to grand gestures that create crises of conscience in the wider public, it may lead to acts of subversion that are only recognized by a few, or it may go completely unnoticed (that is, we might engage in direct action all the time without thinking of it as such).

The Occupy movement took direct action with the tactic of occupation, as a way of seizing space in which participants could "act as if they were already free." In those reclaimed spaces, they drew upon the tradition of direct, participatory democracy. It was *direct*, because each individual spoke only for themselves and questions

---

[6] Graeber 2009, p. 203.

about how to reorganize our political lives were directed to one another, not to those in power; it was participatory, because its structures were open to anyone who devoted the time to help create them. Occupy wove together in public a concept of democracy that, for many, has been buried in history, with an ethos of direct action.

Historical Thread #3: Prefigurative Politics

A third important historical thread that influenced the Occupy movement is the idea of *prefigurative politics*. This is a political strategy that demands that we not separate our means from our ends. If we want to create a democratic society that overcomes the oppressive relations of this one, then the changes we want to see should be reflected in the way we organize ourselves to change the world.

Since at least the 1960s, radicals have been experimenting with ways of modeling in their own organizing the kinds of social relations they ultimately want to see in the wider world—relations free from racism, sexism, classism, heterosexism, and other forms of oppression and hierarchy that we want to see changed. It must be said immediately: this is a long and difficult process, one that demands a willingness to challenge our own assumptions about what counts as "political" activity. The personal work of recognizing how one is privileged from their race, class, gender, or sexual background (for example, the privilege afforded to being a straight, white, middle-class man in our society) becomes an integral component of the political work of struggling for justice. Prefigurative politics is a form of direct action: it is about struggling to create the kinds of relationships we think we would have in a world free from oppression.

This political strategy became central to many groups in the New Left—the student-led movement of the 1960s—but it has changed dramatically since then. At that point, prefigurative politics was directed mostly against hierarchical leadership structures, and even against the leadership of radical organizations like SDS. Like many organizations, there were drastic differences between the experience and aims of those in positions of power versus those at the margins. According to many in the SDS leadership, the New Left failed to create a politically effective revolutionary movement because it was unable to create sustained organizational structures, and so its base got diverted into alternative "culture" rather than getting into the rough and tumble of politics. But according to New Left historian Winnie Breines, such a criticism misses the key point of what was really going on:

> Prefigurative politics was based on suspicion of hierarchy, leadership, and the concentration of power. The movement was not unconsciously unruly and undisciplined. Rather it was experimenting with antihierarchical organizational forms. Prefigurative politics was what was new about the new left. (Breines 1981, p. 5)

What appeared from the outside as unruly and apolitical were, from this perspective, deeply political acts of experimentation, which have yielded tremendous insights into the nature of oppression over the last few decades. If the aim is to create a radically democratic society, one in which participation is as wide and as deep as possible, then prefigurative politics is a powerful way to begin the process of understanding what that might be like—and that many of the challenges to its creation lay not just in the large, powerful institutions, but in our everyday habits of privilege: whose perspectives do we listen to, and why? Who gets ignored? Who has the ability to participate in struggle and who doesn't? In a nutshell, the strategy of prefigurative politics can be summed up in the old saw: the ends do not justify the means. If we accept that, then we're going to have to struggle to allow our ends (a society free from oppression) to be reflected within our means.

Reflecting on experiments in prefigurative politics and the resistance to creating organized "structures" in the women's movement, in 1970 feminist activist Jo Freeman wrote a widely-read and still inflential essay entitled "The Tyranny of Structurelessness." In that essay, Freeman argued that women's groups that claimed to be without any hierarchy in fact created informal hierarchies of cliques, friendships, and influential individuals. Because the groups were "officially" without any hierarchies, the actual power dynamics were more difficult to identify, to challenge, or to hold accountable. Freeman argued that so-called "'structurelessness' becomes a way of masking power," because "the rules of how decisions are made are known only to a few and awareness of power is curtailed by those who know the rules, as long as the structure of the group is informal." Freeman's suggestion was not to give up on prefigurative politics nor on participatory democracy, but rather to recognize that there was no such thing as "structurelessness." There are either explicitly adopted formal structures or implicitly influential, informal structures. Between these options, democratic values require that "the rules of decision-making must be open and available to everyone, and this only happen if they are formalized."[7]

Historical Thread #4: Formal Consensus Process

The consensus process used by the Occupy movement was developed in part as a response to the kind of critique posed by Freeman. It is both a formal structure that makes the rules of decision-making available to all. Though it was unknown to most radical groups in 1970 when Freeman was writing, formal consensus processes have been used by Quakers for generations.

While there are drawbacks associated with consensus, it does avoid some of the important problems with votes and surveys. Posing a question as either "yes" or "no," votes and surveys simply measure people's current opinions, without engaging them in a creative process of generating new proposals and potentially changing their views through discussion. Rather than being an active process of community creation, they end up drawing battle lines. Further, the consensus process adopts the key points of Ella Baker's participatory democracy, emphasizing not the power of leaders or even selected spokespeople, but promoting the concept of "leader as facilitator."

The formal consensus process was introduced into contemporary social movements by anarchist Quakers working with a group called Movement for a New Society. The process fit in with a strategy for nonviolent revolution—radical transformation of society that was based not on seizing state power (as many revolutionary socialist movements had previously attempted), but on creating a living alternative community from the bottom-up:

> Rather than a cataclysmic seizure of power, they [Movement for a New Society] proposed the continual creation and elaboration of new institutions, based on new, non-alienating modes of interaction— institutions that could be considered 'prefigurative' insofar as they provided a foretaste of what a truly democratic society might be like.

---

[7] Freeman 1970.

Such prefigurative institutions could gradually replace the existing social order. (Graeber 2009, p. 235)

While the long-term aims of this strategy are an open question, Graeber's own experience as described in his book *Direct Action: An Ethnography*—and most people's experience in the Occupy movement—attest to the power of these processes in communicating such a "foretaste." The *Consensus* video mentioned in Chapter 2 was meant not just to describe the techniques of the process, but to give viewers a sense of how those participating in it were coming to think and feel about the experiment they were engaged in. As one speaker puts it,

> Because I know what it's like when somebody honors my viewpoint when it comes from an unpopular place, I rejoice in the opportunity to honor somebody else's very different viewpoint. And there have been some decisions made that maybe I don't agree with. But because I was part of the process and because I saw how it was made and I saw how good the intentions were, I honor the decision even if I don't agree with it. (Meerkat Media Collective 2011)

Throughout the video and in occupations that were experimenting with consensus process around the country, there is this mood that is often described as "religious." There is good reason for this: consensus was a *spiritual practice* for the Quakers. It was both a way to make decisions, and a form of worship. The idea is that the community would gather in order to discern what decision reflected God's will. This is done *not* through listening to a priest or some other leader interpret the scripture, but through quiet reflection in which any member of the congregation is free to speak if they truly believe they are moved by "the spirit" to do so. The guiding assumption is that the will of God will be what's best for all members of the community, and that the concerns raised by any member—when they come from a place of true reflection on what is best for all—may potentially be inspired guidance of the divine.

Now we don't need to accept all of that in order to be moved by the dynamics of a consensus process. But we don't need to dismiss it either. We might even entertain the idea that such a religious practice, grounded in the experience of participants, is actually another way of describing the same political concerns that are often discussed in secular terms. When those of us more inclined toward secular language speak of "the will of the people," we should note that "the people" is an abstraction that no one has ever encountered in experience. Perhaps religious people of the past were using the word "God" to stand in for "the loving, peaceful, just community," and attempts to "discern the will of God" were actually attempts to figure out what was demanded of individuals and the group in order to bring that community into existence. In *Direct Action*, Graeber flirts with a similar idea after an old Quaker points out to him that meetings are not conversations, but rather sacred events:

> I reflected for a moment . . . whether there was some significance to the fact that the 'process' anarchists are so obsessed with is always, elsewhere, seen as partaking as the sacred. Creating accord is the creation of society. Society is god. Or, perhaps, god is our capacity to create society. Consensus is therefore a ritual of sacrifice, the sacrifice of egoism, where the act brings into being that very god. (Graeber 2009, pp. 129–130)

Such concerns may seem unrelated to the Occupy movement, but they are not. If we are to understand both the radical transformation of experience as well as the (sometimes contentious and deeply irrational) attachment that Occupiers felt to their process, we have to consider the fact that participation in such a process responded to a sense of alienation and desire that went deeper than mere "politics." It went to the root of what it means to share a world with others.

One of the first large-scale experimentations in prefigurative politics with formal consensus process was by a group called the Clamshell Alliance, a network of affinity groups organizing against the construction of nuclear power plants during the 1970s and early 1980s. An "affinity group" is a small group of activists who know and trust each other enough to plan actions independently and work together in high-stress situations. The "Clams" organized a series of occupations of sites on which state and corporate officials planned to build nuclear power plants. This movement is largely erased from mainstream memory, but was very influential both for putting the issue of the dangers of nuclear power on the map and subsequently stopping the progress of the industry, as well as for their inspiring commitment to prefigurative, democratic political organizing.

The "Clams" were a national network of affinity groups operating with consensus-based direct democratic practices in order to engage in coordinated direct action. The most famous of their actions was an occupation of a proposed nuclear power site in Seabrook, New Hampshire, in 1977. The occupation had over two thousand participants, 1,414 of whom were arrested for engaging in non-violent civil disobedience.[8]

Significantly, the Clams refused to break with their consensus-based, democratic processes even once they were arrested. Although they were packed into the local armory for two weeks, the practices they had developed in order to engage in direct action allowed the Clams to continue their prefigurative practice while imprisoned:

> "The authorities were always coming in and saying we had to make some decision now," Meg Simonds recalled. "We would say, that's not enough time. We're going to use our process. That they had to allow us to do what we wanted. The officers said, 'We want to talk to your leader.' We said no, we have a committee of two men and two women, which will rotate daily; that's who will speak with you. The first time we said it the officers walked out. But several hours later they came back and said okay." (Elizabeth Boardman, quoted in Epstein 1991)

After this initial triumph of an insistence on democratic practices in the face of the authorities, the imprisoned activists began organizing workshops and support groups among one another. "One group was singing, another gave lessons in journal writing. We were as busy and organized as you please, running around and taking our lessons" (p. 68). This powerful demonstration of self-organization and its capacity to forge a community of resistance even in conditions of imprisonment managed to become a media event in itself that drew even more attention than the issue of nuclear power. In the coverage of the Seabrook occupation and the activists' imprisonment, "there was likely to be one paragraph about nuclear power in thousands of inches of coverage."

It might seem, then, that "the process" and direct democratic aspect of the action was a "distraction" from the core issue of

---

[8] Epstein 1991.

nuclear power. But that is not how many Clams saw it. Reflecting on the experience in 2013, some Clams affirmed that creating a media spectacle in which a different form of human organizing and decision making could be shown as effective was just as important to them as resisting nuclear power. If such modes of democratic decision making were more widespread and powerful, the Clams thought, nuclear power would be off the table because of the dangers it posed. Nuclear power was being pursued because corporate interests stood to profit and because those who suffered the most risk were politically impotent.

For the Clamshell Alliance, the growth of the nuclear power industry was connected with a more fundamental political concern for democracy. Some former Clams described their contribution in this way:

> Other factors—including legal challenges and serious accidents at Chernobyl and Three Mile Island—contributed to a suspension of nuclear power plant construction in the U.S. But it was the Clamshell's effective and inspiring exercise in grassroots democracy that made nuclear power a widely debated public issue. Without that debate, a serious imbalance in power around the issue of atomic energy would not have been addressed. In fact, the Clamshell was born out of frustration with a lack of democracy around nuclear power; frustration with nuclear regulators who dozed during public hearings; and with official ignoring of the voters of Seabrook who repeatedly opposed the plant. (To the Village Square 2006)

Social movement historian Barbara Epstein credits the Clamshell Alliance with being "the first important political expression of an anarchist/countercultural tendency that emerged from the movements of the sixties and flowered in the seventies." While they were successful in having contributed to the movement that stopped the construction of new power plants, they also succeeded in contributing to the process of democratic experimentation in social movements. For Epstein,

> The greatest contribution of the Clamshell [Alliance] . . . lay not in containing the growth of the nuclear power industry, but in the creation of a mass movement based on nonviolent direct action and infused with a vision of a better world, which it attempted to prefigure in its own practice. (Epstein 1991, p. 59)

The Clamshell Alliance, with its emphasis on formal consensus process as a means for realizing a participatory democracy, combined with the act of occupation as a means of direct action, is a clear predecessor of the Occupy movement.

The Zapatistas

Arguably the most inspirational social movement in recent history for those promoting prefigurative politics, direct action, and direct democracy has been that of the Zapatistas—an armed indigenous uprising in Southern Mexico that has strategically engaged with the global media as a means of declaring and maintaining an autonomous region in which people practice a form of direct democracy rooted in their Mayan cultural practices. The Zapatistas and their masked spokesperson Subcomandante Marcos have been an inspiration to people around the world because they represent a living alternative to the global neoliberal economy. Rooted in the wisdom tradition and governing practices of a people who have been resisting colonialism for five hundred years, the Zapatistas rose up as a people who had been written off by those in power.

On January 1st, 1994, the North American Free Trade Agreement (NAFTA) went into effect. Trade agreements like this are a cornerstone of neoliberalism. They allow for corporate products and cash to flow across borders with as few restrictions as possible, resulting in outsourcing of production to places where labor is cheaper. NAFTA played a role in the shipping of US-based industrial production to Mexico, resulting in job-losses in the US. Further, it made it easier to flood Mexican markets with US-grown corn, creating a situation where it is often cheaper for Mexicans to buy corn grown in the US than from farms in their own area. This has devastated many Mexican agricultural communities and has played a role in the mass immigration of Mexicans to the United States without documentation.

Free Trade Agreements are often negotiated behind closed-doors by corporate lawyers and governments interested in serving corporate interests. Countries that are signatories to such agreements must then adjust their domestic laws in order to fit the terms that have been agreed upon. In the case of NAFTA, one of the terms insisted upon by the corporations and government agencies involved in drafting it was the elimination of Article 27 of the

Mexican Constitution. Emiliano Zapata, one of the leaders of the Mexican Revolution (1910–1920), had written into the constitution a provision for the protection of communally held indigenous land. This meant that indigenous communities held their land in common (in an *ejido*), and no individual member could sell it off to an outside power (such as a transnational corporation) without the consent of the whole group. NAFTA threatened to destroy this constitutional safeguard that protected Mayan communities. This meant that communities in Chiapas would no longer be able to practice their traditional ways of production and forms of social organization. Like so many indigenous peoples around the world, they would be displaced from their land and likely forced to migrate to city slums.

So on the day NAFTA went into effect, thousands of people of Chiapas said "Ya Basta!"—*enough already!* They seized public squares and engaged in a four-day-long armed insurrection declaring a region with around five million inhabitants to be an autonomous zone no longer subject to the rule of the Mexican government. There was so much popular support for their cause around Mexico that they were able to call a cease-fire and hold their ground. Though there have been many attacks upon them, and the Mexican government has violated a number of agreements they made with the Zapatistas, they fought for their survival and have managed to maintain a network of autonomous indigenous communities for two decades.

It's hard to imagine they could have done this without the careful media work of people around the world and Subcomandante Marcos. Not of indigenous descent, Marcos is rumored to have been an academic and radical from urban Mexico, who moved to Chiapas and became committed to aiding the indigenous struggle to defend the rural people's form of life from the onslaught of neoliberal globalization. Marcos's face has never been caught on camera, because Zapatistas cover their faces with either black masks or bandanas when they are around cameras. They do this both for protection—so that they are less easily targeted by the Mexican government—and also for symbolic reasons. According to journalist Naomi Klein, one of the many influential activists inspired by the Zapatista movement,

> Marcos, the quintessential anti-leader, insists that his black mask is a mirror so that "Marcos is gay in San Francisco, black in South Africa,

an Asian in Europe, a Chicano in San Ysidro, an anarchist in Spain, a Palestinian in Israel, a Mayan Indian on the streets of San Cristobal, a Jew in Germany, a Gypsy in Poland, a Mohawk in Quebec, a pacifist in Bosnia, a single woman on the Metro at 10 P.M., a peasant without land, a gang member in the slums, an unemployed worker, an unhappy student, and, of course, a Zapatista in the mountains."

"In other words," Klein continues "he is simply us: we are the leader we've been looking for."[9]

The black mask quickly became a worldwide symbol of Zapatista resistance. Another Zapatista, Subcomandante Ana Maria describes the importance of the black mask in this way:

Behind our black mask, behind our armed voice, behind our unnamable name, behind what you see of us, behind this we are you. Behind this we are the same simple and ordinary men and women that are repeated in all races, painted in all colors, speak in all languages, and live in all places. Behind this we are you, brothers and sisters of all races. (Eichert et al. 1999)

The mask is both a mirror and a way of symbolically rejecting the narrowness of "identity politics," which focuses on achieving political or material gains for a particular oppressed group. The Zapatistas, though they are mostly Mayans resisting neoliberalism, are inviting people around the world to connect their struggles with their own in order to confront and challenge a global economic and military system.

The Zapatistas also engage in a form of direct democracy and prefigurative politics. Not only "building a new world in the shell of the old"—a classic slogan of the radical labor movement—the Zapatistas are rescuing features of the *older* world for the sake of constructing a new one in territory reclaimed from the current order. This strategy, like that of the Quaker-inspired movements in America, seeks a revolution, not by seizing the power of the state, but by making it irrelevant.

At certain points in their discussions with the Mexican government, the Zapatistas gave the world a lesson in the different pace of democratic politics. Naturally, whole communities couldn't

----

[9] Klein 2002.

attend meetings with government officials. Rather than electing representatives, however, the Zapatistas used the tool of "instructed delegates" to relay the thoughts and concerns of the communities they came from. These delegates are only able to carry with them decisions on questions that have been already been discussed and agreed upon by the community they represent:

> If new questions arise, the delegates will be obliged to return to their constituents. Thus, in the midst of the negotiations [with the Mexican State after their initial uprising] mediated by Bishop Ruiz early in 1994, the Zapatista delegates said they would have to interrupt the talks to consult the villages to which they were accountable, a process that took several weeks. The heart of the political process remains the gathered residents of each village, the *assemblea*. (Lynd and Grubacic 2008, pp. 5–6)

Such a process demands a much slower politics—and this is by design. Very often the demand for urgent decisions serves as justification for trampling on the rights and objections of others, sidelining concerns about democracy in the interest of "getting things done." From the Zapatista perspective, and from the perspective of many participatory democracy activists inspired by them, to give up on democratic processes and considerate attention to the concerns of all to participate is to split off your means from your ends, and once you've done that you've already lost the fight. In the face of the government's complaints about their slow process, one Zapatista commented: "this is the speed of democracy."[10] Against the constantly sped-up world of the global economy, the Zapatistas demand a human pace for decision-making.

What did the Occupy movement have to do with the Zapatistas? On the surface, one could say "not much." After all, what do a bunch of (predominantly white, predominantly young) people camping out in public squares around the United States have to do with an indigenous struggle waged against the Mexican government that sees itself as continuous with more than five hundred years of colonial oppression?

The Zapatistas rebelled against a world that had no place for them, a world that was being transformed by forces they had no say in, forces interested in controlling the land and spreading their tentacles of control with the sole interest in generating

---

[10] Wild 1998.

profit. In opposition to this, they claimed their need for *space* to live in their own way—and nothing else. They wanted nothing from the Mexican government other than to be left alone to make decisions for themselves. This was certainly not the perspective shared by all participants in the Occupy movement, it was what was implied by their organizational practices of consensus-based direct democracy, direct action, and prefigurative politics.

For Occupiers, the act of occupation was an assertion of collective power over a sliver of space in which people could experiment with a different form of self-governance, and in particular with social relations that did not involve money and therefore were not as easily subject to the control or influence of the wealthy. Such a perspective on the Occupy movement allowed for people to see themselves as engaged in the same struggle against the forces of global capitalism as the Zapatistas.

The Global Justice Movement

But there was also a historical connection with the Zapatistas, since the rebellion of indigenous Mayans was partially responsible for inspiring the Global Justice movement. Prior to the Occupy movement, the Global Justice movement was the most recent public resurfacing of these same historical threads in North America. Thousands of activists cut their teeth in the Global Justice movement, learning practices of consensus-based direct democracy and mobilizing large demonstrations against neoliberal globalization.

The Global Justice movement staged massive protests at major meetings of international government and economic elites, most notably those of the World Trade Organization (WTO), the International Monetary Fund (IMF), and the Group of Eight (G8) summits in which economic powerhouses meet. These summits consisted in official meetings where decisions were made affecting the lives of millions around the world by a small group of corporate-friendly politicians. In other words: the opposite of democracy. The Global Justice movement pioneered a carnivalesque style of protest, and planned its movement events using direct democratic organizational forms that participants hoped could prefigure a form of decision-making between groups that were from different places yet focused on a common end. This is also the movement in which the Black Bloc—masked activists who sometimes destroy property or engage in self-defense against the police—first made its appearance on the US media stage.

In national media coverage the movement was consistently referred to as the "anti-globalization" movement, and some of those involved accepted that name. Many others, however, insisted that the movement was not against "globalization" as such—indeed, the movement itself was arguably a form of globalization: a worldwide network of activists organizing grassroots resistance. To capture this perspective, some activists argued that it should be called the "alter-globalization" movement, one which envisioned an alternative form of global connectedness, a form that was not just about allowing money and commodities to flow across borders. It is now most commonly referred to as the Global Justice movement, a name that emphasizes activists' claim that the current process of globalization is problematic not simply because it is global, but because it is *unjust*.

As with Occupy, each event in the Global Justice movement was a point of convergence for countless causes and struggles. This contributed to the festival atmosphere of the protests, because different groups would autonomously organize themselves to present the cause they were working for and wanted to put on the map of other activists and the public at large. Despite the huge variety of causes, there was a common focal point: the transnational institutions of the WTO and the IMF, and their complicity in a corporate-centered globalization that was driving poor nations into debt. This national debt was then used to justify the selling off of public resources, instituting regimes of private property, cutting public services, and enacting austerity measures favorable to transnational corporations. A succinct description of the WTO goes like this:

> The WTO is a global governing body consisting of trade ministers from countries around the world. They are appointed to the WTO by government leaders and typically represent the corporate sector. The WTO has its own hierarchy and subsequent conflicts. Decisions are made behind closed doors that can challenge the sovereignty of local, state, and national laws if such laws are considered by the WTO as deterrents to international trade. (Thomas 2000, p. 8)

It is a group of unelected officials who make decisions that can overturn those of local communities and even elected officials. In order to qualify for loans through agencies like the International Monetary

Fund, poorer countries will have to join the WTO. This means they will have to strip back on whatever legislation might have been put in place to offer labor, environmental, or consumer protection. But this is not just the case in poorer countries. Even in the United States, the laws made by states can be over-ridden, not by the federal government, but by the demands of a trade deal that was negotiated by unelected political appointees and corporations.

The WTO is a transnational legal structure set up to defend the supposed "rights" of corporations against "discrimination." By 'discrimination' they mean the attempt to put legal restrictions on dealing with regimes or corporations that have a history of human rights or environmental abuses, nullifying such laws. According to Article III of the WTO, it is

> *unlawful* for a government to discriminate against products that are manufactured, harvested, or produced in ways that are destructive to people and/or the environment. For instance, if one country uses child labor to make toys and another country doesn't, there can be no discrimination in trade. According to WTO law, the toy made by an underage kid working long hours in an unsafe factory for low wages has every right to the marketplace. (Thomas 2000, p. 53)

While there are technically exceptions to this rule, this is generally how the WTO law has operated. The WTO created a legislative body that is higher than that of nations—a structure of global governance that is answerable only to the interests of transnational corporations, to which nation-states had to conform.

The Global Justice movement created a series of high-profile demonstrations at WTO summits and other meetings of the global economic elites. The most renowned of these was Seattle in 1999. Demonstrations were marked by the use of large puppets, dancing, and music in the streets, as well as human blockades and acts of planned civil disobedience. There was a large black bloc present (I discuss black blocs in detail in Chapter 6 below). The protesters were divided on the issue of black blocs and had numerous arguments among themselves. However, the destruction of property by the black blocs (a few broken windows) undoubtedly raised the media profile of the demonstration and made many more people aware of it.

The Global Justice movement gave rise to other internal debates as well. One such debate centered on the tension between "local organizing" and "summit-hopping," in which activists would flood into a city because of a meeting or a convention, organizing themselves for a few intense days of protest and celebration, only to leave without having created any lasting structures or observable changes for the people being exploited by the global economy. The movement often emphasized the creation of inspiring spectacles meant to offer momentary proof that, as the movement's most famous slogan put it, "another world is possible." Criticizing this approach, Bhaskar Sunkara writes that

> After an "inspiringly-poetic" protest, the movement . . . leaves virtually no trace behind. There is an unmistakable enamoring of pageantry as opposed to concrete social transformation—that which can be examined empirically. . . . It was sustained by sentiment alone. (Sunkara 2011)

This judgment may be a bit unfair. The Global Justice movement was self-critical, and undergoing a learning curve that was ultimately cut short by 9/11 and the Iraq war.[11] There were internal debates that could have generated new strategies and tactics, but for the chilling effect on activism after the September 11th, 2001, attacks on the World Trade Center and the Pentagon. In the subsequent months, with the passing of the US Patriot Act and the widespread suppression of dissent in the American media as the Bush administration beat the drums of war, the Global Justice movement largely morphed into the Anti-War movement. First, smaller numbers turned out to protest the war in Afghanistan. And then, in late 2002 and early 2003, many who had been involved in the Global Justice movement staged the largest global protests in history against the invasion of Iraq.

The Iraq War Protests Revisited

In Chapter 1, I described my experience of attending a protest against the Iraq War. I described it as an alienating experience, one in which the protest itself seemed ineffective, like a ritual performance that none of us really expected to work. Only years later, in the wake of Occupy, would I come to appreciate the depth of my ignorance.

After 9/11, activists in the Global Justice movement faced a new political context, one in which opposition to US policy was more eas-

---

[11] See Thompson 2010.

ily painted by authorities as "support for terrorists." There was widespread repression within activist communities, particularly the "Green Scare" which targeted environmentalists.[12] There was also a movement developing against the proposed war in Iraq that drew in many people opposed to the war, but who otherwise were not interested in radical politics. The national coalitions against the war were led by organizations of a more traditional Leftist approach, which were not interested in the prefigurative politics and experimentation that informed the Global Justice movement.

When I marched in Washington DC on that cold day in February, I wasn't aware of the internal debates and decisions that had shaped that day, nor the different approaches others around the country were taking. For example, there were protests taking place outside of these more rigidly organized marches, which involved

> street blockading, sit-ins and occasional street battles with the police. Although these protests were certainly attended by those who had organized and attended the mainstream marches and rallies, they represented an attempt to actually resist the war machine, not just oppose it. Perhaps the most militant and directed of these protests took place in Olympia and Tacoma, Washington, where protesters blocked shipments of military Stryker vehicles bound for Iraq. (Jacobs 2013)

I was unaware that such tactics were being practiced at the time. But more importantly, I was unaware of the very existence of a radical movement opposing not just the war, but the basic structures of economics and politics that continually generate such wars. Without knowing it, I was living at "the end of history," and the set of assumptions I held made it difficult for me to imagine any other form of opposition to a war that struck me as fundamentally unjust.

Horizontalism

Though the growing Global Justice movement was derailed in the United States by 9/11 and the wars in Iraq and Afghanistan, and a large group of people critical of US policy and corporate power, people who may have been inspired by a social movement gave up their aspirations for changing the world, this was certainly not the case

---

[12] See Potter 2011.

everywhere. In Argentina, for example, 2003 was a year of massive and widespread experimentation in participatory democracy in response to the collapse of their economy. This experimentation went on under the banner of a new term: *horizontalidad,* or "horizontality."

Marina Sitrin, an activist with the Global Justice movement who would later participate in the NYCGA and Occupy, was also in Argentina during the period of street protests, factory and workplace occupations, and neighborhood assemblies in the wake of the 2003 economic crisis. Her book, *Horizontalism: Voices of Popular Power in Argentina,* is a collection of interviews and reflections from Argentinians reflecting on the movement's discoveries. The term "horizontality" attempts to grasp how people in the movement were trying to relate to each other in a way that did not make demands of governmental institutions and did not create party structures, but rather emphasized looking to one another to solve collective problems and building mutually supportive relationships. As Sitrin puts it,

> People describe *horizontalidad* as a relationship that helps to create other things, but it is also a goal: the goal is to be more participatory and more horizontal by using the tools. It is about how one changes in the process of participation. People spoke of how this new relationship with their communities changed them, that the idea of 'I' changed as it related to the 'we', and this 'we' changed again in relation to the 'I'. (Sitrin 2011, p. 10)

The process of everyday people giving up hope in their leaders was also a process of changing the way people saw one another:

> Que se vayan todos! Que no quede ni uno solo!" (*They all must go! Not one should remain!*) And they did go: the country went through five governments in two weeks. At the same time, the people in the streets began to look around, to look to one another, to find and see one another for the first time. (p. 10)

"Horizontality" did not flow from any pre-given "theory" of social change. Rather, once people had stopped looking "vertically" toward those who held official power and started instead looking toward one another, "they created assemblies. People called it the most "natural" thing in the world, to seek out those harmed, just like you, and together begin to see if you can find solutions" (p.

10). In the absence of any legitimate vertical power structure, holding these horizontal collective assemblies simply made sense.

Which leads us to the social movement that was perhaps most directly influential on the organization of the Occupy movement. *Not* the Arab Spring—though that movement's power to stir the sense of the possible in people around the world can't be discounted. Far more directly influential, however, was the 15M movement, or the *indignados*, of Spain. In the Spring and Summer of 2011, Spanish cities saw public squares turn into encampments, or *acampadas*, that experimented with very similar forms of direct democracy that would, come Fall, fill the public squares of cities in the US and around the world under the banner of Occupy. The *indignados* rallying cry was for *Democracia Real Ya!* or "Real Democracy Now!"

The parallels between the *indignados* and the Occupiers abound: both movements claimed that the structures of representative democracy currently operated exclusively in the interests of the wealthy and powerful, and both therefore refused to identify with or explicitly support any existing political party; both movements undertook the tactic of public encampment, physically seizing space in order to engage in public experiments with a form of participatory democracy that broke with the prevailing structures of representation; both movements refused the creation of "leaders" or a formal leadership structure, preferring instead to have rotating facilitators valued in accordance with their capacity to remove their own personality from their function in a group; both movements spread rapidly and employed social media; both movements had particular appeal for unemployed or "underemployed" college graduates in their twenties and thirties, though also resonated with the wider population.

For participants in the NYCGA, as well as activists who helped organize Occupy encampments around the country as the movement spread, the *indignados* were a major reference point. Indeed, the ethos of the Global Justice movement still prevails: a globalized economy serving the rich and powerful requires *a globalized resistance of people attempting to forge a new way of organizing themselves,* a way that is intrinsically inconsistent with the demands of an oppressive economy and structure if government; a way that is more thoughtful, slower, more attentive to the needs of human beings and less concerned with simply producing commodities or transforming human labor into narrowly conceived "economic growth."

The history of participatory democracy is a history of experimenting with such forms of organization, and the Occupy movement was, for the first time in around a decade, the moment when this radical vision of another world burst into the awareness of the people in the United States. As a result, the illusion that we are living in "the end of history" was unmasked for thousands around the country. The historical threads of radical politics that have always been present, beneath the surface, were suddenly being woven together in collectively reclaimed spaces by many people who were largely ignorant of the traditions of rebellion and experimentation informing their practices.

4

What Is Our One Demand?

The Occupy movement engaged in public encampments as a form of direct action to create politically charged spaces to experiment with direct democracy. In so doing, participants managed to expose thousands of people to a fundamentally different ideal of political life, that of horizontal power structures, and to prefigurative politics as a strategy for spreading the practices required for realizing this ideal. But when we think we're living our ideal, problems can arise. For instance, we can fall in love with ourselves.

And this tendency can be exacerbated if everyone else seems to be in love with us. Soon Occupy encampments around the country received visits from established intellectuals and activists, offering encouragement in their experiment. On October 6th, journalist Naomi Klein visited Liberty Plaza and declared Occupy Wall Street to be "the most important thing in the world right now." Klein emphasized that Occupy was prefiguring a society that operated on a different set of values from today's, in which money speaks louder than principles:

> I am talking about changing the underlying values that govern our society. That is hard to fit into a single media-friendly demand, and it's also hard to figure out how to do it. But it is no less urgent for being difficult.
>
> That is what I see happening in this square. In the way you are feeding each other, keeping each other warm, sharing information freely and providing health care, meditation classes and empowerment training. My favorite sign here says, "I care about you." In a culture that trains people to avoid each other's gaze, to say, "Let them die," that is a deeply radical statement. (Klein 2011)

For Klein, the Occupiers were doing everything right: they were targeting Wall Street, they were maintaining a disciplined nonviolence, they were supporting one another, and they were staying put with no end in sight. This last point concerning the occupation itself was particularly important, she noted, because "only when you stay put can you grow roots." She praised the horizontal and direct democratic practices, and encouraged Occupiers to maintain these principles through the "hard work of building structures and institutions that are sturdy enough to weather the storms ahead."

In Chapter 2, I mentioned Slavoj Žižek's speech at Liberty Plaza, in which he praised the occupation for "giving us red ink." But Žižek's speech also contained a warning: "There is a danger," Žižek said, through his characteristic twitches and sniffles, "Don't fall in love with yourselves. We have a nice time here. But remember, carnivals come cheap. What matters is the day after, when we will have to return to normal lives. Will there be any changes then?"

In the years since Occupy Wall Street, no less than during the wave of occupations itself, one criticism sounded loud from both the mainstream media and the traditional Left: "But they have no demands!" Over and over this accusation was made and, in the wake of Occupy, it has, for some, come to signify that the Occupy movement fell into the danger of which Žižek warned, and failed to grow the roots for which Klein had hoped. Doug Rossinow sums up a general impression that I and others have encountered: "'We are the ninety-nine percent' was and is a brilliant rallying cry. But those five words were the essential contribution of Occupy, and they came at the start. After that, it became about celebrating activism."[1]

Specifically, for many, the Occupiers' inability or unwillingness to formulate demands has been taken as a mark of political immaturity. The prefigurative space of the occupation that Klein and Žižek celebrated was also seen as the limitation that sealed the fate of the movement, creating a space that was too inward-gazing. The most forceful of these critiques from the Left comes from Thomas Frank, who argued that Occupy made a serious tactical error in not issuing demands, falling in love with its own horizontal process and squandering its potential.[2]

---

[1] Rossinow 2013.
[2] Frank 2012.

No doubt there were cases of people "falling in love with themselves." Many newly radicalized people in Occupy assumed they had figured it all out, and gave in to the temptation to assume everyone else had simply not yet seen the light. But the criticism that Occupiers fell in love with themselves and therefore made serious tactical errors overlooks the way the encampments themselves became sites for education in the complexities of our current social and political landscape. Occupiers were not only *not* issuing demands—we were *doing* something else, which the selection of a single demand would have obstructed. The encampments were spaces in which people were being changed, developing a deep analysis of the power structures of the dominant society, skills to challenge it, and fragments of a vision for a more just, sustainable, and liberatory world. We were not simply falling in love with ourselves, so much as coming to better understand ourselves and our society.

Further, the criticism of Occupiers' failure to issue demands misses something important about where people were at in their political consciousness. As I've suggested, most people in the US tacitly conceive of themselves as living at the 'end of history', largely because they have been cut off from the tradition of radical struggle. Because of this, people are generally ignorant of the history of struggles for justice, as well as the injustices experienced by various social groups. But without such an understanding, "demands" will likely be shallow or privilege the interests of some particularly vocal group within a movement.

Here's another way to put it: every demand can only be issued relative to some grievance, and people in the US have a lot of very different grievances. A demand looks for a change in policy, a grievance clarifies why such a change is needed. But Wall Street and the political power that sustains it affect many of us in many different ways, and so our grievances with the current system are sometimes very different: some have been kicked out of their homes, some are buried in student debt, some in medical debt; some are serving decades-long sentences for non-violent drug offenses, some are working three jobs and unable to spend time with their children, some are dying of cancer from exposure to toxic chemicals; some are concerned about the future of the planet, ravaged by climate change; some about the future of their neighborhood, ravaged by high-priced condos that are driving up the rent; some are unemployed and some are working jobs they think are fundamentally unsafe and hazardous, simply because they need the money. This list could go on—and when we take into consideration the experiences of the *global* ninety-nine percent, for instance the people of the global south living under repressive regimes that have been supported and sustained by the US government's commitment to support the economic interests of corporations, the list grows even longer.

In encampments across the US, we weren't there to make demands so much as to formulate and connect our grievances; we were learning to understand a system that divides and separates its population in very different ways. While many people were drawn to occupations because they were convinced that "We are the ninety-nine percent," what they learned upon arrival is that it is not so easy to determine what "the ninety-nine percent" needs— or rather, that "the ninety-nine percent" needs a lot of different things. Perhaps surprisingly, the Occupy movement made some significant progress in understanding our shared grievances, how they are connected, and how we might get out of this mess.

The Demand for Demands

It is ironic that the movement became so widely associated with a lack of clear demands, since the initial *Adbusters* call to Occupy Wall Street on July 13th 2011 was crystal clear in its message: the proposed occupation should decide upon and articulate one simple demand. The call to action starts by mentioning the encampments in Egypt's Tahrir square and the public squares of Spain, and refers to the "beautiful new formula" those movements have hit upon:

> . . . we talk to each other in various physical gatherings and virtual people's assemblies . . . we zero in on what our one demand will be, a demand that awakens the imagination and, if achieved, would propel us toward the radical democracy of the future, . . . and then we go out and seize a square of singular symbolic significance and put our asses on the line to make it happen. (Adbusters 2011)

At least on the Internet, the initial call to occupy Wall Street then was basically a call to come up with a demand. This was the strategy that had inspired *Adbusters'* idea in the first place. Even the image of the ballerina balancing on the Wall Street bull carried with it the question: "What is our one demand?" So what happened?

During their pre-occupy planning sessions, the NYCGA decided that articulating demands would be the wrong approach. As Marina Sitrin put it, "We discussed and debated the question of demands and what would define the movement, but we agreed not to use the framework of demands at all." Rather, as we've seen, the aim was "to open space for conversations—for democracy—real, direct, and participatory democracy." Sitrin goes on to frame this as, itself, a kind of "demand":

> Our only demand then would be to be left alone in our plazas, parks, schools, workplaces, and neighborhoods so as to meet one another, reflect together, and in assembly forms decide what our alternatives are. And from there, once we have opened up these democratic spaces, we can discuss what sort of demands we might have and who we believe might be able to meet these demands. Or, perhaps, once we have assemblies throughout the country, the issue of demands upon others will become mute. If there are enough of us, we may one day only make demands of ourselves. (Sitrin 2011, p. 8)

For Sitrin and those in the NYCGA that shared her perspective, the refusal to issue demands to those in power was a kind of deeper double-demand: a demand, on the one hand, to be left alone by those in power and a demand, on the other hand, for everyday people begin the process of deepening their collective responsibility among themselves.

Still, in the early weeks of OWS, it seemed obvious to mainstream commentators that occupiers were going about things all wrong. In an article for *The Guardian*, Graeber sums up this criticism and responds:

> Almost every time I'm interviewed by a mainstream journalist about OWS, I get some variation of the same lecture: "How are you going to get anywhere if you refuse to create a leadership structure or make a practical list of demands? . . . You're never going to reach a regular, mainstream American audience with this sort of thing!" It is hard to imagine worse advice. After all, since 2007, just about every previous attempt to kick off a nationwide movement against Wall Street took exactly the course such people would have recommended—and failed miserably. It is only when a small group of anarchists in New York decided to adopt the opposite approach—refusing to recognize the

legitimacy of the existing political authorities by making demands of
them; refusing to accept the legitimacy of the existing legal order by
occupying a public space without asking for permission, refusing to
elect leaders who could then be bribed or co-opted; declaring,
however non-violently, that the entire system was corrupt and
they rejected it; being willing to stand firm against the state's
inevitable violent response—that hundreds of thousands of
Americans from Portland to Tuscaloosa began rallying in support,
and a majority declared their sympathies. (Graeber 2011)

Occupy was so inspiring and contagious in large measure because
it refused to play by the rules of the game, and came prepared with
a set of practices of its own.

Speaking broadly, there were two very different ways Occupiers
could have been against making demands to those in power. The
first position, which Graeber, Sitrin, and others held, was that to
make demands of existing political structures was to acknowledge
their legitimacy and thus distract from the aim of rejecting their
power and beginning to create an alternative—or at least inspire
others to believe that an alternative was possible. The second position, which Thomas Frank and others held, was that while a period
without demands was clearly a great way to rally many people to
the cause, "the failure to generate demands was a tactical mis-
take."[3] For the first camp, the aim was to call into question the
legitimacy of current political and economic structures; for the second camp, the aim was to organize a political body that could
directly engage those structures in order to change or win conces-
sions from them.

The Occupy encampments were experimenting with values and
forms of power that are different from those values and forms of
power with which both corporations and state power operate: horizontal power, as opposed to hierarchical, or vertical, power. The
problem with "demands" is that issuing them seemed to contradict
the commitment to horizontal power; demands look "up" to those
who have the resources or power to distribute them, while horizontal power looks "out" to everyday people and asks, "how do
we stop supporting the power from above?" Without support from
below, vertical power can't function.

---

[3] Frank 2012.

But there's another reason why demands were felt as counter to the spirit and practice of the movement: once we had a sense of all the wide variety of problems that drove people to the encampments and to participate in assemblies, it became increasingly difficult to select just one problem without risk of unduly marginalizing others. Even making a "list of demands" would seem to prioritize some grievances, would insinuate that some were up for negotiation, and would inevitably exclude others. To put the matter bluntly: demands require *specific* problems, but most of the people drawn to Occupy were not motivated by some one specific concern. The problem was *general*, a sense—articulated with various degrees of precision—that there was an *entire system of values that needs to be rejected or transformed*.

Often when people are upset about a whole value-system, a whole conception of what human life is about, they will select one thing at which they direct their anger. "Demands" play into this tendency, and serve as an attempt to translate a group's dissatisfaction with a whole situation, a whole structure of power, into terms that can be understood by and solved within that very structure of power. Chris Hedges, who saw the Occupy movement as a revolutionary response to what he termed a "corporate *coup d'état*" that had taken place in America, put his criticism of making demands in this way:

> All revolutionary movements, at their inception, demand that the corrupt and decayed power elite be removed. And that demand is unpalatable to that elite because, of course, it would mean their dissolution. And the elites can't respond to that demand. So when you see outside forces tell you "what are your demands?" "make demands!" "do you want to revoke corporate personhood?" "Do you want finance reforms, regulations?" Do you want campaign finance reforms?"—what they are attempting to do is *funnel you back in that dead system*. And the power of the Occupy movement is that it won't go there. It realizes a fundamental truth about American politics, and that is: there is no way to vote against the interests of Goldman Sachs. (Hedges 2011. Italics added)

For Hedges, it serves this current system if our dissatisfaction with it can be translated into a single demand that the system can appear to address. Hedges saw the Occupy movement's absence of demands as a refusal to fall into this trap—as an expression of popular desire, in the words of Argentinians, to "que se vayan todos," to "throw them all out"—not *just* congress and party politicians, but the corporations and financial institutions that actually run the show.

Grievances, Not Demands

All the media focus on the Occupy movement's absence of a clear demand distracted attention from one of the most important document produced by Occupy Wall Street: the list of *grievances* found in *The Declaration of the Occupation of New York City*. This short pamphlet can be read as a response to the demand for demands, shifting the conversation from demands to grievances.

This shift of focus from demands to grievances is appropriate for a movement based on horizontal, direct democracy: before we go about saying what we *want*, we first need to get clear about what our various problems are with the current state of things. Too often, people came to the occupations with a pre-conceived set of ideas about what was wrong with America or the economy, and thus what the appropriate solutions would be. When working well, the democratic structures of the General Assembly effectively ran counter to this attitude, opening a space for people to listen to grievances affecting people from different backgrounds. Here is the *Declaration,* passed by the NYCGA on September 29th 2011:

> As we gather together in solidarity to express a feeling of mass injustice, we must not lose sight of what brought us together. We write so that all people who feel wronged by the corporate forces of the world can know that we are your allies.
>
> As one people, united, we acknowledge the reality: that the future of the human race requires the co-operation of its members; that our system must protect our rights, and upon corruption of that system, it is up to the individuals to protect their own rights, and those of their neighbors; that a democratic government derives its just power from the people, but corporations do not seek consent to extract wealth from the people and the Earth; and that no true democracy is attainable when the process is determined by economic power. We come to you at a time when corporations, which place profit over people, self-interest over justice, and oppression over equality, run our governments. We have peaceably assembled here, as is our right, to let these facts be known:

- They have taken our houses through an illegal foreclosure process, despite not having the original mortgage.

- They have taken bailouts from taxpayers with impunity, and continue to give Executives exorbitant bonuses.

- They have perpetuated inequality and discrimination in the workplace based on age, the color of one's skin, sex, gender identity and sexual orientation.

- They have poisoned the food supply through negligence, and undermined the farming system through monopolization.

- They have profited off of the torture, confinement, and cruel treatment of countless animals, and actively hide these practices.

- They have continuously sought to strip employees of the right to negotiate for better pay and safer working conditions.

- They have held students hostage with tens of thousands of dollars of debt on education, which is itself a human right.

- They have consistently outsourced labor and used that outsourcing as leverage to cut workers' healthcare and pay.

- They have influenced the courts to achieve the same rights as people, with none of the culpability or responsibility.

- They have spent millions of dollars on legal teams that look for ways to get them out of contracts in regards to health insurance.

- They have sold our privacy as a commodity.

- They have used the military and police force to prevent freedom of the press.

- They have deliberately declined to recall faulty products endangering lives in pursuit of profit.

- They determine economic policy, despite the catastrophic failures their policies have produced and continue to produce.

- They have donated large sums of money to politicians, who are responsible for regulating them.

- They continue to block alternate forms of energy to keep us dependent on oil.

- They continue to block generic forms of medicine that could save people's lives or provide relief in order to protect investments that have already turned a substantial profit.

- They have purposely covered up oil spills, accidents, faulty bookkeeping, and inactive ingredients in pursuit of profit.

- They purposefully keep people misinformed and fearful through their control of the media.

- They have accepted private contracts to murder prisoners even when presented with serious doubts about their guilt.

- They have perpetuated colonialism at home and abroad.

- They have participated in the torture and murder of innocent civilians overseas.

- They continue to create weapons of mass destruction in order to receive government contracts.*

To the people of the world,

We, the New York City General Assembly occupying Wall Street in Liberty Square, urge you to assert your power.

Exercise your right to peaceably assemble; occupy public space; create a process to address the problems we face, and generate solutions accessible to everyone.

To all communities that take action and form groups in the spirit of direct democracy, we offer support, documentation, and all of the resources at our disposal.

Join us and make your voices heard!

These grievances are not all-inclusive.

(NYCGA 2011b)

This list of grievances did not receive much press—many who complain that the movement had no demands have never even heard of it. But it stands as a clear (though not all-inclusive!) statement and catalogue of various forms of corporate oppression, enabled by state-sponsored corporate control over contemporary life. It is a collection of facts, gathered within the democratic space of the occupation, that sets aside broader political interpretations of how these problems are generated. That is, the list of grievances makes no reference to political ideologies, nor to "solutions." Instead, like the *Declaration of Independence*, it names an oppressor, enumerates injustices, and appeals to rights that are more fundamental than any system of government.

Since any demand must be in response to some grievance, the *Declaration of the Occupation of Wall Street* accomplished a collective action that could be seen as more fundamental than issuing

demands to those in power: it outlined the enormity of our grievances against a power structure that affects people around the
world in very different ways. Perhaps most importantly, the
Declaration conceives its authors and its audience not in our status
as "citizens" issuing demands to our government. Rather, we are
addressed *by* mere people, peacefully assembled, *as* mere people,
who might also assemble. Occupiers were reaching beneath our
identities as citizens of this or that nation-state, sounding an alarm
to the "people of the world" in order to remind us all that we are
the true locus of political power.

All Our Grievances Are Connected

Shortly after the *Declaration of the Occupation of Wall Street* was
passed by the General Assembly, Rachel Schragis showed up at
Liberty Plaza. Schragis is an artist who had for some time been
attempting to take complex ideas or long lists and turn them into
conceptual flowcharts. When she saw the *Declaration*, she was
immediately struck with the sense that this was the list she had
been waiting for, and that a flowchart would be a helpful way to
visualize the document. At the time, according to Schragis, "people kept saying that the movement isn't about anything, but the
problem is that it's about *everything*. The problem is its very complicated, there's not one punchy sentence."[4]

She contacted the working group that had compiled the list for
the *Declaration* and they went to work trying to find a way to visu-
ally represent the list of grievances. Once they had decided on a
structure of concentric circles with the list of grievances at the center circle, Schragis took a draft of the chart to Zuccotti Park and
asked people what they thought was missing and, specifically,
whether their own struggle was represented on the chart. She kept
doing that until she didn't get any new answers. According to
Rachel, though she had a strong hand in shaping the chart, "there
were a couple hundred people who participated in making it."

The construction of a list of grievances was an effective way to
express many different complaints against and oppressions committed by "the corporate forces of the world," without privileging
any one of them. The flowchart of the *Declaration* managed to

---

[4] Personal interview, August 2013.

perform a second, equally important step: it clearly illustrated links between the various forms of oppression experienced by people in different groups that make up the ninety-nine percent. The *Declaration* lists grievances that affect a variety of different groups and individuals; the flowchart shows how "all of our grievances are connected."

More than just presenting the grievances in an interconnected way, the flowchart gives us the sense of a whole system of values that the Occupiers were attempting to turn on its head with their prefigurative, horizontal power. It is a map of the world from which the occupations were attempting to break away.

The *Declaration* and this flowchart illustrate that the *absence* of demands from the Occupiers was not simply a matter of lack of discipline or unwillingness to get serious about political change.

Rather, the reluctance to make demands came from both fundamental questions about the legitimacy of the political institutions to which demands would be addressed, and from the fact that Occupiers were trying to do something different, something deeper. They were trying to wake us up to our common life together, to the intersections and overlappings of our various problems. On the left side of the flowchart, it reads: "engage your community in any way you believe forges a more just world!" The occupations weren't the kind of political bodies that wanted to make demands of those in power—they were a wake-up call that was trying to make demands of us all.

The Demand for Justice

The occupied spaces, then, were about something other than issuing demands to those in power. Still, it seems that the activities Occupiers engaged in could be seen as having some kind of *implicit* demand—that is, a demand that their own actions pointed toward, even if it wasn't always articulated.

One way to think about the possibility of an implicit demand in the Occupy movement is to consider how Occupy engaged in what political scientist Bernard Harcourt has called "political disobedience." Harcourt contrasts this with "civil disobedience," which "accepts the legitimacy of the political structure and our political institutions, but resists the moral authority of the resulting laws."[5] For civil disobedience, one need only think of Martin Luther King Jr.'s approach to direct action, which emphasized that breaking an unjust law was, in reality, "the very highest respect for the law" because it challenges the existing law to live up to its own highest ideals.

In contrast to this, *political disobedience* "resists the very way in which we are governed." The struggle, in this case, is not against some particular unjust law, but against, for instance,

> the structure of partisan politics, the demand for policy reforms, the call for party identification. It rejects the very idea of expressing or honoring "the highest respect for the law." It refuses to willingly accept the sanctions meted out by our legal and political systems. It challenges the conventional way in which political governance takes

---

[5] Harcourt 2013, p. 46.

place and laws are enforced. It turns its back on the political institutions and the actors who govern us (p. 47).

Political disobedience, then, is a kind of protest that resists not some particular set of unjust laws, nor does it respond to some particular horrendous act, but expresses a discontent or outright rejection of the governing institutions and the processes by which they make and enforce laws. The Occupy movement not only broke laws and ordinances relating to curfews and municipal camping, but also engaged in practices of self-organizing and decision-making that broke sharply with the representative system by which the United States government is supposed to operate. This was not an appeal to the ideals of representation, but rather the insistence on a different ideal, one of democracy that did not rely upon those representative mechanisms. Clearly this was political disobedience.

But it was also something more than that: Occupy was performing a different kind of politics, and this performance was an implicit demand for a different way of thinking about *justice*.

Too often, we assume that we have figured out what justice is. That is, we assume that the decisions of courts, for example, reflect it. But the idea of justice extends beyond the current structures of governance. In a sense, we could think of any particular form of government as one attempt to answer the question, "What is justice?" To assume that the contemporary United States has hit upon the best of all possible answers is a bit hubristic. It assumes that we are currently at "the end of history." If those who have struggled for democracy throughout history are right, then the only just foundation for governance is the consent of the governed—we are all, as living beings, owed the right to assent or dissent from the attempt of another to govern us. Further, as socialists and anarchists have argued, justice is not merely a matter of subtracting governance, but of rectifying material inequities arising from sexist, racist, colonialist, and capitalist class oppressions. The Occupiers, with their practice of assemblies based on consent, and with their practices of mutual aid, were modeling a fuller, more democratic, conception of just governance. They were demonstrating how far from real democracy the current structures of governance actually are.

This demand for justice at the heart of Occupy was articulated well by Arundati Roy, the world-renowned novelist, staunch critic of the global capitalist Empire, and advocate of radical democracy. Roy gave a speech at Occupy Wall Street the day after the park was first evicted:

> Yesterday morning the police cleared Zuccotti Park, but today the people are back. The police should know that this protest is not a battle for territory. We're not fighting for the right to occupy a park here or there. We are fighting for Justice. Justice, not just for the people of the United States, but for everybody. What you have achieved since September 17th, when the Occupy Movement began in the United States, is to introduce a new imagination, a new political language, into the heart of Empire. You have reintroduced the right to dream into a system that tried to turn everybody into zombies mesmerized into equating mindless consumerism with happiness and fulfillment. As a writer, let me tell you, this is an immense achievement. I cannot thank you enough. (Roy 2011)

For Roy, what's so significant about the Occupy movement is its articulation of a demand for justice that breaks out of the normal framework of "human rights," pushing further into an implicit demand for equality and a critique of global corporate power. Roy emphasized that Occupy's demand for justice was not limited in its scope to justice for the people of the United States, but rather was based on a recognition that, since corporations and nation-states operate at a global scale, what happens in the United States affects and is affected by what happens elsewhere. Fighting for justice in the US requires joining and supporting the struggles for justice elsewhere. And moreover, struggling for economic justice—the major mainstream focus of the Occupy movement—cannot be construed as separate from the ongoing struggles for justice against racial, sexual, gender, ableist, and other forms of oppression.

Tensions and Fractures in the Ninety-Nine Percent

On these fronts, the democratic spaces of the encampments were by no means perfect. But it was often the emphasis on direct democracy and consensus building that helped reveal tensions within the ninety-nine percent, and helped generate internal criticism of Occupy. These tensions and criticisms were not only based on political ideologies, but also based on the different experiences of those who participated. In some cases, these tensions led to fractures: groups broke off, declaring the inadequacy of the Occupy movement's practices for dealing with and recognizing the problems of their communities. Often these fractures were not based on a critique of the horizontal, direct democracy of the encampments as such, so much as the naivety of those who were engaging in these practices without a deep enough understanding of the way privilege, power, and even acts of violence were being reinforced within the space of the encampments.

Perhaps the most widely cited problem in the encampments were the acts of sexual assault that took place. OWS's Safer Spaces Working Group both provided support for the survivors of the assaults of which they became aware, and issued a statement about this support and how it fit in with the aims of OWS.

Within this statement, Safer Spaces criticized segments of the media who have "attempted to use this incident as another way to disingenuously attack and discredit OWS." They note that OWS exists within a broader culture where sexual assault is egregiously common: someone in the US is sexually assaulted every two minutes, most assaults are never reported, and most rapists are never held to account. We live in a culture of violence in which sexual assault is often ignored, condoned, excused and even encouraged.[6]

In opposition to these tendencies of mainstream society, OWS's Safer Spaces strove to model a better support process for survivors of sexual assault. This process included providing the survivor "with the time and space to carefully review the options available to her. Following two days of discussion with family, friends, supporters and anti-violence advocates, the survivor decided to make a report to the police and to push for a criminal investigation and prosecution" (p. 138). This is itself significant. Even though many involved with OWS had themselves been assaulted by the police, and perhaps would have liked to leave the NYPD out of their processes entirely, those working with Safer Spaces wanted to model a form of support that took the survivor's wishes as primary:

> We are working for an OWS and a world in which survivors are respected and supported unconditionally, where they are supported to

---

[6] Safer Spaces Working Group 2012, p. 139.

come forward, and where every community member takes responsibility for preventing and responding to harm. (p. 139)

This process was not perfect, but it was pointing in a different direction from powerful trends in this society. And it should be noted that this orientation toward supporting the agency of the survivor was hardly an OWS invention. Rather, it is drawn from practices of those social workers, therapists, and others who tirelessly work to support survivors of sexual assault in their everyday lives and work, but who often find themselves either lacking the means to do so and fighting against a tide of entrenched practices and cultural habits that engage in victim-blaming (asking, for example, "well, what was she wearing?" as if there were a way to dress that justified the actions of a rapist). With this issue, as with others, OWS was not re-inventing any wheels, so much as trying to practice and model the better tendencies within the wider society.

Sexual assault was just one particularly acute way in which Occupy encampments failed to fully live up to their ideal of creating a space in which all felt safe to participate and in which their concerns were being heard. At encampments around the country, women grouped together to issue statements and organize around the fact that many felt marginalized by newly radicalized white men, whose privileged position in society tended, sometimes unconsciously, to lead them to assume positions of visibility and responsibility in the movement. For example, the Women's Caucus of Occupy Boston interrupted their General Assembly on November 18th 2011 to deliver a message about the sexism that they had experienced at the encampment. Though not all the men had behaved in a sexist way, the Women's Caucus applied the kind of systemic critique that Occupiers made of Wall Street to the situation of Occupy Boston itself:

"A few bad apples" can't exist without a community that condones their attitudes and behaviors. Oppressive language and behavior are an effort to limit our participation and silence our voice.

We chose to disrupt the GA because those with privilege have avoided spaces devoted to anti-oppression, when they are the ones who most need to hear this.

As the 99%, we must actively break down the systems which divide us. (p. 128)

This intervention into the Occupy Boston General Assembly illustrates an important point: a better world cannot simply be created by declaring some space an "occupation" and utilizing a set of horizontal organizing tools. Since we enter such spaces from a world in which privilege and oppression condition our habits of thought and action, we cannot expect to simply shed those tendencies without struggle. Indeed, the struggle against oppression and privilege must itself be pursued within such spaces. Still, such interventions were enacted in the name of the horizontal principles that Occupiers were attempting to model.

Another line of tension that was revealed in the Occupied spaces was racism. For people of color, racism is a pervasive experience within contemporary US society—in the workplace, on the streets, in encounters with police, in social settings, and so on. But just as the sexism experienced by women is often invisible to men, so too is much racism invisible to white people. As the benefactors of racial oppression and inequality, white people often don't see the way it functions—they have the privilege to remain ignorant of this harsh reality. Racism, as a structural feature of US society, was unavoidably present in Occupy encampments, and, in many cases, it was challenged by people of color and their allies.

Reporting on his experience, longtime activist Bruce Dixon noted that some Occupiers claimed that "the concerns of immigrants and black people had no place in the Occupy movement because they were 'divisive'. They said this to me in an Atlanta park that the Occupiers shared with a hundred homeless black men" (Dixon 2011, p. 145). Dixon's experience was in no way unique, and revealed clearly the political danger of an over-simplified concept of "the ninety-nine percent." If the aim was to unify the ninety-nine percent behind some one set of demands, then the specific oppression faced by people of color may have looked like divisive issues that distracted from the main goal.

But this desire on the part of some Occupiers to marginalize racial concerns was also taken as an opportunity for some people of color to intervene, and call-out white activists on their privilege. As social justice lawyer Tammy Kim suggested to people of color who avoided occupied spaces because of their perceived (and often very real) whiteness, "If you don't agree with the messaging, it's on you to change it. If you feel it's not diverse enough, add your body to the mix. In this consensus-based process, participation is our most valuable critical faculty" (Kim 2011, p. 161).

Of course, simply telling people they ought to participate isn't quite enough—one must acknowledge that there were real limitations and fears unique to people of color. As Dixon suggests,

> *If the first occupiers in Zuccotti Park had been young and black,* they'd instantly have been branded a street gang and arrested en masse, with or without violence, but certainly with little media play or sympathy. If the first occupiers were black, and blathering about the ravages of finance capital and how neither of the two parties are worth a damn, they certainly would not have been endorsed by what passes for the preacher-infested local leadership of black communities. (Dixon 2011, p. 143)

The ability to engage in an occupation, which usually involves a collective act of law-breaking, itself implied a certain amount of privilege. Those who went down to occupations for the most part understood that to do so was to risk arrest. But because of the racist nature of the current criminal justice system, in which people of color receive disproportionately harsher sentences for the same crimes committed by white people, an arrest can mean a more serious set of consequences for people of color and immigrants than it does for white activists.[7]

There were lots of other tensions that were brought to the surface in the Occupy encampments: distinctions developed between those who had been experiencing homelessness long before the occupations, and those who were newly engaged with sleeping outdoors; between trans-gender women and women-only groups that excluded them; between those who wanted to beat drums all night, who thought of themselves as the heartbeat of the movement, and those who wanted to sleep. The encampments were both spaces of love and support, and also spaces of conflict, tension, and, from time to time, resolution.

But even when resolutions were not or could not be forthcoming, the occupations were places where people expanded their experience. The encounter with conflict, in other words, was an

---

[7] See Alexander 2012.

opportunity for participants to understand that some people have far deeper critiques of the current social and political order than others, where "deeper" means that they are more sensitive to the experiences of those whose voices are marginalized or ignored in mainstream society. Perhaps the best example of this depth of criticism came from those for whom the term "occupy" was itself deeply problematic. Indeed, many members of Occupy Oakland, influenced by the challenges put forward by indigenous groups and people of color, referred to the movement as "Occupy/ Decolonize" to emphasize that the United States itself was occupied territory seized through a long history of genocide and broken treaties with indigenous people.

If we look at Occupy encampments as sites of radical education, then the Occupy movement's "success" came not despite these critiques and limitations, but *because* of them. Throughout the fall of 2011, thousands of white people from middle class backgrounds were opening up their eyes and *beginning* to see the US and corporate power from a lens that poor people, people of color, and indigenous people have seen it for a long time. This was deep, educational work, and like all such work, only bears its fruit with time. But this slow process was pushed along through internal conflicts and courageous interventions within the encampments themselves.

An important instance of this kind of growth occurred during the drafting of the "Declaration of the Occupation of Wall Street." Manissa McCleave Maharawal is an activist of South Asian descent who was curious but hesitant about Occupy Wall Street in its early days, largely because she did not see many people of color present. As Maharawal tells the story, however, the democratic space that was opened up in Zuccotti Park impressed her, and she brought a number of other South Asian friends to the park. They happened to be there on the evening when the *Declaration of the Occupation of Wall Street* was up for approval in the General Assembly, and they were struck by a line at the very start of it. The initial draft of the *Declaration* announced the Occupiers were speaking as "one race, the human race, formerly divided by race [and] class." Writing about the experience later, Maharawal said this line "hit me in the stomach with its naivety and the way it made me feel alienated." In her essay, "So Real It Hurts: Notes on Occupy Wall Street," Maharawal elaborates:

This movement was about to send a document into the world about who and what it was that included a line that erased all power relations and decades of history of oppression. A line that would de-legitimize the movement, this would alienate me and people like me, this would not be something I could get behind. And I was already behind it, this movement, and somehow I didn't want to walk away from this. I couldn't walk away from this. (Maharawal 2012, p. 158)

In a General Assembly with hundreds of people, she and her close friends yelled "mic check" and said they would block the document unless this language was changed. She blocked because if the document had gone through as written, she would have left the movement. Her changes were accepted, even though the person who had written the line, a white male with good intentions but little awareness of the reality of racism in US society, had questions about the changes. After the General Assembly, she spoke with him about OWS speaking on behalf of "one race, the human race":

But it's 'scientifically true' he told us. He thought that maybe we were advocating for there being different races? No, we needed to tell him about privilege and racism and oppression and how these things still existed, both in the world and some place like Occupy Wall Street.

And so, as happened countless times at occupations around the country, Maharawal and her friends conducted a spontaneous seminar that lasted well into the night:

there in that circle, on that street corner, we did a crash course on racism, white privilege, structural racism, oppression. We did a course on history and the Declaration of Independence and colonialism and slavery. It was hard. It was real. It hurt. But people listened. We had to fight for it. I'm going to say that again: we had to fight for it. But it felt worth it. . . . It felt worth it not only because, while standing in a circle of twenty, mostly white, men, and explaining racism in front of them—carefully and slowly spelling out that I as a woman of color experience the world way differently than the author of the Declaration [of the occupation of New York City], a white man, that this was not about him being personally racist but about relations of power, that he needed to, he urgently needed to listen and believe me about this—this moment felt like a victory for the movement on its own. (p. 159)

Maharawal wrote about her story and shared it in the *Consensus* video, and it was used as way of illustrating the consensus process and to highlight the danger of speaking on behalf of others, making grand generalizations about "the people." Her story emphasized that those who were often most vocal and most comfortable speaking at the occupations were not the experts on everyone's experience, and that race, gender, and class divisions—among others—exist within the ninety-nine percent and must be challenged. Maharawal's story also demonstrates both the courage such challenges require and the compassion and commitment it takes to educate others about experiences to which they have been privileged enough to remain oblivious.

Particularly after Occupiers were evicted from their encampments many tensions led to fractures and in-fighting. Without the shared space of a park, it was much easier for people to go their own separate ways. Occupy forged spaces of spontaneous community, creating previously non-existent relationships of mutual dependence. These weren't going to last, and very early on many Occupiers began bringing the organizational forms they were so excited about back into their own communities and neighborhoods. But rather than criticize the occupations for their fleetingness, I think it is more important to stress how the presence of tensions and differences within the occupations resulted in a serious education for many who had come to Occupy with a starry-eyed idea of "the ninety-nine percent." The activists' standing up for themselves and for the different experiences and historical oppressions of groups with which they identified was an effective form of political education for many who were being newly injected into the long struggle for fundamental social change. They were demanding that Occupy live up to its own ideal of justice.

The Ninety-Nine Percent as Productive Illusion

In Chapter 1, I suggested that the idea that "we are the ninety-nine percent" was a bit more complex than it sounds. On the one hand, if we look at the distribution of wealth and income since the 1970s, there is certainly a drastic difference between the rise experienced by the top one percent and the ninety-nine percent. So from a very simple breakdown of where the benefits of economic growth have gone, it would seem that it would be effective to divide people up into "the one percent" and "the ninety-nine percent." But I noted also that, although the ninety-nine percent might be said to exist as an economic reality, prior to Occupy Wall Street, no one would have said that they *feel* or even *think about* themselves in those terms. I suggested that, between the encampments and social media sites, the ninety-nine percent was being *produced*. People were learning how to conceive themselves as having something very important in common with others who appear quite different: they were struggling while a privileged few were making off like bandits.

But it is not even clear that it is good idea to consider. ourselves "the ninety-nine percent." There was a process of radical education going on in Occupy encampments for which the idea of "the ninety-nine percent" was only the starting point, and this process of education was intimately related to the idea of "demands." In a sense, "the ninety-nine percent" was a productive illusion: it conjured an illusory sense of unity, one which set people up to learn something important when that illusion was challenged. In discovering that the ninety-nine percent was too simplistic a concept for making sense of their experience in the encampments, participants learned something important about the various ways power and privilege, oppression and exploitation, function within contemporary US society. By coming down to Occupy sites around the country with the idea that "we" were finally waking up as "the ninety-nine percent," many soon learned that this "we" was actually much more fraught and complex than they had imagined. In this sense, Occupy encampments were sites of real education in power relations, and this education was sometimes difficult and painful, and often resisted by those who were most excited and enlivened by the occupations.

For the sake of clarity, I want to spell out this "process of radical education" in steps. These are simply a helpful way of walking through a process that was in fact not so clearly articulated, and was happening for many people at different paces and in very different ways, just like any lesson. This process didn't follow any necessary order—this is just how it looks to me with hindsight.

Here are the "steps" that I have observed:

1. *Prior to Occupy*: many would-be Occupiers generally thought of themselves as either "liberals" or "Democrats," with

some identifying as "Libertarians" or "Independents" and even a few as "Republicans." What each of these political categories share is the belief that politics only occurs through the official structures of the state and that the capitalist economy is to be taken for granted (though the central question of politics is to what extent the state should be involved). From each of these positions, if we do not want to engage with those state structures, they are considered apathetic or apolitical.

2. *Upon encounter with the rhetoric and images of Occupy Wall Street*: participants gained a language to conceive of their political identity not simply as either Republican, Democrat, or something in between, but in terms of wealth distribution. We are the ninety-nine percent, and both parties are mainly serving the interests of the one percent. Occupy rewrote the political landscape in economic terms.

3. *Upon participating in Occupy events*: people came thinking that they were part of the ninety-nine percent, and that they were going to organize in those terms. This suggested to many that they, the ninety-nine percent, should as such make demands as such against the political and economic elites of the one percent.

4. *Through participation in the horizontal space of the occupations*: participants encountered or observed racism, classism, sexism, gender privilege, ableism, and, of course, abuse at the hands of the police (who were, as many noted, "part of the ninety-nine percent"). If they did not observe these phenomena, they encountered more experienced activists who vocally criticized and highlighted these tensions, connecting them to the way power operates through privilege and oppression in the mainstream of US society. For many, what it meant to be a "part of the ninety-nine percent" became less clear.

5. *Through reflection on these various forms of privilege and oppression*: participants realized that the economic power of the one percent oppresses the ninety-nine percent in very different ways, and that the attempt to issue a single demand would necessarily privilege some. Not everyone thought this was a bad idea, but it introduced a real difficulty: when dealing with a system of oppression, how do you select a

demand that addresses the various grievances held by different oppressed groups?

I've suggested that the list of grievances in the *Declaration of the Occupation of Wall Street* was a brilliant attempt to negotiate this difficulty. These grievances all shared the "corporate forces of the world" as a common target, but the *Declaration* didn't prescribe any solution. Rather, it offered an invitation to the people of the world to get together, share their grievances, and develop their own local practices and processes to address them. The flow-chart of the *Declaration*, which exhibited how "all of our grievances are connected," revealed a system of power that affects different groups differently, but which is nonetheless part of an interlocking network of corporate power. It's an image of the often-unnoticed connections of economic and state power, showing how the various facts documented by the *Declaration* connect with wider forces and tendencies in a global system.

This process of coming to a shared understanding of the way Wall Street and the corporate forces of the world are involved in a global system of oppression was some of the important work going on in the Occupy movement. Such work is a condition of articulating demands that could, perhaps, challenge that system. Those who criticize Occupy for not coming forth with demands risk ignoring the radical education that many movement participants were undergoing through the movement. We were not just "in love with ourselves"—we were changing ourselves.

5

Is Occupy Anti-Capitalist?

The question "Is Occupy anti-capitalist?" is a bit more difficult to answer than it seems. It was a matter of intense debate within the occupations themselves between those who believed that the issues raised by Occupy were consequences of a capitalist economy and those who believed that capitalism, as we know it, has merely gotten "out of control" and needs to be reformed, not abolished.

One forceful articulation of the anti-capitalist position comes from Mark Bray, author of *Translating Anarchy: The Anarchism of Occupy Wall Street*. Bray gives a straightforward description of what, in his judgment, Occupy wanted:

> The destruction of capitalism and the construction of a classless, environmentally sustainable, democratic economy characterized by mutual aid and solidarity that prioritizes the fulfillment of human need. The development of forms of participatory and direct democracy grounded in local communities, groups, and bodies that empower individuals and collectivities. The elimination of all hierarchical social relations, whether founded in concepts of sexuality, race, gender, or any other.
>
> That is what Occupy Wall Street wanted (and much of what anarchists want too).
>
> Or at least that is what the vast majority of OWS organizers envisioned as the ultimate goal of their political struggle.
>
> Not the Volker Rule. Not a Robin Hood tax. Not the Glass-Steagall Act. Not ending corporate personhood. Not an increased capital gains tax. Not repealing Citizens United. And certainly not re-electing Obama. (Bray 2013, p. 39)

According to Bray, at its core the Occupy movement was an anti-capitalist movement that strove to create an egalitarian society. It is part of a longer revolutionary struggle to overcome capitalism as a historical epoch.

This understanding of what Occupy wanted, however, appears to be contradicted by at least one study of Occupy participants. Conducted at the May Day 2012 demonstration in New York City, researchers surveyed over seven hundred marchers. Of those surveyed, only 9.3 percent claimed to be against "capitalism as a system." By contrast, 47.5 percent said they were against "wealth inequality/the one percent" and 25.5 percent said they were against "money in politics."[1] Presumably, those who answered they were against one of these latter issues but not against "capitalism as a system" believed that the problems of wealth inequality and money's influence on politics could be solved without fundamental changes to economic life (perhaps, through higher taxes, campaign finance reform, or any of the policy proposals Bray mentioned).

But this survey targeted a large demonstration rather than those who were actively participating in Occupy encampments. As with any social movement, there were layers of participation in Occupy—some people may have simply showed up for the May Day march without having any previous encounter with the practices of horizontal direct democracy that characterized the movement. Simply asking people a multiple choice question on a single day of their lives misses what I have been suggesting was the most important part of the Occupy movement: the way participants were changed through their experience, the way the practices of the movement were educational and tended to cultivate a radical critique of the power relations of US society.

Bray also has a survey of his own, which speaks in favor of his conclusion about what Occupy wanted. He interviewed 192 organizers with OWS—people who were deeply involved in creating and sustaining the movement, not just people who showed up for a march. He found that 78 percent of those core organizers held explicitly anti-capitalist politics. Of those he interviewed, 72 percent identified as anarchist or "anarchistic" anti- capitalists, and the remaining 6 percent as Marxists.[2] Anarchism and

---

[1] Milkman, Ruth, et al. 2013.

[2] Bray 2013, pp. 41–44.

Marxism are, of course, two historical movements that have had different strategies for opposing capitalism.

There are two ways we can claim that Occupy was an anti-capitalist movement, in spite of the fact that the majority of those who identified with Occupy enough to turn out for a march did not think of themselves as anti-capitalists. The first way is more often associated with Lenin's version of Marxism, the second with anarchism. In this fashion, we could claim that those 9.3 percent surveyed on May Day and those interviewed by Bray are the *vanguard* of the movement, or the pool from which the vanguard will emerge. According to this view, these are people who have connected the dots and understand that the issues of wealth inequality and money's influence in politics can't be solved without fundamental, structural change to the economy—a revolution. It's the vanguard's job, as the most 'advanced' members of the revolutionary class, to build a party which both educates everyone else in the need for revolution and concocts a strategy for seizure of power. From the perspective of the vanguard, Occupy could become anti-capitalist if participants were to organize themselves for the aim of taking over state power, because it is only after power is seized that 'the people' can begin to uproot capitalist society. Historically, many debates among the anti-capitalist Left have turned on this question of "vanguardism," with socialists advocating for vanguardism and anarchists denouncing it.

The other way we might claim that Occupy was an anti-capitalist movement is more in line with the anarchist and "anarchistic" politics of those making up the majority of Occupy organizers. From this perspective, Occupy was already anti-capitalist, because it was an antagonistic crack in capitalist rule. Occupy's anti-capitalism was rooted in what they were doing in the here and now. This approach suggests that through participation in an experiment that illegally seized public space, forming encampments, sharing resources, and practicing direct democratic self-governance, participants in Occupy were anti-capitalist *in practice*, regardless of how they identified politically. Rather than demanding or not demanding the overthrow of capitalism, Occupiers were performing non-capitalist social and material relationships. In contrast to the vanguardist approach, then, the aim is not to create a party of leaders who can seize power, but rather to spread anti-capitalist practices that undermine capitalism through the creation of relationships that are intrinsically antagonistic to its ability to function.

Capitalist Realism

It is easier to imagine the end of the world than it is to imagine the end of capitalism.

—Sometimes attributed to Slavoj Žižek, sometimes to Frederic Jameson

I mentioned in Chapter 3 that most people in developed Western countries today believe, often unconsciously, that we are living at "the end of history," a time when all the basic questions about economic and political life have largely been asked and answered. In 2009, theorist Mark Fisher developed a concept that adds something helpful to this widespread ideology, and diagnoses one of the main obstacles that those opposing capitalism today continually run into. He named it "capitalist realism."

According to Fisher, capitalist realism is "the widespread sense that not only is capitalism the only viable political and economic system, but that it is now impossible to even *imagine* a coherent alternative to it."[3] There are various ways this thesis is expressed, but usually it is related to the claim that capitalism is "natural" or that nature itself operates by capitalist principles. The point, however, is that capitalism appears so obvious to many of us that we think it is impossible that things could be any other way.

Lurking behind capitalist realism, there is usually a version of history that runs something like this: for most of the twentieth century, there appeared to many people to be two options for how human economic life could be organized. On the one hand, there was capitalism, which meant private ownership of the means of production (land, factories, heaps of money, and everything else that produces wealth), and, on the other hand, socialism, which meant state ownership of those same means of production. The socialist option, taken by the USSR, East Germany, China, Cuba, and a few other countries, led to a totalitarian state, and eventually, to either internal collapse (Russia and East Germany), becoming capitalistic (China), or . . . well, Cuba is usually left out of consideration alto-

---

[3] Fisher 2009, p. 2.

gether in this version of history, or quickly dismissed as too horrible and oppressive to consider. This blind spot regarding Cuba is aided by the fact that the US government has made it difficult for its citizens to travel there and check it out for themselves. On the other hand, the capitalist option, pursued by the United States, Western Europe, Japan, and others, while not perfect, at least provided a measure of freedom for its citizens, produced large amounts of material wealth, and has outlasted the socialist experiments.

This story, then, works like an argument for capitalist realism: there were two options, and the socialist option didn't work, can't work, won't work. So there's really only one option: capitalism. The idea that capitalism is the only plausible option has been an important aid to the current era of neoliberal globalization—the creation of a transnational legal structure that allows for corporate money, commodities, and factories to flow freely across borders while people cannot do so unless they are very skilled, very wealthy, or willing to do so illegally.

Capitalist realism, then, is the conviction that capitalism is not only the best system, but the only possible or at least, the only "realistic" one. Capitalist realists base this conviction on the idea that capitalism is either somehow founded in nature, or because everything else has been tried and failed. In the United States, this is a widespread, often unconsciously held assumption by many people. It is particularly appealing to those whose political consciousness was shaped during the Cold War, when the world perhaps really seemed to be divided between two contradictory systems, and one seemed to fail. But there is reason to suspect that many in the generation born after 1980 are not so narrow in their assumptions about what is possible economically and politically. Indeed, Occupy can be seen as a straightforward attack on capitalist realism. Where it says that "capitalism is the only world possible," Occupiers attempted to simply create a world that operated by non-capitalist principles right in the symbolic center of capitalism: Wall Street.

What Is Capitalism?

Capitalism is a social system that encourages the constant growth of capital. Capital is not merely tools and machines or even human skills (as in "human capital"). Rather, capital is a *way of relating* to tools, machines, human skills, the natural world, and sums of money. When we relate to these things as capital, we evaluate them in terms of money and see them as opportunities for trade and production in order to make more money. This constant demand to transform one sum of money into a larger sum of money is the basic necessity undergirding capitalist society. From the perspective of capital, all questions of human need—whether that is for food, shelter, clean water and air, education, healthy communities, and so on—take a back seat to the one fundamental question: how can we make money?

This demand to constantly "grow" the economy (in terms of money) has consequences for our work lives, our social lives, our politics, and our environment. Capitalism achieves this growth through market exchange, which requires the institutions of private property (backed by the State) and the power of money. The focus of capitalist society on market exchange leads some to talk about "the economy" as if it were something separate from the rest of social life. In fact, the economy is one aspect of social life—the aspect that involves money transactions. The economy, therefore, relies upon vast amounts of human activity that is not measured in money—the labor of housework, birthing and raising children, caring for friends and family, and thousands of other forms of labor that are not performed for a wage. Without all this unpaid labor (sometimes called "reproductive labor") that is not counted as part of "the economy," the money-economy could not function. All profits in capitalism are made possible by the millions of unpaid tasks that make a money-economy possible.

In order to examine some features of capitalism, let's take a tour through some signs that were held up in Occupy encampments. A little elaboration on these one-liners can serve as a helpful way to introduce some basic dynamics of contemporary capitalism:

DEAR 1%. WE FELL ASLEEP FOR A WHILE. JUST WOKE UP.
SINCERELY, THE 99%

Income inequality in the US has increased to levels not seen since the Gilded Age, which preceded the Great Depression.[4] Almost all economic growth since the 1970s has gone to the top one percent.

----

[4] Saez 2013.

This is no accident. There has been a massive restructuring of economic and social life, often referred to as neoliberal globalization. This is a political project for stripping government regulations on capitalism, cutting funds for social services like education, opening markets around the globe for corporations to gain access to cheaper labor and natural resources, and promoting an increasingly dominant role for finance in the economy. This has amounted to a massive funneling of wealth into the hands of a very few people.

One way this occurred was through increased exploitation of workers: wages for workers have remained stagnant while their productivity has increased. According to Richard Wolff:

> Basically, it's been the best thirty years that capitalists in this country have ever had because they have been in the wonderful position to get more and more from their workers—rising productivity—without paying them more.
>
> The business community enjoyed their profits, but they told a completely different story than the one I just did. The story they told was a kind of folklore mythology. That the reasons their profits were so big was because their executives were geniuses. . . . They had books written about them as if they were icons of some magical, mystical productivity that accounted for the profits.
>
> Well, let me tell you, as an economist, it's embarrassing to read. I know and every other economist who looks at the numbers knows where the profits came from. They stopped raising their workers' wages, and they kept getting more out of them. There it is. No mystery here. They didn't suddenly become genius executives. (Wolff and Barsamian 2012, p. 29)

Starting with Margaret Thatcher in the 1970s UK, and then with Ronald Reagan in the 1980s US, there was a concerted effort of corporations and right-wing politicians to destroy the labor movement. This was effected by many means, including the "outsourcing" of factory production to other countries where labor could be more cheaply exploited, the formation of right-wing think tanks and lobbying organizations that could influence and even write legislation favorable to corporate profits and increase in roboticization of manufacturing, permanently replacing workers with machines.

This highlights one of the fundamental conflicts in capitalist society: the conflict of interest between owners of the capitalist firms and the workers who run them. The boss wants to get the most out of workers, while paying them the least. This exploitation is one main source of capitalist profit, which is why corporations are always looking for ways to "cut labor costs"—for them, workers are just another cost, which they want to trim as much as possible. If workers look like they are getting emboldened, and the cultural tide is turning against capitalist power, then capitalists, as a class, fight back. They've done this by creating a situation in which people feel so lucky to have work at all that they are less likely to stand up for themselves in the face of exploitation.

While wages have remained stagnant, cost of living has continued to rise. The gap has been made up with a regime of debt— the "product" created by the financial services industry. Increasingly, corporate profits in the US come from interest and fees collected on debt. This accounts for forty to fifty percent of corporate profits nowadays. This is a wonderful scheme for the rich: poor people take out debt in order to get a house, or a car, or a diploma—things they need in order to live and work in today's economy. Then, if they're lucky, they find a job, where their labor is exploited. Then they use a huge chunk of the money they earn to pay back the financial institutions that gave them the loans so they could work. This scheme has been remarkably effective at making rich people richer, and keeping poor people so desperate that few even consider fighting back. But, as the sign says, we're waking up.

I Can't Afford a Lobbyist

In the 1960s and 1970s, emboldened and radicalized through the Civil Rights and Anti-War movements, people around the country were standing up to both the authority of the State and the power of capital. A new common sense was taking root, and those in power fought back. One of the ways they have done so is a through a concerted effort to reshape political life.

This may sound implausible, even conspiratorial. But it's quite reasonable if you think about it: those with lots of wealth and power usually believe they are entitled to it, and they organize to defend it. Today, that happens through many different channels, but one obvious way we see it is through corporate lobbyists. As people hired to represent the interests of corporations in Washington, they are agents of a class conspiracy against the those who don't benefit from the constant increase in corporate profits—that is, the rest of us. Since politicians today are constantly on the prowl for campaign donations, lawmakers have sympathetic ears to lobbyists with deep pockets.

But lobbying wasn't always as common a practice as it is today. The modern regime of corporate lobbying was kickstarted in the years after an infamous memo written in 1971 by Lewis Powell. Powell was director of the Chamber of Commerce and a corporate lawyer sitting on the boards of eleven different corporations. His "Confidential Memorandum: Attack on the Free Enterprise System" was distributed to CEOs around the country, warning that

> what now concerns us is quite new in the history of America. We are not dealing with episodic or isolated attacks from a relatively few extremists or even from the minority socialist cadre. Rather, the assault on the enterprise system is broad based and consistently pursued. It is gaining momentum and converts. (Powell 1971)

Powell points to the college campus as the most dangerous source of attack on capitalist values, and outlines a plan—both intellectual and economic—for changing the conversation on college campuses. Powell also recommends that corporations start flexing the political muscle that their tremendous wealth affords them. In the next decade, the number of registered lobbyists in Washington skyrocketed: "in 1971, only 175 firms had registered lobbyists in Washington, but by 1982, nearly 2,500 did."[5] Two months after his memo, Powell was appointed to the Supreme Court by President Nixon.

Powell's memo was particularly well-placed to have an influence, but it has to be seen as a sign of the times: in response to a tumultuous decade of social struggles in which the ideological foundations of capitalism were being threatened, corporate leaders geared up to fight back against the social movements that had been effectively transforming American society. And they used their wealth to gain political influence that reshaped American society. It is one fine smoking gun in the class war that has been in high gear since the 1970s.

---

[5] Hacker 2012.

I Am a Human Being, Not a Commodity!

Under capitalism, production occurs for the sake of creating commodities, or products to be sold on the market. But capitalism also creates a "labor market," in which human labor is treated as a commodity, something bought and sold. Under slavery, people were bought and sold as commodities. Capitalism should be seen as an innovation in this oppressive relationship: rather than buying and selling whole human beings, what is bought and sold is their labor power. Rather than being *owned*, you are *rented* for the day. "You" are not a commodity, but your labor power—your time and energy—is. Capitalism, then, relies upon a peculiar fantasy that "you" can be separated from your own labor. When we engage in labor that seems like it is not our own, when we seem to separate our selves—our thoughts, feelings, aspirations—from our work, we are engaged in *alienated* labor.

Alienated labor is a sign that we are being coerced, and the workplace is typically a site of hierarchical and coercive relationships. Workers have to take orders from above, or risk losing their job—which means suffering for them and their family. The standard response from those who support capitalism is, "if you don't like it, quit and work somewhere else." This shows just how removed from working-class reality those who defend capitalism actually are. If you quit your job, your only option is to go and find another job, where you are similarly subjected to the rule of a boss. In order to earn a wage, you have to find someone to sell yourself to. This is why it is sometimes said that capitalism relies upon "wage-slavery," and this need to earn a wage leads us to put up with hierarchical and exploitative relationships in the workplace that, in another context, we would recognize as oppressive. As Noam Chomsky puts it:

> It's ridiculous to talk about freedom in a society dominated by huge corporations. What kind of freedom is there inside a corporation? They're totalitarian institutions - you take orders from above and maybe give them to people below you. There's about as much freedom as under Stalinism.

Even if there are some hip corporate offices that promote the self-exploration of their employees, these workplaces are the exception to a global economy in which people elsewhere are trapped in the relations Chomsky describes. Managers have realized that the production of software or marketing occurs best in an environment where workers feel free—but the computers they are programing and the products they are selling are still produced under conditions of coercion.

Under capitalism, our working days are turned into commodities. Hours of our lives are bought and sold, during which we behave like the tools of those above us. Capitalist society has taught us that this is called "freedom." In this so-called "freedom," most people have to spend the majority of their lives carrying out the will of others for the sake of keeping them rich, or risk getting kicked out of their homes or not being able to care for themselves and those they love. This "freedom" is wage-slavery, in which human life becomes a commodity.

HUMAN NEED, NOT CORPORATE GREED

Greed is a moral vice—the desire to hoard more and more for yourself at the expense of others. Not all capitalists are greedy in this sense. Many are decent human beings, especially with their family and friends. Criticisms of the one percent as "greedy" are inadequate because they give the impression that all that is needed is to reform a few bad people. But capitalism isn't just the bad behavior of a few: it is a social and economic system, a set of rules for how we relate. The problem with capitalism is that its rules *encourage and reward greedy behavior.*

Capitalist businesses reward those employees and managers who make them money, moving them up the corporate ladder and giving them bonuses. Firms that make the most money gain more power to expand and compete with other firms. The demand to constantly increase profit creates a situation where greedy people are rewarded with more power and social status. On the job, workers may be encouraged to cooperate and to empathize with customers—but only in the interest of making money. If someone were to *really* act from empathy to the extent that it interfered with the firm's profits, they would be fired. In capitalism, all human values are made subordinate to the demand for profit. Smiles, concern, and all other signs of human affection are turned into instruments for making profits.

People have to participate in these practices even if they are not otherwise bad people. They are simply doing their jobs, forced to turn off emotions and second-thoughts for the sake of earning a paycheck. Those who can most effectively turn off their moral reservations and become ruthless for the sake of the corporation will likely be rewarded within it. The capitalist corporation, while a "person" under the law and thus able to own property, has one purpose only: profit. Everything a corporation "does" is oriented toward this one goal, no matter what public-relations image it puts forward. The corporation is a rigidly hierarchical structure that traps the labor of people through wage-slavery, steering their activity toward its own aim of gaining more and more money. Greedy people rise to the top. But since people working within the corporation must train themselves to put the profit ahead of everything else, the corporation functions as a social machine for manufacturing people who put the power of money above all when they're on the job.

ARE WE REALLY GOING TO LET A BUNCH OF GREEDY, SELFISH FOOLS DO IN THIS WHOLE PLANET?

Capitalist firms exist for the creation of profit, and subordinate every other value to this end. One of the ways this is showing up today is in ecological crises. Put bluntly: capitalism is destroying the ecological basis of life on the planet. Repairing the ecological systems of the Earth requires that we break with capitalism, and fast. Climate change is caused not simply by "humans," but by specific human activities that rely upon the constant increase in the extraction and combustion of fossil fuels. The demand to constantly expand the economy lies at the root of this process. Chemical contamination of water and soil, habitat loss through deforestation, and the warming of global temperatures are some of the main contributors to the loss of thousands of species each year. Since these ecological relationships are not directly productive of money, they are ignored and exploited by those looking to simply produce commodities.

Ecological systems are dense networks of relationships between species and their environments. Sustaining them requires attention to these connections, and an understanding of how our actions have effects that cannot be calculated in terms of money. But capitalism puts profit above all else, and looks at all these systems as merely a stock-pile of resources to be extracted, reshaped, and sold. This attitude and the practices that follow from it are devastating the earth.

In order for capitalism to get off the ground, a wealthy class of people first needs to create wage-slaves by destroying peoples' ability to produce for themselves. Capitalism has spread around the world through colonialism, which robbed communities of resources and kicked them off the land through *enclosure,* turning this land—and sometimes the people—into "private property." These massive acts of deprivation, which included the kidnapping of African slaves, the burning of peasant villages, and the genocide and mass dispossession of Native Americans, stand as the historical basis of capitalism. It was acts like these that created the proletariat —masses of people with no choice but to sell themselves for a wage.

Besides the brutality and injustice of this process, it has also had consequences for the environment: when people are separated from the land and incorporated in the wage system, the social relationships of money appear more relevant for survival than the ecological relationships that actually sustain their lives. Knowledge that allowed indigenous cultures to live in sustainable and mutually beneficial relations with the non-human world comes to be seen as irrelevant compared with the knowledge that allows us to accumulate money. As a result, most of us have no understanding of the basic processes and ecological relationships that sustain our lives, and so we are largely unable to help rebuild those ecosystems, or even recognize how they are being destroyed.

SHIT IS FUCKED UP AND BULLSHIT

This sign, which popped up at occupations around the country, captures the sense of complete disgust with an entire social system. Often, it's difficult for us to examine social and political problems, because our thoughts quickly spiral into an overwhelming web of fears and problems beyond our control. The whole thing can lead to a crushing anxiety and depression. It shouldn't be surprising, then, that rates of depression and anxiety are so high in the contemporary US. Much of the work we do in capitalist society is meaningless for our lives and controlled by others. Depression is a natural response to this kind of situation. We are constantly under pressure to compete, whether in the workplace or in a social life saturated with images calculated by marketing firms to induce the sense that we aren't beautiful enough. Anxiety is a natural response to this kind of situation. These feelings overwhelm us when we don't understand them as resulting from an oppressive social system, and pharmaceutical companies make tremendous profits off convincing us that these problems are simply "chemical imbalances" that need to be fixed with one of the drugs they have for sale. In fact, depression and anxiety are responses to a social world that is not meeting our needs for a cooperative, ecologically sustainable, and just society. When we are pitted in competition against each other for basic resources, when our economic activity is destroying our future, and when things are fundamentally unfair, we *feel* bad, even if we don't let ourselves acknowledge why.

Much of the tremendous energy and excitement that exploded in Occupy encampments stemmed from the fact that a situation was created in which people could finally admit to themselves and others how terrible things actually are. They connected the problems together and learned to see their rage, depression, and anxiety as not merely personal problems, but as their own intuitive understanding of a system of upside-down values, a system that puts profit above the dignity of human beings and the health of the planet.

How Occupy Was Anti-Capitalist in Practice

If capitalism is a set of social relationships—of ways of interacting with each other and with nonhuman things—based on the legal structure of private property, the wage, the power of money, and the demand for constant increase in profit, then Occupy encampments around the country were places where these kinds of social relations were suspended and other kinds of relationships were practiced. By "suspended," I mean that they were halted momentarily and within a limited space—predominantly within the parks, but also extending out through networks of mutual aid that supported and sustained the encampments.

First, the very act of occupation itself was an affront to the legal structure of private property, as well as that of state (or "public") property. Occupiers seized space, often exploiting legal ambiguities in ownership. Zuccotti Park, for example, was a "privately owned public space," which means that although it was owned by a private corporation, it was legally required to be open to the public twenty-four hours a day. Still, as soon as the occupation started to gain momentum, the owners of the space tried to shut it down by claiming it posed a sanitation hazard. Confrontations like this occurred throughout the country, where the use of violence (the police) was threatened to remove occupiers from the space they were claiming for their assemblies.

In taking public or private space for political experimentation and the construction of a mini-society, Occupiers were reclaiming the tradition of "the commons": land or resources that are neither controlled by private owners nor the state, but rather are managed collectively by those who use them. Within the encampments, personal belongings were—apart from instances of theft—respected, but the rule of private property, as a legal structure that excludes others from the use of things they need, was not. Further, through participating in encampments, many personal belongings (computers and media equipment, tents, blankets, food, art materials, cigarettes) were shared, and people's skills and labor were offered freely in the form of health clinics, massage tables, teach-ins, and other forms of care-provision.

Second, as I mentioned in Chapter 2, in Occupy encampments, people engaged in labor that was outside of the wage relationship and thus unswayed by the power of money. The occupations were intensely productive places, where people were freely organizing themselves to care for one another and constantly planning and mobilizing support for both the occupation and outside struggles. All this occurred not because someone was issuing orders or because participants stood to gain money, but because the occupations provided a space in which people felt they were working on behalf of their collective self-interest. Bonds of solidarity were forged both within individual encampments and with the wider movement, and people saw their own actions as contributing to a larger struggle in which they had a stake, but not one they expected to personally profit from at the expense of others.

Within the occupations, the power of money was largely eliminated. One young Occupier described to me how, when he first arrived in Zuccotti Park and received a plate of food from the kitchen, he asked where he could pay for it. The kitchen crew just laughed at him. This is important, because it demonstrates that the predictability of money's power was broken within the encampments: if within capitalist society, one can be sure that their money will result in some people taking orders from them, as soon as one

entered the encampments, all bets were off. If you wanted someone to do something for you or with you, you would have to convince them that it was the best thing they could be doing at the
moment. When the power of money is suspended, the hierarchical
relationships on which capitalism relies no longer function. As will
be discussed in the next chapter, when money loses its ability to
reliably coerce the behavior of others, those in power have to
resort to the violence of the police in order to get their way.

Third, the productive activity of the Occupy movement was not
oriented toward making commodities for the sake of selling them
to turn a profit. Occupiers produced artwork, writings, events, acts
of civil disobedience; they produced gardens, meetings, electric
generators, images, and friendships; they produced joy and anger
and insight and songs. But they didn't produce commodities to be
sold on the market. Or rather, if they did, they were betraying the
spirit of the movement and trying to do what capitalists always do:
attempting to take something that was freely offered (in this case,
the image and excitement of a social movement) and turn it into a
commodity. As they wrote in the Principles of Solidarity,
Occupiers wanted to "redefine how labor is valued." This means
recognizing that the production of commodities is an inadequate
measure for the work that is really done to create and sustain satisfying and joyous human experiences. Which is, of course, what
we all want.

But like capitalism, Occupy was bent on expansion. And this
too, was part of its being a real anti-capitalist practice. Those who
respond to capitalism by taking to the hills to form a commune are,
in a way, trying to find a path of adaptation within capitalism, trying to carve out a comfortable, communal life within its structure.
Occupy, through performing anti-capitalism in public and actively
attempting to spread the non-capitalist social relations on which it
relied outside of the confines of its parks, was trying to alter the
social relationships that sustain capitalism. Occupiers encouraged
people to stand up for themselves in all areas of their lives, and
encouraged them to get together with their neighbors and friends
and begin to practice the radical democracy they were modeling.

This practice of radical democracy was, in fact, the core of
Occupy's anti-capitalism. Since capitalism is ultimately a system of
hierarchical relations sustained by, first, the power of money and,
when that fails, the power of state violence, the commitment to

practice horizontal decision making for all is an inherent obstacle to the power of capital. This is not to say that there aren't ways capitalist firms incorporate horizontal decision making into their own management. But when they do so, it always comes with limits: there are always people whose voices matter less or not at all (whether those people are the workers or the people who live next door to the factory). In encouraging everyone, everywhere, to start looking to themselves and one another, and to begin solving their problems in ways that benefited everyone, Occupy was pointing toward a democratic economic life, a world in which every legal claim to private ownership of some necessary resource is up for discussion about how it could be managed in a way that benefits all who need it.

Within the occupations, then, a new common sense was born regarding why people labor and how people should relate with material goods. Anyone who assumed that people only labor for money and that people are naturally opposed to sharing with others—psychological assumptions that are often made to support capitalist realism—would only need to step into an occupation to see just how wrong they were. The best argument against an ideology as deeply rooted as capitalist realism is simply the demonstration of an alternative, which Occupy, in the time it was allowed, managed to achieve.

Creating Cracks, Reclaiming the Commons

Capitalist society is controlled by the dictates of capital—it is tyranny of the demand for profit. But a tyrant's power is rooted in the rest of us:

> Everything that the tyrant has comes from us and from his exploitation of us: we have only to stop working for him and he will cease to be a tyrant because the material basis of his tyranny will have disappeared. We make the tyrant; in order to be free, we must stop making the tyrant. The key to our emancipation, the key to becoming more fully human is simple: refuse, disobey. *Resolve to serve no more, and you are at once free.* (Holloway 2010, pp. 6–7)

But this does not seem so "simple": how would we "resolve to serve no more"? Holloway proposes that capitalist society has "cracks" in it—spaces where the rules break down, if only for a moment. There are moments when we say "No, in this space, in this moment, we are not going to do what capitalist society expects of us. We are going to do whatever we consider necessary or desirable." This refusal creates a "crack," in which "we take the moment or space into our own hands and try to make it a place of self-determination, refusing to let money (or any other alien force) determine what we do" (p. 21).

Holloway argues that opportunities for such cracks abound, and that they are becoming more frequent:

> Humanity (in all its senses) jars increasingly with capitalism. It becomes harder and harder to fit as capital demands more and more. Ever more people simply do not fit in to the system, or, if we do manage to squeeze ourselves on to capital's ever-tightening Procrustean bed, we do so at the cost of leaving fragments of ourselves behind, to haunt. That is the basis of our cracks. . . . (p. 9)

Occupy was an extraordinary crack, a crack that rippled throughout the globe. The cracks were created by a collective refusal to move, and sustained by horizontal organizing practices. In opposition to the social relations that sustain capital, Occupiers created *commons* in the cracks they opened up.

In August of 2011, while the NYCGA was meeting in Tompkins Square Park organizing for the occupation of Wall Street, a seminar was being conducted at 16 Beaver Street, a radical art space in the financial district of Manhattan. Led by Silvia Federici, George Caffentzis, and David Graeber, the seminar was entitled "Beyond Good and Evil Commons."[6] These thinkers, all of whom were highly influential participants in OWS, were reflecting upon the meaning and potential of reclaiming the commons as a means for generating both resistance and alternatives to capitalism.

The term "commons" historically refers to the fields and forests collectively managed by peasant communities. In England, for example, it was the commons that were seized through the Acts of Enclosure, which was the brutal land-grab that displaced peasants and created the English proletariat. Many contemporary anti-capitalists, having recognized that enclosure is not merely a one-time event in the pre-history of capitalism, but an ongoing part of cap-

---

[6] Federici et al. 2011.

italist expansion, emphasize that commons too are perennial features of human existence, and sites of struggle against capitalist social relations.

"Commons" are not merely shared resources, but social relationships between people for the collective use and care of those shared resources. As Massimo De Angelis puts it, "to pose the question of commons is simply to recognize the social character of our doing, the fact that individuals are *social* and hence they *must share something* (language, land, sea, air, values, etc.); and, at the same time, what is shared is the result of social co-production."[7] This is the broadest meaning of commons: though capitalist social relations encourage us to think of ourselves as isolated economic units, calculating our own personal gain, in fact we are participants in a shared world, and all our action involves the co-operative use of what we share together. "Reclaiming the commons" is an attempt to reclaim space and activity based on the recognition of this fact of our shared, common world, a fact that capitalist society tends to cover over with private property and money relations.

In the contemporary United States, as well as other developed countries, it often feels like there are no commons left to defend. Nearly every aspect of our lives—or at least the aspects of our lives we think most often about—is enclosed—access to resources is restricted to those with money, and those without money are subject to violence if they use those resources. The Occupy movement was thus about *reclaiming* the commons. First, it was about reclaiming resources, most notably *time* and *space* for democratic self-management. Second, Occupy was about reclaiming *the very idea* of the commons, which has been obscured today by capitalist realism, which leads us to think of private property as "natural." Reclaiming the commons reasserts the possibility of life and activity in cracks created within the world of private property and state control.

Again, the commons isn't solely about "resources," but about social relationships for managing them. The state is formed of social relationships of hierarchy, in which those with a monopoly on the perceived legitimate use of force are able to give orders that are backed by the threat of violence (the police and military). Capitalism too relies upon hierarchical social relationships, in

---

[7] De Angelis 2007, p. 243

which those who have money are able to give orders because of the deprivation of others, and this condition of deprivation is sustained by the state's protection of property rights through threat of violence. Creating the commons occurs through making processes of democratic self-management, in which decisions are made by those who have a stake in a resource for the purpose of making it widely available, rather than for the purpose of depriving it from others for the sake of money.

The challenge of those who attempt to create the commons is to come up with schemes whereby resources can be provided to all who need them and managed by all who use them. This is not always easy—but neither is it always easy to come up with a scheme whereby resources can be taken from people and sold back to them at a profit! To demand the commons, then, is to demand that we use our creativity to figure out new and innovative ways to provide for one another's needs directly, rather than spending our energy trying to figure out new and innovative ways to profit off the needs of others.

Occupy reclaimed a commons, and therefore called into question the basic assumptions of capitalist social relationships through suspending those relationships and creating different ones based on direct democracy. None of this, obviously, was communicated with the slogan "We are the ninety-nine percent." Even if these elements of Occupy were reported on, they were unlikely to make much sense outside of a direct experience with them. Occupy, as a practice of seizing space for collective self-management, was not just "anti-capitalist" in the sense of being ideologically opposed to capitalism (though many Occupiers were and are). Rather, it was actively, practically un-capitalist in the social relationships it forged and attempted to spread. It was a crack in the facade of capital, and was the death-knell for capitalist realism among its participants; it unlocked the radical imagination. And once that box is open, so is the future.

But Is This *Really* a Challenge to Capitalism?

If you're asking yourself whether the strategy of occupying public parks and prefiguring a non-capitalist world is really enough to challenge a whole global system, your doubts are well founded. Capitalism is, ultimately, a system of control backed by the power of the police and the military, and it is not so easily toppled. My contention, however, is not that Occupy was "the revolution," but that it opened a crack, and with that the possibility of imagining a revolution by combating the widespread assumption of capitalist realism. While Occupy was hardly the end of capitalism, it was a moment of collective learning that *did* effectively transform people who were, for a variety of reasons, dissatisfied with the current structures of government and economic life, into people committed to creating a world based upon principles like those Bray described above.

The experiments in reclaiming the commons with democratic principles that took place in Occupy camps were far from perfect. And it makes sense that they would be, not just because nothing is perfect, but also because if the commons is about learning how to relate with one another in egalitarian ways, we have to understand that this process of learning takes time. If capitalism is a set of social relationships, it is also a set of habits of interacting with both others and the world. While in moments of exhilaration, habits can be broken, the process of really changing and reconstructing habits does not happen overnight. A public experiment in creating the commons has to keep in mind that the social relationships for maintaining it are new to many of us—co-operation requires skills that many of us have not spent much time developing. As a result, being thrust into an environment where we have to co-operate feels very intense. This intensity can be enlivening, but it can quickly start to feel like too much. People get burned out, don't take care of themselves, and end up fighting one another rather than those who rule the world. Suspending capitalist relations is, for many, emotionally challenging, and this fact points to the need for a process of cooperative education that allows us to develop our skills for working together.

Another question should arise: doesn't reclaiming the commons sound like a pretty normal thing? Isn't that what we do at a potluck, for example? Is this really a challenge to capitalism?

Well, yes and no. One of the important features of the anti-capitalist analysis that takes reclaiming the commons as its point of departure is that it *is* something many of us have some experience with. Potlucks and camping trips and, really, any moment when people are making decisions among equals about how to use or produce something, are moments that prefigure this kind of struggle. But the essential point that is missing in such moments is the element of *struggle*. If, for example, a community were to arrange a potluck to support striking workers, then the pot-luck would be playing a role in a struggle against certain entrenched capitalist forces. What was anti-capitalist about Occupy was its demand that the commons be generalized, its own attempt to grow as a movement that was both antagonistic to capitalist ways of relating and modeling horizontal relationships.

But this raises the question of the limits of an experiment like Occupy. If the relations that compose capitalism are indeed backed by the power of state violence, then any prefigurative experiment in creating a non-capitalist world is limited, because it will become the target of state violence. Which is what happened. This fact raises the vexed issue of violence, which was hotly debated within the Occupy movement.

6

Violence and the Occupy Movement

It's March of 2012, and Occupy St. Louis is hosting a convergence of Midwest Occupy groups. We plan to re-occupy a park on the south side of the city as part of an effort to bring the movement back into public for the Spring. A few hundred people have come in from out of town, and we gather at Compton Reservoir Park. Some people have built a structure that can best be described as a small house and assembled it, providing shelter from the evening's rain. The police have surrounded the park and inform us all that they will be enforcing a curfew at 10 p.m.

The Occupiers, armed with nothing more than a mobile stereo system pumping hip-hop and a thirty-foot long banner that reads POLICE STATE, refuse, at first, to leave the park. When police reinforcements come and it's clear that remaining in the park will mean trouble, we all leave, marching from the park with the intention of going down the street as we did so many times in previous months. As we march out of the park past the police and begin heading down the street, a wave of armed men in blue overtakes us. I'm thrown to the ground by five officers and handcuffed. Chaos erupts as some shout at the police and others are chased down side streets, where there are no cameras to record what the police do to them.

As we were being piled into the police van with hands turning blue from zip-ties, the officer who was loading us in said, "You know, I agree with what you are all protesting. The banks screwed this country. But you have to obey the law. You can't go blocking traffic." At the station, as a young guy working there was scanning my finger prints into an FBI database, he asks me what we were protesting. "Inequality and how corporations run the world," I say, thinking this a useful way to sum up everything. He says, "The way I see it, the police are just one more gang with a lot of guns and a lot of money."

A year later, I'm found guilty of disobeying an officer and disorderly conduct after the police construct a fantastical and untrue scenario in which Occupiers engaged in a standoff with them in the middle of the street, refusing to leave the intersection where they attacked us. In the police version of events, they kindly asked us to leave the road and gave us ample time to do so before they reluctantly arrested us. After this farce, I am left alone in the courtroom with the judge for a strange moment. Since the verdict is already in, I figure there is no harm in letting him know that the police, one by one, lied to his face. I ask if I can speak and he cuts me off, going into a speech of his own: "You know Mr. Smaligo, I am not unsympathetic to what you all are doing. The banks and these corporations run this country. They take everything for themselves, they break and ignore laws, and they own the political system. It is a terrible mess we're all in, and I am not unsympathetic to your cause. I wish you and your friends a lot of luck."

During each of these encounters, I'm left with a terrible impression that the law is a machine operating on its own, without anyone actually believing in it. Where are the passionate defenders? Why are all these people who are putting people in cages doing so for reasons they don't seem to believe in? Then I recall a moment at the police station in the holding cell, when one of the cops responsible for beating three friends bloody was pacing around making fun of us whike we were being processed. Someone accused him of beating up our friend and he tells us all, proudly, "as long as I get my paycheck, I don't give a shit."

"So you're evil?" I say.

"What?"

"You don't care what happens to others, as long as you get paid. That makes you evil."

I notice a slight pain in his expression, like I've actually struck a nerve. Soon his demeanor changes and he is concerned about my blue hands. He offers me water. I refuse. Another cop marches us all into a full holding cell and, when he opens the door, informs the mostly black men inside that we are a group of white supremacists and they should do whatever they like to us. When we get inside, a friend says, "Look, we all know it's the cops that are the fascists. They beat up our friends and now they want you to beat us up." The tension is immediately relieved and we all try to get comfortable.

Hours later, a friend shows up with two black eyes, a row of staples in his skull, and a head swollen to almost twice its normal size. A black man in the holding cell, picked up for something else, says "Damn, the cops are beating up white kids now?"

"Violence" in Occupy

In the winter of 2012, a debate about "violence" tore through Occupy circles, centering on the phrase "diversity of tactics." The Occupy movement was not planning on using lethal weapons, or engaging in kidnapping or any other form of harm against human beings. Rather, "diversity of tactics" refers to a framework for protests that acknowledges from the outset that there will be some who choose to struggle in ways that are more rowdy and confrontational with the police, and that while not everyone agrees this is the best approach, it is either futile or undesirable to try to stop them or publicly condemn them for it.

From the beginning, this was a contentious issue within Occupy, but one which nonetheless was pursued successfully for the first few months. This was, admittedly, largely because there were very few instances of property destruction or fighting with the police in the early months of the movement. But as the police became more effective in suppressing Occupy, some involved with the movement responded in turn, and the tensions that had been present all along crystallized into an internal crisis for the movement.

In this chapter, I describe the development of this crisis through a special focus on Occupy Oakland and the debate spurred by Chris Hedges's notorious article "The Cancer in Occupy," which painted a picture of "Black Bloc anarchists" as trying to destroy the movement from within. Black bloc is not a particular group of people, but a tactic that various people have engaged in. Those engaging in this tactic wear all black, conceal their faces, group together during demonstrations, and sometimes (though not always) engage in property destruction, vandalism, and self-defense against police aggression. During Occupy, black bloc was demonized, often by people who did not listen to why those who engage in it think it is a good idea. In order to avoid this pitfall, I try to present what I think are some often overlooked arguments for why some think black bloc is an important component of contemporary protests. The question of violent and confrontational tactics that arose within the Occupy movement is not going away, and I hope this discussion will help those involved in future protests to avoid rehashing the same debate that Occupy encountered—or at least allow that debate to be slightly more informed.

But it's important to focus first on the real sources of violence during Occupy. If we use the term "violence" in the strict (perhaps too strict) sense of meaning physical harm against other human beings, then by far the most violence that was committed during the Occupy movement was enacted by the police against protesters.

There were countless examples of police violence during Occupy, but among the most striking was the incident of Pepper Spray Cop at University of California Davis. On November 18th 2011, students participating in Occupy UC Davis sat down to link arms to resist the eviction being carried out by campus police in riot gear. After being told to leave and refusing to move, UC Davis police officer Lt. John Pike unleashed a thick stream of pepper spray onto the faces of the seated demonstrators. After this point-blank deposit of chemical agents onto the eyes of people who posed no physical threat to anyone, the police proceeded to arrest them all—just as they could have without the spraying. What was so despicable about this incident was the complete absence of malice on the part of Lt. Pike. He was clearly just doing his job, as if being on the clock released him from all the burdens of conscience for his actions.[1] He later won $30,000 in worker's compensation for psychological damage incurred by the shaming that followed.

Incidents of police violence like this took place all around the country, and were, at first, beneficial to the movement's popularity. In order to suppress the movement without generating more sympathy for it, police needed to change their tactics.

Evicting an Idea

Early in the morning on November 15th 2011, police attacked and removed Occupy Wall Street from its home in Zuccotti Park:

---

[1] The incident can be viewed here:
https//www.youtube.com/watch?v=WmJmmnMkuEm.

At one in the morning, hundreds of police in riot gear . . . stormed the plaza, shining floodlights and tearing down tents. Sanitation workers loaded Occupiers' belongings into garbage trucks, including thousands of books from the People's Library. Truck-mounted, "less-lethal" LRAD sound cannons were on the scene, and five police helicopters hovered high overhead, where airspace was closed to media aircraft. Occupiers locked arms around the kitchen area, facing pepper spray and batons for doing so. Reporters and elected officials who managed to get into the middle of it came out bloody with the rest. (Schneider 2013, p. 101)

The police had put the surrounding area on lock-down, shutting down subways, telling local residents not to leave their buildings, and erecting barriers throughout the surrounding blocks and only letting in those with official press credentials—but even they did not fare well once inside the militarized zone. Media were shoved around by police, a *New York Post* reporter was put in a choke-hold and some journalists were arrested.[2] One can imagine how those who attempted to resist the eviction were treated. Proudly taking responsibility for the actions of the NYPD, Mayor Michael Bloomberg provided an Orwellian justification for the night raid: his aims, he said, were "guaranteeing health and safety, and guaranteeing the protesters' First Amendment rights."[3]

Weeks earlier, a similar scene had unfolded at Occupy Oakland, where on October 25th police stormed the encampment, trampling upon and destroying everything in their path and firing tear gas and "flash-bang grenades." One of them struck Army veteran Scott Olsen in the head, nearly killing him. One survivor of the police assault noted that "there were young people in these camps and children, infants in a lot of the tents and this was just . . . completely out of whack with the situation."[4]

The brutality of this first attempt to evict Occupy Oakland only emboldened the movement. Occupiers in Oakland reassembled the next day, held a GA and declared themselves ready for a General Strike on November 2nd, what was perhaps the most impressive single action of the Occupy movement. But on November 14th, the Oakland PD swept in again and succeeded in clearing the encampment.

---

[2] Stelter and Baker 2011.
[3] Lockwood 2011.
[4] Street 2011.

In fact, the police cracked down on encampments in more than a dozen cities during that week in November, and this was probably no coincidence. As Oakland Mayor Jean Quan let slip during an interview with the BBC, she had participated in a conference call with eighteen other mayors about how to suppress the movement.

In discussing Occupy Oakland, Mayor Quan assured "We will continue to be vigilant and ensure that public safety remains our first priority."[5] Months later, a set of leaked emails between the Oakland Police Department and the Mayor's office gave a much different perspective. As Rebecca Solnit reports:

> While the camp was in existence, crime went down 19% in Oakland, a statistic the city was careful to conceal. "It may be counter to our statement that the Occupy movement is negatively impacting crime in Oakland," the police chief wrote to the mayor in an email. . . . Pay attention: Occupy was so powerful a force of nonviolence that it was already solving Oakland's chronic crime and violence problems just by giving people hope and meals and solidarity and conversation. (Solnit 2012)

Public safety apparently had little to do with the need to crush Occupy Oakland. Indeed, the police chief was worried that the public might learn that Occupy was actually reducing crime, since it was contrary to their public message.

Many Occupiers who were new to activism were shocked by both the violence of the police crackdowns and the revelations that their own government would go to such lengths as to spy on them and co-ordinate their eviction. Those who had some experience with protest, however, were less surprised. While many people—particularly those who are white and middle to upper class—in the United States grow up with the sense that police are there to "serve and protect" everyone, those with a sense of how past social movements have struggled to change the world often conclude that the fundamental function of the police in the US is and has always been to maintain the current power structures. Police are defenders of the current legal structure, no matter who that legal structure benefits. They are people who employ force for a paycheck.

---

[5] Street 2011.

The Occupy movement exposed for a new generation the relation between police and the wealthy. And in a time when public funds have been stripped and cities are in debt, this relationship has become even more pronounced. For example, it turns out that many of the New York Police Department officers who were working around Occupy Wall Street were not working as officers of the law at all. Rather, they were "moonlighting" as security guards for banks while in their official uniforms. According to Naomi Wolf:

> A nontransparent program called "Paid Detail Unit" has been set up so that private corporations are actually employing NYPD officers, who are in uniform and armed. The difference is that when these "public servants" are on the payroll of the banks, they are no longer serving you and the impartial rule of law in your city—despite what their uniform and badge imply. (Wolf 2012)

The wave of evictions of Occupy encampments in the fall of 2011 was followed by vigilant prevention of re-occupations in the spring of 2012. Occupy's tactic of seizing and holding public space had struck a nerve, and the veneer of the First Amendment, which supposedly protects both freedom of speech and peaceable assembly, was peeled back to reveal the strong arm of the state and its unquestioning support for the powerful. Beyond the egregious instances of excessive force by a few officers, what the evictions of the Occupy movement revealed was something much more important: the *structural violence* that maintains both the power of corporations and that of the state.

Structural Violence and Changing the World

Structural violence is the violence—or the threat of violence—that maintains the dominant institutions or social relations of a given society. When I argued in Chapter 1 that the power of money relied upon the fact that people need money to gain access to what they need (or think they need) in our society, I mean to claim that the power of money relies upon structural violence. If you don't have any money, you have every reason to believe you will suffer in this society, whether physically or through some other deprivation of your dignity. The peculiar thing about structural violence, as opposed to some individual violent act (like, say, an armed robbery of a bank), is that structural violence, for most people involved, *doesn't appear as violence at all.* It appears as "peace" or "order." Whether through force or through ideas and rituals that justify the current distribution of power and wealth, structural violence appears as "just the way things are," as "natural" or as "the law."

When something appears natural or just a matter of the law, we tend not to condemn it as "violence." So it doesn't seem like "violence" every time someone has to go to work at a job they think is meaningless or degrading just in order to pay rent or feed their kids. It just seems like "the way things are." It doesn't seem like "violence" when the company lays off a thousand workers in order to remain profitable, even if this means people lose their homes, their medical care, or have to move across the country and leave behind people they love—it just seems like "the economy." It doesn't seem like "violence" when oil and gas drilling operations like "fracking" leak toxins into the water table, or when coal power plants raise rates of asthma in surrounding communities, or when sea levels rise due to climate change. All of the human activities that cause these effects are seen as simply "business." But challenge any one of these conditions, and you likely find yourself face to face with the agents of structural violence: the police.

When people stop believing in the ideas that justify the power of a ruling class (whether those are oppressive religious ideas, as they were during the Middle Ages, or oppressive economic ideas, as they are today), they often start imagining how the structures of that society could be different. What if everyone had a right to housing, just like they have a right to a library card? What if there were food carts just like there were water fountains? What if we made our number one priority the construction of communities that lived in a mutually enhancing relationship with the ecosystems that sustain them, rather than the production of profit? Start proposing any of these eminently plausible ideas and you will find yourself up against "the realities of the economy." Decide you aren't interested in the economy's version of reality, and you want to live in accordance with a different set of principles, and again, you'll soon encounter the police.

Once you know the world can be different, everyday oppressions have a new sting to them. But there is a long history of people recognizing a shared sting and turning it into collective action to change their conditions. As soon as people who have given up on ruling-class illusions, whether those are economic, racist, homophobic, misogynistic, and begin to organize against their oppression, they discover—if they weren't already aware—that there was a threat of violence behind those illusions all along.

Those newly introduced to activism through Occupy were perhaps more ignorant than most about the role of the police and the threat of violence in changing the world. Many Occupiers were raised in white and middle-class environments, where it is easy to grow up thinking police are more or less there for the benefit of all, even if there are a few bad apples in their ranks. In part, this view is aided by the warped history we inherit—a history of great men changing the world—that ignores or downplays the struggles of everyday people. This means ignoring or downplaying the role the state and its agents of violence have played in repressing them.

What does it mean to "change the world"? The world is changing every day. Every new product claims to be a "revolution" of one sort or another. What distinguishes social movements from new commodities is that social movements are collective attempts to challenge the structural violence on which a particular society relies. When a social movement seeks to change the world, it inevitably confronts and provokes this violence. As those who have taken an oath to defend the laws of the land as they stand, the police are the hired enemies of social movements. It is the police who beat up black people trying to desegregate the South. It is the police who raided gay bars like Stonewall in 1969. It is the police who beat up striking workers when they were fighting for an eight-hour day. Look throughout the history of struggles for liberation and you will find that at every moment, the police are on the wrong side. Some individual cops might be particularly kind-hearted, turning the occasional blind eye or even openly refusing to do their job and enforce an unjust law. These individuals may show themselves to be good people, but only by showing themselves to be bad at their job as cops.

Police and Protest Strategy

Over and over during the Occupy movement, one heard the phrase that "the police are part of the ninety-nine percent." Slogans and signs were used to communicate to the police that they too were being harmed by rampant inequality, and that the target of the movement's protests were the mega-wealthy and financial institutions, and not people from working class backgrounds. Many Occupiers offered police water and food and tried to engage them in conversations about inequality.

More experienced activists tended to argue that, just as "the ninety-nine percent" covered over distinctions between lower class and middle class people, just as it covered over racial and gender oppression, it also ignored the role of the police as defenders of the status quo, as the teeth behind structural violence. The main job of the police in a given protest situation is to enforce "order," often with little concern for the law. Usually the police don't have a very good grasp of the law, and will simply follow whatever orders their higher ups hand down, even if they don't result in convictions.

Kristian Williams, an activist and scholar of the history of policing, offers a framework for understanding the relation of police to social movements since the 1960s.[6] Williams describes three police strategies under the headings of Escalated Force, Negotiated Management, and Strategic Incapacitation. Escalated Force was the typical police crowd control strategy of the Civil Rights era, in which they responded to demonstrations with overt violence, "not just arrests and billy clubs, but fire hoses, police dogs, and sometimes live ammunition" (pp. 210–11). Civil Rights demonstrations that relied on a strategy of nonviolent civil disobedience were tailored to the expectation of this police response, intending to lure out such violence in order to expose the brutality of an unjust order. The police, in turn, updated their own strategy to one of Negotiated Management, which they tended to use throughout the eighties and nineties. In this approach to dealing with protests,

> rather than prohibit them, the cops sought to regulate them through permit requirements and agreements with responsible protest leaders. The cops would allow demonstrations, and even accommodate certain forms of civil disobedience; but in exchange, protesters were limited—or, more often, they limited themselves, to types of action that were minimally disruptive. (p. 211)

---

[6] Williams 2012.

This was simply another approach to the police's goal of undercutting the strength of social movements: the police's "strategy changed, but their ends remained the same. They moved from hard tactics to soft ones because the soft tactics seemed like a better way of controlling, and therefore neutralizing, social movements."

The Global Justice movement developed a range of tactics that more or less successfully, challenged the police's strategy of Negotiated Management. In the 1999 Battle of Seattle, protesters engaged in a range of different demonstrations and marches, some permitted, some unpermitted, and co-ordinated to disrupt the flows of traffic and the functioning of the city. Included within this— though it was not supported by all participants—was a black bloc march which engaged in destruction of storefronts and property symbolic of transnational corporations. The police response to this "new paradigm of disruptive protest"[7] was a new framework called Strategic Incapacitation. According to Williams, this strategy involves unilaterally dictating the acceptable limits of the demonstration, applying Escalated Force to specific groups that do not abide by those rules, as well as "extensive surveillance; the management of space to restrict movement and contain public assemblies; the sharing of information between police departments (and other agencies); and, focused campaigns to shape public perception of the protests through the news media" (p. 213). With Strategic Incapacitation, the police themselves apply a "diversity of tactics" toward containing and undercutting the power of social movements.

One of the most successful tactics the police employ is the creation of a division within the protest itself between the "good" and "bad" protestors. This division can be used by authorities to obscure the real perpetrators of violence in protest confrontations—the police themselves. Then the police can say that they are in support of the "peaceful" demonstrators, where "peaceful" means those who abide by the rules the police themselves have imposed on the situation. The police can claim that they only needed to respond with force to those elements within the protest that were rowdy and unco-operative. When they succeed in framing the events in these terms, too often the supporters of nonviolent actions join the police in condemning those protesters who

---

[7] Quoted in Williams 2012, p. 212.

broke the police-imposed rules—as if the police would have allowed the movement to succeed in its aims if it weren't for those few bad apples. In the wake of Seattle in 1999, internal debates sparked by the black bloc and the awareness of this police strategy led activists to develop the protest framework of a "diversity of tactics." The aim was to respect the fact that different people struggle in different ways, and while we may not all agree about the wisdom or effectiveness of others' tactics, we have to acknowledge that the police's aims are contrary to that of the movement and agree not to aid the police in their creation of divisions between legitimate and illegitimate protestors.

For Kristian Williams, the police response to Occupy was surprising because it seemed to play into the classic strategy of civil disobedience, producing media images of brutality that sparked widespread sympathy for the movement. The police's actions were so outrageous, it was as if they had forgotten what they'd learned in past decades. Williams credits the tactic of occupation with challenging the police's practice of dictating when and where demonstrations or assemblies can occur. According to Williams:

> Though the camps were, by any sober assessment, purely symbolic and no real threat to anyone, they had positioned themselves outside the police-regulated framework of managed protest. In a sense, they represented a rejection of the cops' right to dictate the conditions under which free speech occurs, and at the same time, they embodied the public's right to control urban space. (Khatib et al. 2013, pp. 213–14)

Williams downplays the power of the symbolic threat Occupy posed. What needed to be rooted out of public space *was* the symbolic threat Occupy posed, because it is symbols that sustain the legitimacy of the powerful. At Occupy encampments, people were withdrawing their consent from the symbols of government and corporate power, and when those illusions no longer function for a particular group, the powerful resort to brute force against them. Still, he rightly notes that the tactic of occupation "switched the game" on the police, creating situations they were not trained to handle. And in such situations, they lash out.

During the Occupy movement, the main police justification for shutting down protests was appeals to "health and safety." Needless to say, "safety" was not their concern, as they demonstrated by batons, tear gas, and a number of other harmful weapons. But neither was "health." If city authorities were truly interested in supporting Occupiers' right to peaceably assemble, but were concerned about inadequate access to clean toilets, they would have simply used the money they spent on militarized evictions to install port-o-potties. If they were concerned about mental health and stress to those in encampments, they surely have the resources to hire therapists and masseuses. This seems absurd, of course. But only because we all know "health and safety" was merely a front for creating a situation where it was perceived as acceptable to brutally crack down on a movement that was openly challenging the power of corporations in dominating contemporary life.

Nonviolence as Strategy versus Nonviolence as Ideology

In their preparations for Occupy Wall Street, the NYCGA, composed mostly of anarchists and other radicals, decided to take an approach of Gandhian nonviolence for strategic purposes. While some of them may also be pacifists—support nonviolence as a matter of principle and a way of life—many adopted a nonviolent framework out of the practical concern that to engage in any kind of actions that damaged property would result in a brutal police response.

The vast majority of participants in the Occupy movement maintained a disciplined nonviolence throughout their involvement. In response to police aggression, they remained as calm as possible. Some intentionally engaged in civil disobedience—for example, through sit-ins at banks or government buildings, or defending their encampments through linking arms and refusing to move. To a large extent, the strategy of nonviolence, combined with the political disobedience the Occupiers showed through their prefigurative experiments, was successful in revealing the brutality of the structural violence that the police uphold.

This strategic conception of nonviolence, however, must be distinguished from what is sometimes called the "ideology of nonviolence."[8] By "ideology" here I mean a set of ideas that are useful for sustaining—rather than challenging—the structural violence of a society. Strategic nonviolence follows from an analysis of

---

[8] Meyers 2000.

the particular context in which a social struggle occurs. For example, the decision to engage in nonviolent action for Occupy Wall Street came out of the aims of those organizing it to create not merely a confrontational march, but a space for political experimentation. They believed this would in no way be allowed if protesters were perceived as aggressive.

By contrast, nonviolence becomes an ideology when its advocates—sometimes unwittingly—help the police in their efforts to divide and stifle social movements. Often those who are advocating nonviolence denounce other demonstrators, sometimes handing them over to police (who then use violence against them). In other circumstances, nonviolent ideologues blame those who step out of line for the violence that the police commit. This is a really wonderful situation for police, since they can simply issue arbitrary rules, and some protestors will then take it upon themselves to enforce those rules in the name of "nonviolence," even if the actions others take are in no way "violent"—like, say, marching on the street rather than the sidewalk. Then when the police beat up or arrest someone who stepped out of line, those who entered the street are condemned for provoking the violence of the police!

Those for whom nonviolence has become an ideology usually claim that it is the way the social movements of the past have been effective. Just as those who see history as being created solely by "great statesmen" or through electoral reforms, the claim that nonviolence has, on its own, won freedoms in the past relies upon a terribly selective historical memory. As anthropologist James C. Scott writes,

> most of the great political reforms of the nineteenth and twentieth centuries have been accomplished by massive episodes of civil disobedience, riot, lawbreaking, the disruption of public order, and, at the limit, civil war. Such tumult not only accompanied dramatic political changes but was often absolutely instrumental in bringing them about. (Scott 2013, pp. 16–17)

The point is not that nonviolence is completely ineffective, nor that riotous tumult is the only way social change occurs. Rather, Scott is emphasizing that past movements have always involved multiple groups engaged in a variety of different tactics. Even the nonviolent movements led by Gandhi and King did not occur in a vacuum, but were one tendency within wider movements that often employed or threatened violence. Rather than a liability, this was an asset for those movements, since it gave those in power an incentive to listen to the nonviolent wings of the movement to prevent emboldening the more rowdy or violent tendencies.

CrimethInc.'s Open Letter to the Occupy Movement

In the early weeks of the Occupy movement, a pamphlet was circulated at encampments across the country by CrimethInc. Ex-Worker's Collective entitled "Dear Occupiers: an Open Letter from Anarchists." Excited by the sprouting of occupations around the country, CrimethInc. offered their letter in a spirit of solidarity. They also answered the question, "Why should you listen to us?":

> In short, because we've been at this a long time already. We've spent decades struggling against capitalism, organizing occupations, and making decisions by consensus. If this new movement doesn't learn from the mistakes of previous ones, we run the risk of repeating them. We've summarized some of our hard-won lessons here.

Here are some of those hard-won lessons:

> **Police can't be trusted.** They may be "ordinary workers," but their job is to protect the interests of the ruling class. As long as they remain employed as police, we can't count on them, however friendly they might act. Occupiers who don't know this already will learn it firsthand as soon as they threaten the imbalances of wealth and power our society is based on. Anyone who insists that the police exist to protect and serve the common people has probably lived a privileged life, and an obedient one.

> **Don't fetishize obedience to the law.** Laws serve to protect the privileges of the wealthy and powerful; obeying them is not necessarily morally right—it may even be immoral. Slavery was legal. The Nazis had laws too. We have to develop the strength of conscience to do what we know is best, regardless of the laws.

> **To have a diversity of participants, a movement must make space for a diversity of tactics.** It's controlling and self-important to think you know how everyone should act in pursuit of a better world. Denouncing others only equips the authorities to delegitimize, divide, and destroy the movement as a whole. Criticism and debate

propel a movement forward, but power grabs cripple it. The goal should not be to compel everyone to adopt one set of tactics, but to discover how different approaches can be mutually beneficial. (CrimethInc. 2011)

Responses to this pamphlet varied, but it was widely distributed and sparked numerous discussions among Occupiers about both the system they were opposing and the role of police in upholding it—just as was intended. Though the pamphlet did not explicitly mention engaging in black blocs, for many the phrase "diversity of tactics" was read here as a position that encouraged acts of property destruction and self-defense against police. Perhaps it was this subtext that led Rebecca Solnit to refer to the pamphlet as a "screed in justification of violence," when such an interpretation is clearly not warranted by the text itself. Encouraging a diversity of tactics and discouraging "internal policing" of the movement was equated very early on, by many, with active support for violence.

The Oakland Commune

We can't understand the violence debate as it erupted in Occupy without looking at Occupy Oakland more closely. Oakland has a deep radical history that has not been forgotten by its current residents, and this history influenced the development of Occupy Oakland. The Black Panther party was founded in Oakland in 1966 by Huey Newton and Bobby Seale. Oakland remained one of the most active chapters of the Panthers throughout their existence, organizing community defense against police violence and various programs for the alleviation of poverty, including their popular free breakfast program. Prior to its being an important site in the black freedom movement, numerous important labor struggles occurred in Oakland, including the 1946 General Strike, which started with women retail workers at the intersection of Broadway and Telegraph Avenue before spreading to shut down the whole city for fifty-two hours. This was the last General Strike to have occurred in America—until November 2nd 2011, when Occupy Oakland succeeded in shutting down most of the city's businesses and the Port of Oakland.

In recent Oakland history, the most influential events on the occupation in recent Oakland history were the 2009 police shooting of Oscar Grant and the subsequent riots that swept the city. As one participant-analyst writes, "I'm going to insist as stubbornly as possible, that if there was a fundamental source, not for the *presence* of Occupy Oakland, but for its peculiar *radicalism* and the mantle of national leadership it assumed, this source was to be found in the Oscar Grant rebellions and the political lessons these rebellions contained" (Ciccariello-Maher 2012, p. 41).

In the early morning of January 1st 2009, Oscar Grant, a twenty-two-year-old black man who worked as a butcher in a local supermarket, was shot in the back by transit officer Johannes Mehserle. Grant was held in handcuffs, lying on the ground when Mehserle shot him. Critically wounded and about to die, Mehserle and his fellow transit cops confiscated the cell-phones of eye-witnesses in a futile attempt to prevent footage of the incident from leaving the scene. Many who filmed the shooting hid their phones and later uploaded videos to the Internet, where they went viral. Mehserle was not arrested, and escaped the need to answer questions about the matter by quietly resigning his post. For about a week, it looked as if a white man in a uniform could execute a black man in Oakland among dozens of eye-witnesses and suffer no repercussions.

A week later a rally was held at 14th and Broadway, which quickly became uncontainable by those who had apparently organized it. Hundreds broke through downtown Oakland, smashing windows and burning cars. This was the first Oscar Grant rebellion. A week later, another march was planned:

> As the date of the promised January 14 follow-up march approached, and as the threat of another riot-rebellion became tangible, the wheels of political power in the state, county, and city, groaned reluctantly into motion. Under pressure from the state Attorney General and the Mayor, Johannes Mehserle was arrested, and he was arrested *to prevent a second riot*. (Ciccariello-Maher 2012, p. 40)

The radical community of Oakland learned from this experience: sometimes riots work. An unruly show of popular force can sometimes be required to obtain even the most basic standards of justice—that someone who openly kills another person should be arrested and charged. When, on the night of the second riot, the Mayor of Oakland took to the streets to condemn the property destruction, he was rebutted by one of the protestors:

Fuck the car, someone DIED! Do you know the difference between a LIFE and a Lexus? Did you see the person get killed? He was lying down and they shot him in the back! A car is not the same as a human life. I'm sorry you don't understand that. You're lucky it was just a car! ONE CAR! (Anonymous Pamphlet 2009, p. 17)

When we hear the word "riot," we generally have an image of thoughtless violence and an every-man-for-himself ethos, in which aggression is directed without reason or direction. A document produced by participants in the riots provides a very different image, and one which foreshadows the descriptions of Occupy Oakland two years later:

If we must stress anything it is that the rebellion is tender. We make quick friends with one another: we share laughter, water and tips on police maneuvers, saving all rage for the police and the city. We care for one another in ways Oakland never sees on a day-to-day level. We hope we don't sound trite, but a rare public solidarity exists this night between us all. (Anonymous Pamphlet 2009, p. 12)

This comment gives a glimpse into something not often noted in media and even most activist discourse on "riots"—there can be a care and tenderness cultivated among those who put themselves at risk together to face oppressive forces.

Two years later, as the Occupy movement offered a new opportunity for Oakland to rebel against the persistent effects of economic and racial inequality, one of the first acts of the Oakland General Assembly on October 11th 2011 was to rename the park outside of city hall where their encampment had been created: what was Frank Ogawa Plaza became Oscar Grant Plaza. And from day one, no police were allowed.

The history of Oakland, recent and more far reaching, was there to draw upon as a resource for the occupation. And not just of Oakland. With an eye toward the Paris Commune—the 1871 insurrection in which the working people of Paris seized control of the city for two months before being crushed in a bloody battle—Occupy Oakland declared itself "the Oakland Commune," and set about trying to provide direct material support to those suffering on the streets of Oakland. As one visitor put it:

This is what I found inspiring from the beginning: in a community as utterly divided by class, race, politics, language and gender as

Oakland, people reflecting so much of that variety of difference were getting together to hammer together some kind of common and communal purpose, to declare that everyone who inhabited the same space was, in an important sense, *there* together. We ate together, we listened together, we spoke together, and we were teargassed together. In the days when Frank Ogawa Plaza became Oscar Grant Plaza, that tiny stretch of Oakland was perhaps the least segregated neighborhood in the city, and the *only* place in the city where I would ever have the conversations I had with the people I did. (Bady 2012, p. 209)

While such experiences were present at encampments around the country, by all accounts Oakland was special.

The police descended upon the encampment on the night of October 25th, using excessive force to destroy the kitchen, tents, and the fruits of the Oakland Commune's energetic self-organization. The Oakland Commune was not deterred by the eviction, and set up camp again the next day, removing the tall metal fences surrounding Oscar Grant Plaza and neatly stacking them on the side of their reclaimed territory. Often, in the face of police repression, Occupy encampments were tempted to respond by jumping through legal hoops in order to get on the right side of the law. Such an approach was fueled by a belief that the law will actually allow for a space for a social movement to grow and be effective, as long as we play by their rules. Occupiers in Oakland had no such illusions, and their response to police violence was to take the opposite approach: to reassert their encampment and escalate their tactics. The evening after the first eviction, the Oakland General Assembly passed a resolution to hold a general strike the following Wednesday, November 2nd. The proposal won with 96.9 percent support in a GA of over 1,500 people.

Many organizers and activists, especially those involved in labor struggles, were taken aback by this declaration. For them, a general strike—the total shutdown of a city, the complete withdrawal of human activity from wage work—is the nuclear weapon of labor struggles, and as such it isn't something to be declared lightly. But it is just that boldness, the willingness to push the limits of what was possible, that marked what was so inspiring about the Oakland Commune. As one participant put it, during the early discussions of the strike,

speakers made clear that this is merely a first attempt at a general strike, which when they occur are usually the culmination of a period of heightened class struggle. Using the rhetoric of an offensive counter-attack [for the eviction] was a popular sentiment that came up naturally. We knew we were planting the seeds of an idea that would take further, more intense, struggles to truly bear fruit. (Hieronymous 2012, p. 174)

Those who called for a strike cast a spell on the city, and they had no idea what would come of it. All they knew was that they had a lot of work to do. The *communards* of Oakland began spreading the word, printing flyers, constructing signs, and planning the actions for the day.

Among the actions planned for the General Strike was an "anti-capitalist march." The march was not organized through the Oakland General Assembly, but instead by an affinity group that promoted it through posters and flyers that made clear their intentions to shut down those businesses that were not participating in the strike. The subtext was: black bloc event—if you aren't down with a rowdy march, don't come.

On the day of the march, this sentiment showed itself early on in the march, where the familiar Occupy chant *We. Are. The Ninety-Nine Percent!* morphed into the more class-conscious *We. Are. The Proletariat!*—the latter chant pleasingly taking up the same cadence as the former. Soon after, the chanting switched to *Occupy! Shut it down! Oakland does not fuck around!*

Despite the tone set by the promotional materials and these militant chants, there were a number of people on the march who objected to the acts of vandalism (which were limited to spray painting, breaking windows, and knocking over tables and chairs outside businesses that remained open). Some of these objections were very vocal and confrontational, leading to a number of scuffles between protestors on the march. Frustrated shouts of *peaceful protest!* and *non-violence!* were directed at hooded demonstrators, and more than a few attempts to physically confront them were captured on video. At one point, a protestor opposing the property destruction confronted a videographer who was apparently wearing a mask, yelling in their face: "Why do you wear a mask, if you really want to send them a message, show your face! Show them that you are a person!"

The "anti-capitalist march" was just one event throughout the day—and hardly the most economically destructive one! By far the most economic damage caused to the rich and powerful came from the seven-thousand-strong march that effectively shut down the Port of Oakland. Causing approximately $4 million in lost profits—without damaging a single window and while generating droves of positive media coverage. This is a curious tension: the act that is *more* obstructive for capital—the Port shut-down—was celebrated, while the act that was relatively trivial economically (causing perhaps a few thousand dollars worth of damage), was demonized as violence, performed by people who, as one observer put it, "have no values."

Move-in Day

On January 28th 2012, over a month after their definitive eviction from Oscar Grant/Frank Ogawa plaza, members of Occupy Oakland planned for an action that was both a logical outcome of the ideas of Occupy and a tactical escalation: to take an unused city building and turn it into a community center and base for Occupy Oakland organizing for the winter. They advertised the act in simple terms:

> It's cold outside. Like millions of people in this country, Occupy Oakland has no home. And yet, all over the city, thousands of buildings stand empty. On January 28, we're going to occupy one of those buildings and turn it into a social center. We're going to fill the space with a kitchen, first aid station, sleeping quarters, an assembly area, libraries, free school classes, and hundreds of uses yet to be determined. Let's establish our new home, defend it, and adapt it to Oakland's needs. We get what we can take. (Occupy Oakland 2012a)

All of the major occupations had either been aggressively evicted or run into the many practical problems that made a full-time, outdoor encampment impossible, but the Occupy movement was still alive in the minds of its participants. The activist and community networks it had formed were still active—in short, though there were few people sleeping outside, planning for the movement was still going strong. Warm weather was a few months away, and dreams for an American Spring seemed possible. We felt like we were winning.

Occupy Oakland's plan to reclaim an unused building for a community center was an exciting prospect to say the least. They had been empowered by the Oakland General Assembly with specific guidelines concerning the building to be seized:

> The building will have sufficient office space for all of the Occupy Oakland committees and an auditorium large enough to hold Occupy Oakland general assemblies and adequate sleeping space. It will be a vacant building owned either by a bank, a large corporation of the 1% or already public. (Occupy Oakland 2012b)

The Move-in Assembly, the group assigned responsibility for selecting the building and planning the action, identified a number of buildings which fit this criteria. But like the initial occupation of Zuccotti Park, the potential locations had to remain secret until the actual event to avoid police barricades. Despite the secret location of the actual proposed community center, the Move-in Assembly had clearly taken the time to plan in accordance with the "diversity of tactics" framework, creating zones corresponding to participants' different levels of comfort with police confrontation. They advertised this as a family-friendly event, and agreed with the Occupy Oakland Children's Village that they would break-off from the march before reaching the proposed building until space was secured. There were plans to make clear announcements about where to be depending on your comfort level and before the building was locked down so that no one would be trapped in the building unwillingly. In short, the event planners did their best to follow the Diversity of Tactics framework.

Unfortunately, things didn't go as planned.

Those intent on occupying the unused Kaiser Convention Center were met with riot cops who prevented their entry. Some protesters had come prepared to defend themselves and others against the police, with shields made from trash cans, furniture on wheels to hide behind, and light barriers made from corrugated metal with the words "Cops move out" and "Commune move in" painted on them. These defensive measures proved incapable of withstanding the police barrage.

Occupy Oakland saw the occupation of an unused building as a natural extension of the tactic of occupying a public park. They planned their action on the principle that people should have free space to assemble and organize, to experiment with creating the world they wanted to see. And they came up against the main obstacle to that principle: the police. Those who were "bloc'd up" on that day were not engaging in property destruction, so much as they were prepared for defending both themselves and other movement participants in pursuing a course of action that everyone had agreed to—the occupation of an unused building to transform it into a community center. Though this event resulted in images of people dressed in black facing-off with the police, it was hardly the same kind of action as a march with the explicit intention of smashing stuff.

After being beat up, gassed, and thwarted by the police, in their plans to find a new home for the Oakland Commune, an angry group broke into city hall, trashing it. They took two American flags and burned them on the front steps.

Hedges's Critique of Black Blocs

In response to the images and reporting that came out after Oakland's Move-in Day, Hedges wrote the article that crystallized tensions over the black bloc and diversity of tactics within the movement. The article contains a number of wild inaccuracies: it continually suggests that there is a group called "the Black Bloc" that shares a single ideology, when in fact black bloc is a tactic that many different anti-capitalists sometimes think it is a good idea to engage in; Hedges suggests that those who participate in black blocs are against all forms of organization, when many who engage in black blocs are also organizers involved in various other projects that don't involve smashing things or dressing in black. For many readers, however—particularly many of those with more mainstream liberal politics who had been inspired by Occupy's having drawn attention to wealth inequality—Hedges's article reinforced their fears about radicals in the movement. Those who covered their faces and were unwilling to respect police authority were described as saboteurs of the movement, which, according to Hedges, required mainstream appeal for its success.

Hedges's article argues that the black bloc is a "gift from heaven for the surveillance state," since its activities would be used to justify increased surveillance and repression of the Occupy movement. Further, he suggested that it was "hypermasculine," requiring participants to destroy all feelings of empathy within themselves and give over to the destructive and aggressive impulses of a thoughtless mob. He also accused it of being not only a strategically bad idea, but carried out by people who are explicitly against any strategic thinking—while at the same time suggesting that they were carrying out a strategy to destroy the Leftist organizations they deemed to be less ideologically pure.

Nathan Schneider summarizes the effect Hedges's article had:

> The effect in OWS's Direct Action Working Group (DAWG), one of the movement's most vibrant quarters, was catastrophic. "Chris Hedges really screwed us," says Chris Longenecker, who has been with DAWG since day one. "It's anarchists that are driving this movement." So many of OWS's most cherished institutions—the general assemblies, the leaderless structure, the diversity of tactics—have roots in anarchism, and have been maintained by anarchists who'd been practicing them long before the movement began. They include both self-described pacifists and members of black blocs. Within a few days of Hedges's article, there was a proposal at the General Assembly to create an anarchist caucus, a measure usually reserved for marginalized identity groups. It failed to reach consensus. Some people quit the movement in frustration, others in tears. (Schneider 2012)

There was a rapid demonization of anarchists in the movement—regardless of whether they had actually engaged in any property destruction. The debate often became more about whether they were willing to argue in favor of such acts or even defend them in principle. In the name of diagnosing a cancer within the movement, Hedges's article deepened divisions and shut down conversations about tactics, excluding some of the most energetic participants on the grounds that they had a different analysis.

Graeber responded to Hedges's article with "Concerning the Violent Peace Police: An Open Letter to Chris Hedges." Graeber argued that Hedges' article is "not only factually inaccurate, it is quite literally dangerous. This is the sort of misinformation that can get people killed. In fact, it is far more likely to do so . . . than anything done by any black-clad teenager throwing rocks." The reason the article is so dangerous, according to Graeber, is that Hedges paints the black bloc as a violent group that cannot be reasoned with, who are all the same and bent on destroying the movement. This characterization of *any* group is a recipe for either forcefully suppressing them or turning them over to the police who will, in turn, forcefully suppress them:

> After all, if a group is made up exclusively of violent fanatics who cannot be reasoned with, intent on our destruction, what else can we

really do? This is the language of violence in its purest form. Far more than "fuck the police." To see this kind of language employed by someone who claims to be speaking in the name of non-violence is genuinely extraordinary. (Graeber 2012)

Graeber's point in his open letter is less to *encourage* the actions of black blocs than, on the one hand, to articulate why some people engage in them and, on the other hand, to address how those involved in a movement should respond to tactics with which they disagree. Graeber notes the purpose of black blocs is not exclusively to engage in property destruction, but to signal an explicitly revolutionary element within a protest prepared for militant action, while also providing a way of distinguishing that segment of the demonstration from those who wish to keep a safer distance from such actions. He also notes that the framework of "diversity of tactics" was born out of a recognition of the futility of internally policing the tactics of a protest. We can often come to common agreements about tactics, but in the moment of the event—especially when people are being gassed and beaten—it is not only impossible, but perhaps undesirable to limit the actions people take to defend themselves.

Regarding how those who disagree with black bloc actions should respond, Graeber emphasizes Gandhi's own mode of response to violent and even terroristic factions within India's anti-colonial struggle. According to Graeber, Gandhi

> was regularly challenged to prove his non-violent credentials by assisting the authorities in suppressing such [violent or terroristic] elements. Here Gandhi remained resolute. It is always morally superior, he insisted, to oppose injustice through non-violent means than through violent means. However, to oppose injustice through violent means is still morally superior to not doing anything to oppose injustice at all.
>
> And Gandhi was talking about people who were blowing up trains, or assassinating government officials. Not damaging windows or spray-painting rude things about the police. (Graeber 2012)

Without explicitly defending the use of the black bloc tactic during Occupy, Graeber nonetheless is deeply critical of Hedges's public condemnation of those who engage in it. Doing so, he argues, does the State's job of dividing and neutralizing a movement for them, and exposes those who engage in tactics you may not agree with to the police violence and potential imprisonment—all in the name of nonviolence.

Better Informed Critics of the Black Bloc

If Hedges was uninformed about both the tactic of black bloc and made a strategic error by publicly demonizing a segment of movement participants, there were other criticisms of the black bloc tactic during Occupy that perhaps hit closer to the mark. One particularly powerful criticism comes from Sunaura Taylor, a participant in Occupy Oakland and a wheelchair user. Careful to note that "the violence perpetrated by protesters was minimal compared to the violence perpetrated by the police," Taylor nonetheless describes how she felt betrayed and endangered by the actions of those confronting police and engaging in property damage. Describing her experience on the night of Occupy Oakland's first eviction, Taylor writes:

> I can't stop thinking about what happened that night. Besides being disheartened once again by the brutality of the cops (who, along with tear gas, shot rubber bullets at people, one of which hit a homeless man), I also felt dismayed and betrayed by some of the protest activity itself. As I watched from a distance it seemed to me that the crowd was largely very young and able-bodied. It is easy for me to assume they were also predominantly white and male (since I was not on the frontlines, I'm not sure. I do know, though, that as a disabled woman and wheelchair user, I felt little of the diversity of people that makes this movement so beautiful and so revolutionary to me. (Taylor 2012, p. 141)

Weighing in on the debate about whether property destruction constitutes "violence," according to Taylor:

> destruction of property has had its place even within nonviolent movements, but it is a tactic that is too often used rashly and dangerously. After all, the one percent were not the ones out in the streets of Oakland the next morning sweeping up the shattered glass or picking up the debris. I do think there is a kind of violence in the way property destruction affects others without their consent. A small group of people making decisions that affect the safety and reputation of the whole movement is not what democracy looks like. That is what violence looks like.

While property destruction might be a useful tactic, as it was employed in Occupy Oakland, Taylor was left with the sense that it was engaged in by those who were privileged by their able-bodies, put others at risk who had not consented to it, harmed—or at least annoyed—people who were not the proper targets, and broke with the spirit of inclusion and democratic process of the movement.

Some of these concerns had been expressed earlier by writer and activist Rebecca Solnit, whose essay "Throwing Out the Master's Tools and Building a Better House" argues that, indeed, the destruction of property can be violent. She states that, in some cases, in some movements, such acts like this as well as even more overt violence are justified. But she is committed—and thinks Occupy too ought to be committed—to "people power": large groups of people co-ordinating nonviolent, disruptive actions that clearly illustrate the moral superiority of protesters and clearly expose the moral weakness of the police and the power structure they represent. She views the temptation to violence as a trap:

> If we were violent, we would be conventionally dangerous and the authorities could justify repressing us. In fact, we're unconventionally dangerous, because we're not threatening physical violence but the transformation of the system (and its violence).
>
> So when episodes of violence break out as part of our side in a demonstration, an uprising, a movement, I think of it as a sabotage, a corruption, a coercion, a misunderstanding, or a mistake, whether it's a paid infiltrator or a clueless dude. Here I want to be clear that property damage is not necessarily violence. The firefighter breaks the door to get the people out of the building. But the husband breaks the dishes to demonstrate to his wife that he can and may also break her; it is violence displaced onto the inanimate as a threat to the animate. (p. 148)

This qualification is important, because it allows her to support, say, those who cut apart and removed the fence around Oscar Grant Plaza to allow for the General Assembly to meet after the first eviction. Though this involved property destruction, it was more akin to the firefighter breaking down a door. Those engaging in black bloc tactics, Solnit suggests, are more like the abusive husband.

Solnit is clearly correct that violence can serve as a threat. But I wonder if her analogy isn't backwards. Are those engaged in black blocs like a husband breaking the dishes to threaten his wife, or more like the wife—the dominated party who is threatened with violence—breaking the dishes to show her own willingness to use force to defend herself? Unfortunately, the answer might be *both*. People who use black bloc may appear one way to the police, and another way to someone like Taylor, quoted above.

Another criticism of the use of black bloc in Occupy comes from Mark Bray, who himself admits to having participated in about a dozen black blocs over the course of a decade. In his discussion of black bloc in *Translating Anarchy*, Bray cautions against a tendency to "transplant tactics from other times and places and expect the same results."[9]

While black bloc has been and is still of use in certain circumstances, he argues that "militant black bloc tactics make sense when they have a clearly expressed social purpose that supports community struggles" (p. 241). He cites a number of examples that he thinks fit this bill, from West Germany in the 1980s (when black blocs were first used to retaliate for the eviction squatted buildings that had wide social support) to Greece in 2008, where black blocs and riots were used in response to the police murder of a fourteen-year-old in the anarchist-controlled neighborhood of Exarchia. And while he notes that he is not necessarily opposed to the way they were used in Oakland, he offers this general summary of their usefulness in contexts like our own:

> Do working class people and people of color tend to look favorably upon property destruction when it's carried out by a group of young, predominantly white, people who they have never known against a target that seems to have been chosen at random at a large demonstration against an abstract international financial institution that they may not have heard of? Usually not so much. (Bray 2013, p. 244)

For his own part, Bray concludes that as he "participated in more and more of them over the years, it became increasingly clear that they rarely accomplish anything, even on a symbolic level. What was once a surprise tactic became very predictable and containable" (p. 246). Instead, Bray thinks the obsession over black blocs came to limit the actual discussions about the diverse tactics that could have been available to demonstrators.

---

[9] Bray 2013, p. 238.

CrimethInc.'s Defense of Black Blocs

Though the Occupy movement did not see many black blocs, they did undoubtably become a cause of great debate—and one must expect they (and other militant tactics) will continue to be a divisive issue in social movements to come. For this reason, it is important that we actually listen to those who defend them, and that we really question the assumptions that have made it so simple for some to dismiss such tactics, while others feel so passionately about them. In response to Hedges's article, CrimethInc. came out with an article of their own entitled "The Illegitimacy of Violence, the Violence of Legitimacy," which offered a critique of the tendency on the part of writers like Hedges and Solnit to use the distinction between violence and nonviolence when describing actions of those engaged in struggle. Further, in September of 2012, CrimethInc.'s B. Traven engaged in a public debate with Chris Hedges on the subject.

Reading Hedges and Solnit, one might get the impression that CrimethInc. is composed of thoughtless thugs interested simply in getting a rush through street confrontations without giving any consideration—strategic or moral—to their actions. I don't think anyone could in good faith maintain such a view after reading "The Legitimacy of Violence, the Violence of Legitimacy"—or any of CrimethInc.'s recent work, for that matter. They are some of the most sensitive and engaged theorists of contemporary social movements, and they are bold enough to follow unpopular lines of thought. In this essay, they start by pointing out that the term "violence" has two, sometimes contradictory, meanings. On the one hand, it can mean the "illegitimate use of force," while on the other hand it can mean any "harm or threat that violates consent." That is, from the perspective of the first definition, the police may harm or threaten people without their consent, because their use of force is perceived as "legitimate." Thus police activity is not perceived as "violence," a fact CrimethInc. confirms by citing lines such as this one, from a Montreal newspaper after a protest: "Violence erupted when protesters began throwing tear gas canisters back at the lines of riot police." The police action of throwing tear gas canisters was not perceived as "violence," but the protesters' act of throwing them back was—even though protesters were acting in self-defense and the police likely had gas masks.

CrimethInc. argues that what is really at stake in social movements is not violence or nonviolence, but *legitimacy*. The police have *legitimacy* when they use force, so it is not generally interpreted as "violent." But legitimacy is something that *we* help give them. CrimethInc.'s aim is to broaden the kinds of actions that are seen as legitimate forms of protest and resistance. This involves consciously pushing the boundaries. This is a strategic act, because it follows from an assessment that we will only be able to confront the structural violence of capitalism and the police power that upholds it by becoming collectively unwilling to play by the rules imposed upon us. The issue of whether an action is "violent" or "nonviolent" tends to obscure what, for CrimethInc., is the more important question: does this or that tactic expand our collective sense of power?

CrimethInc. has provided a number of arguments for why they think engaging in black bloc can sometimes be a good idea—or at least why publicly condemning it is a bad one. I want to focus on three: the power of anonymity, the need to expand our sense of entitlement, and the need to build a movement that can channel the anger and despair that contemporary life forces upon people. Each of these components of the black bloc tactic can be found in other actions, but black bloc brings them together in a way that creates a powerful image and sends a powerful message—which is why it is so controversial.

The fact that some Occupiers wore masks was one of the simplest ways that they were painted as violent, or as engaging in something other than respectable civil disobedience. According to the standard assumption, people who cover their faces in public are engaged in dangerous or criminal activity. Covering faces seems like an unnecessary provocation or, worse, a cowardly act of a protester who is unwilling to actually stand up for her convictions.

In response to this, one must emphasize that we live in an age of mass surveillance, in which almost anyone engaged in protest activity that attracts a police presence, no matter how peaceful, can be almost assured that they will be filmed and photographed and that their identities will be put on file either with the local police department or with the FBI. It's difficult for many people who have not engaged in protest to take this seriously, but this is the sad truth of the current world. Many people, with good reason, would like to be careful about building a record with those institutions.

Moreover, some people are more vulnerable than others to police harassment, or to the consequences of having their image associated with a protest. As Traven pointed out in his debate with Hedges, should someone call in sick to work to attend a protest, and should their face end up on the evening news, they might lose their job. There are myriad other reasons why individuals in this society would be worried about having their faces associated with a radical movement—from employer discrimination to people who have past criminal records. These concerns combined with the reality of police and FBI surveillance make the idea of normalizing masks at protest seem like a good idea to many. The more people who wear masks, the less we can be individually targeted by the authorities. In the debate, Hedges eventually agreed that covering faces wasn't as bad an idea as he had first thought.

In addition to these clear practical concerns, there is also another, deeper element to wearing masks—an element pioneered by the Zapatistas who wear balaclavas and bandanas both to conceal their identities *and* to reveal themselves as potentially anyone. When you wear a mask, you can be almost anyone—someone from any race, gender, class or social position. Anyone can potentially see themselves acting in such a way. The black bloc tactic uses masks in part as a way of communicating that this is something anyone can engage in.

Next, black bloc is about expanding people's sense of entitlement as to how they can act. Just like Occupy itself, which expanded people's sense of entitlement by seizing space and engaging in prefigurative political practice, those advocating black bloc tactics are interested in expanding our sense of what it might take to *defend* such spaces and one another. Many people I've spoken to who participate in black blocs describe how, in moments of police confrontation, it was those dressed in black who helped them, providing relief from tear gas or, in some cases, snatching them from the clutches of the police. Those engaged in black blocs have shown remarkable courage in extremely tense situations, and this has expanded people's sense of how they themselves can act. It turns out, just because the police lay their hands on a friend or fellow protestor, it doesn't always mean they have to go to jail. Black bloc is about spreading an ethos of *ungovernability*, about encouraging people to refuse to cooperate with the arbitrary authority that police use to restrict and contain protests. It is about taking back the capacity to shout and yell at injustice, and about losing our illusions that holding signs within a designated "free speech zone" at a protest that has been authorized and permitted by the police is going to make any difference at all.

From this perspective, the aim is to encourage people to challenge authority, not only by "speaking truth to power," but by actively and physically interrupting and even attacking the symbols of that power. One way this is manifested in the black bloc—and a way that is particularly powerful for those who have participated in such actions—is through attacks on corporate property, on commodities.

Too often critics of the black bloc interpret property destruction as simply an attempt to cause economic damage to the banks and corporations. They then argue that this damage is negligible compared with the billions of dollars they rake in and, after all, it is working folks that have to pick up the glass the next day. If the aim were only to cause economic damage, a black bloc is not the best way to do it. The Oakland Port shut-down, for example, was a far more effective tool for causing economic disruption than any black bloc during Occupy. The aim of black blocs, however, has to be seen not simply as attempts to cause monetary damage to the economy so much as to disrupt the assumptions upon which it is founded, namely, the semi-sacred aura that surrounds commodities and the marketing images used to sell them. Global capitalist society places the value of commodities over the lives of poor people and the ecologies of the planet, and the marketing images used to sell them manipulate us into feeling inadequate unless we purchase this or that new product. In this context, there can be a tremendous feeling of liberation and satisfaction in simply smashing a commodity or a window display. Strange as it looks, doing so can have the effect of setting the world right again—reasserting the dignity of the human over the mere thing, which has been elevated into an idol. And, it must be emphasised, doing so causes no physical harm to anybody.

Moreover, collective property destruction transforms the landscape of a city, revealing the fact that what appears so solid—the walls, the windows, the distinction between street and sidewalk—is in fact quite fluid and open to interpretation. Participants in black blocs describe the sense of possibility that their riotous behavior creates. In a black bloc that engages in riot, people radically alter the world around them and, in so doing, radically alter themselves. Concerning the black blocs of the Global Justice movement, A.K. Thompson writes that these riots transformed participants, opening them up to their own power to transform the world: "the riot yields political subjects that are able to produce the world, subjects that—through the process of transformation that the riot entails—are forced to confront the unwritten future within them."[10] Rather than appealing to those in power to "represent" their interests, those engaged in black blocs found power within themselves collectively to pursue and transform the world around them.

During his debate with Hedges, B. Traven made reference to this potential for collective power with a comment about the Iraq War protests of 2003. Traven noted that the largest mass mobilizations of protesters in history was unable to stop the war. And yet, hundreds of thousands of people in the streets actually *may have been* capable of stopping an invasion—but those present did not use all the power they had to do so. Peaceful marches and appeals to our leaders could have turned into barricades and paralysis of the capacity to move supplies. We could have used "people power" and our power to disable the systems that support and sustain the war machine to actually have prevented the invasion—or at least to have put up a better fight.

What held us back was not uncertainty about the injustice of the Iraq invasion, but rather a shared limitation of tactics, a set of assumptions about how protest should go that amputated our ability to actually make use of our collective power. This collective power need not be "violent," in the sense that it need not intend to cause direct harm to human beings. But it did need to be outside the bounds of what is generally considered a "peaceful protest," in which people follow the rules set by the police and engage in symbolic arrest activity. Because of our unwillingness to use our own collective power at that critical moment, half a million people have died as a result of an invasion based on deception.[11]

There's a final argument in favor of black blocs that I want to touch on. It will likely sound strange, but I think it is perhaps the most important and perceptive argument that CrimethInc. has offered in

---

[10] Thompson 2010, p. 27.
[11] Sheriden 2013.

their defense. In his debate with Hedges, B. Traven puts it this way:

> We live in a time when people are getting increasingly desperate. The question is not whether people are going to revolt. People are going to revolt. The question is: what happens when they revolt? People are going to do things that today we see as illegitimate or crazy. They are going to act out. When this happens, if there is no movement they can participate in to act out against their conditions, they are going to act out in isolation. They are going to join clandestine armed insurgencies. They are going to throw their lives away in a way that is anti-social and unproductive. The question is: how do we make a movement that can make the most of all our despair and desperation, that can create a possibility when we are at our breaking point to push forward in a way that benefits all of us? If we make the black bloc a bugaboo and we say that all those who act out are monsters and are against the movement and are going to ruin it, then we create a situation in which these people can only act out autonomously in a way that doesn't contribute to what everybody else is trying to do. (CrimethInc. 2012b)

Usually, when discussing tactics or what to do, we would like to be able to say what is permitted and what is not permitted with reference to some principle or some set of given ends. The difference here is that Traven is openly acknowledging that, whether or not we decide that violent outbursts should or should not happen makes little difference: they are going to happen. People are going to act out and, Traven is suggesting, it is the responsibility of social movements to provide paths for expressing this rage in a direction that allows it to be a part of the project to change the conditions that are creating it. To support this argument, CrimethInc. cites the London riots of 2011, in which people engaged in massive property destruction, arson, and in which people were killed in an outburst of collective rage that seemed to have no ideological or political motivation:

> The responsibility for this tragedy rests not only on the rebels themselves, nor on those who imposed the injustices from which they suffered, but also upon the activists who stigmatized them rather than joining in creating a movement that could channel their anger. If there is no connection between those who intend to transform society and those who suffer most within it, no common cause between the hopeful and the enraged, then when the latter rebel, the former

will disown them, and the latter will be crushed along with all hope of real change. (CrimethInc. 2012a)

Black bloc, because it performs this rage against commodities and empowers participants to defend themselves and take care of one another while at the same time pushing the boundaries of disobedience, can be a channel for the anger and desperation of contemporary society. Unlike other channels for discontent our society offers—booze, sports, fighting—this is a channel that actually directs that rage toward the structural violence of capitalism, and the commodities that it holds on high.

Again, none of these points in defense of the black bloc are meant to suggest that it is always or even often a good idea. Still, the tactic is likely to stick around, because it has something powerful and frightening about it, so those of us who want to help build the power of social movements may as well understand what those who engage with this tactic get out of it. Reflecting on their debate with Hedges, CrimethInc. described why they decided to take a stand on this issue:

> We have made a point of standing up to those who would demonize the black bloc not because we are invested in that particular tactic, but because its essential components—the willingness to act illegally and anonymously, and to stand up to the force of the state—are precisely what it would take to sustain a movement beyond the impasse imposed by the Occupy evictions. (CrimethInc. 2012b)

In response to social movement tactics, the police adapt and develop new approaches. CrimethInc.'s suggestion is that social movements must be even more agile, and that we can't be seduced into believing that we can repeat the same tactics time and again—be they sit-ins, occupations, or black blocs.

7

Beyond Occupation

The Occupy movement was an eruption of radical politics in the United States, at a moment when such politics had been effectively erased from public view. When such practices burst into the mainstream consciousness, they were difficult for most people to understand, but during the three months of 2011 when Occupy Wall Street and the encampments around the country had national attention, ideas and practices that had been submerged for at least a decade reached the lives of many people who had never been exposed to a radical critique of capitalism or state power.

And almost as rapidly as they ascended, the movement seemed to disappear from public view. We weren't half-way through 2012 before people began to claim the movement had "fizzled" or simply "disappeared." They often failed to recall the brutality with which encampments were destroyed, or at least didn't consider this to be a significant factor in extracting the movement from public view. In fact, as we've seen, the movement and its ideas were ruthlessly evicted from the public view it had claimed. And radical organizing is once again submerged into a world beneath the media's gaze.

But it has left the consciousness of people throughout the United States altered—sometimes without their even recognizing it. The division of the ninety-nine percent and the one percent has become so common, many people don't even recall that it was Occupy that provided this language. Moreover, although many people somehow gloss over the brutality of the evictions from their recollection of Occupy, there is a widespread understanding that protest is a dangerous activity, and that the police and surveillance state are hardly interested in protecting rights to freedom of assembly. Occupy can be credited as demonstrating, in public, that the political freedoms the United States claims to uphold are vacuous. In fact, the US government will treat peaceful demonstrators as potential terrorist threats, mobilizing the vast legal and surveillance apparatus of the post-9/11 era against us all. Occupy dismantled many of our illusions about how the world can be changed. Learning painful truths is progress.

In the period after the encampments and the major public audience, the tendencies that were woven together in public during the Occupy movement have re-submerged. But they have done so with new energy, novel experiences, and countless new comrades. Those who had been working for social, economic, and ecological justice before Occupy made connections with people in their own cities and around the world who are working toward the same ends, and movement networks are more vast and more deep after the experience. The kinds of systemic injustices that Occupy took as its target were never going to go away overnight—no matter how possible that seemed in the heady days of proliferating encampments. It was only going to be a moment of resurfacing, followed by renewed efforts to slowly and patiently continue the work of organizing, of activism, of self-and community transformation. Nathan Schneider quotes Occupier Ravi Ahmad:

> "We've moved out of the spectacular phase," she said. "The main focus of what we do now is day-in, day-out organizing." For her, that part's even more important. And so is a sense of perspective: "The [goal] of Occupy is to smash capitalism," she reminded me. "That's the standard we measure ourselves by." (Schneider 2012)

Such a transformation will be long and drawn out. It may involve many more eruptions like that of Occupy, in which more people encounter radical ideas and practices, in which people step into momentary times and spaces in which capitalist social relations are suspended and they can develop a vision of a more just and equitable mode of human relating.

In this final chapter, I'll point to standouts from the innumerable projects that activists involved in the Occupy movement have been working on—sometimes loudly, sometimes quietly. But first, it's worth examining the major ways in which Occupy has transformed the awareness of non-activists in the United States. There are two fundamental shifts in our collective common sense that Occupy has helped to accomplish: first is the understanding of the problem of wealth inequality and its corruptive effects on politics, and second is the awareness that the US is, in many respects, a police state.

Inequality and the Police State Become Common Sense

When Occupy Wall Street was first appearing on mainstream news outlets, I recall an anchor saying, "They are protesting what they call 'wealth inequality' in America." I remember these words standing out: "what they call." As if it was a mere opinion that some crazies held; as if the division between rich and poor wasn't one of the most obvious social facts. Now, of course, no such qualification is needed. Everyone recognizes that inequality is pervasive—and most understand that it is a problem. Occupy's injection of inequality into the mainstream political discourse has not gone away. Labor studies scholar Penny Lewis was surprised to find that in December 2013, news-media mentions of "income inequality" had risen to even higher than the levels they were at during the height of the Occupy movement:

> We found that news mentions of "income inequality" rose dramatically with the outset of Occupy, and in the aftermath remained substantially higher through the end of 2012 (up about a third from pre-Occupy levels).
>
> I ran the numbers again this week, and I have to admit I was surprised by the results.
>
> As we'd seen before, in the year after Occupy's peak, the numbers stayed higher: 30–50 percent of the pre-Occupy discussion. But beginning in the fall of 2013, the numbers reached Occupy levels again, and this time rising to over 2,000 mentions of the phrase "income inequality" in December 2013—over 50 percent more than Occupy's peak. (Lewis 2014)

Occupy influenced the language by introducing the concepts of the ninety-nine percent and the one percent, giving us a very crude set of concepts to begin to discuss the political and economic problems arising from a situation where a small group of people have control over the lives and environments of many. Occupy initiated a conversation that we all need to be having.

In April of 2014, a pair of political scientists at Princeton published paper with the unexciting title, "Testing Theories of American Politics: Elites, Interest Groups, and Average Citizens." Professors Martin Gilens and Benjamin I. Page drew on data they had collected from 1981 through 2002, analyzing over 1,700 political issues. According to the authors:

> The central point that emerges from our research is that economic elites and organized groups representing business interests have substantial independent impacts on U.S. government policy, they write, while mass-based interest groups and average citizens have little or no independent influence. (James 2014)

This comes as no surprise to most people who went through the experience of Occupy—and to many in the US who don't vote and are therefore accused of being "apolitical" or "apathetic." What's significant about this paper is that it provides social-scientific evidence for what radicals have known for a long time. It should be noted that the data-set being analyzed ended in 2002—long before the Great Recession, which further exacerbated wealth inequality,[1] and the 2010 *Citizen's United* v. *The Federal Election Committee* Supreme court ruling, which interprets spending money as equivalent to "free speech" and therefore prohibits restrictions on campaign contributions. Helpfully then, Gilens's and Page's work bursts any bubbles about "the good old days" before the most recent economic crisis. They demonstrate that US policy is overwhelmingly influenced by the wealthy—that whatever the United States calls itself, in practice it functions as a plutocracy: rule by the wealthy.

Many articles written about Gilens's and Page's work have summarized it as concluding the US is an "oligarchy." Gilens cautions about the use of this term, because "it brings to mind this image of a very small number of very wealthy people who are pulling strings behind the scenes to determine what government does. And I think it's more complicated than that. It's not only Sheldon Adelson or the Koch brothers or Bill Gates or George Soros who are shaping government policy-making."[2] This is an important

---

[1] Cronin 2013.
[2] Kapur 2014.

point, directing us toward an understanding of the systemic way that the power of money functions, and not just toward condemning a few evil and conspiratorial individuals.

Though Page and Gilens had been at work on this research long before Occupy, their work has likely received the attention that it has because it confirms the claims that Occupy injected into our common sense. As Penny Lewis put it: "In the years since the destruction of the occupations, this critique of inequality has only broadened and deepened in the US. Occupy should claim credit for getting it on the map, while political iterations old and new have been keeping it there."[3]

But this is not the only shift in common sense that Occupy accomplished, and the destruction of the occupations itself carried with it a somber political lesson. While this is hardly as often discussed, I don't think it can be underestimated the extent to which Occupy convinced everyday people around the country that any effective expression of dissent challenging corporate power in the United States will be brutally repressed. Occupy made into common sense that the US is a police state, and that activism is dangerous business.

In 2012, the Protest and Assembly Rights Project, a collaboration of numerous law schools and legal clinics, issued a report entitled "Suppressing Protest: Human Rights Violations in Response to Occupy Wall Street." The authors documented numerous police practices that violated Occupiers' First Amendment rights, including:

- **Aggressive, unnecessary, and excessive police force against peaceful protesters, bystanders, legal observers, and journalists**
- **Obstruction of press freedoms and independent legal monitoring**
- **Pervasive surveillance of peaceful political activity**
- **Violent late-night raids on peaceful encampments**
- **Unjustified closure of public space, dispersal of peaceful assemblies, and kettling (corralling and trapping) of protesters**
- **Arbitrary and selective rule enforcement and baseless arrests**
- **Failures to ensure transparency about applicable government policies**
- **Failures to ensure accountability for those allegedly responsible for abuses.** (The Global Justice Clinic et. al. 2012)

---

[3] Lewis 2014.

The report concludes that "U.S. authorities have engaged in persistent breaches of protest rights since the start of Occupy Wall Street," and recommends, among other things, an independent review of police practices during Occupy. No such review has been conducted, and we have every reason to believe that, should another movement take to the streets en masse, the response will be more repression and abuse of demonstrators.

Or worse. On December 31st 2011 President Obama signed into law the National Defense Authorization Act (NDAA) of 2012. The law allows for the indefinite detention of US citizens it suspects of being part of or who "substantially support" those engaged in terrorism. This may not seem particularly relevant, since the Occupy movement did not engage in anything that could reasonably construed as "terrorism." And yet, according to the Department of Defense's own training materials, protests should be regarded as "low-level terrorism."[4] This accounts for the way the network of "Fusion Centers," developed after 9/11 to share information between federal and local law enforcement to counter terrorism, were immediately mobilized against the Occupy movement.[5] From the perspective of government agencies, any political expression that operates outside the narrow confines of the money-saturated electoral system is seen on a continuum with those who murder innocent civilians.

In response to the NDAA, Chris Hedges and a number of other prominent intellectuals attempted to sue Obama. Hedges argued that his own journalistic work has required him to interview and share the perspective of groups that the US government has labeled "terrorists," and that, under section 1021(b) of the 2012 NDAA, this could be construed as providing "substantial support" resulting in his indefinite incarceration without due process. On April 28, 2014, after a number of rulings in Hedges's favor in lower courts, the Supreme Court refused to even hear the case. For Hedges, this refusal to examine the constitutionality of the NDAA is catastrophic:

It means the nation has entered a post-constitutional era. It means that extraordinary rendition of U.S. citizens on U.S. soil by our gov-

---

4 ACLU 2009.
5 Moynihan 2014.

ernment is legal. It means that the courts, like the legislative and executive branches of government, exclusively serve corporate power—one of the core definitions of fascism. It means that the internal mechanisms of state are so corrupted and subservient to corporate power that there is no hope of reform or protection for citizens under our most basic constitutional rights. It means that the consent of the governed—a poll by OpenCongress.com showed that this provision had a 98 percent disapproval rating—is a cruel joke. And it means that if we do not rapidly build militant mass movements to overthrow corporate tyranny, including breaking the back of the two-party duopoly that is the mask of corporate power, we will lose our liberty. (Hedges 2014)

Curiously, Hedges insists that it is "capitalism, not government" that is "the problem." He ties the NDAA and the restriction of rights of protest more generally to the influence of corporate power on government, but for some reason insists that it has to be one or the other—capitalism or government. For anarchists and many influenced by the anarchistic strand of Occupy, the problem is *both* capitalism *and* government. After all, it is only when you have a massive state apparatus with police, military, and prisons, that corporate power can seize it and wield it against the rest of us. At the moment when it seems that Hedges should be most convinced of the horror of state power, he emphasizes the power of corporations. Still, the consequences of the NDAA are frightening, since it solidifies a legal framework in which protest, already regarded as "low-level terrorism," can be crushed without any legal safeguards. Should any protest movement challenging corporate power truly gain the steam it would need to actually shift the structural violence that holds the current system together, we can expect that the US government would begin making use of such powers:

> Our corporate masters will not of their own volition curb their appetite for profits. Human misery and the deadly assault on the ecosystem are good for business. These masters have set in place laws that, when we rise up—and they expect us to rise up—will permit the state to herd us like sheep into military detention camps. Section 1021(b)(2) is but one piece of the legal tyranny now in place to ensure total corporate control. The corporate state also oversees the most pervasive security and surveillance apparatus in human history. (Hedges 2014)

Occupy, of course, is not solely responsible for the spread of the awareness that the US is effectively a police state. It needs to be seen as having helped to prepare the stage on which Edward Snowden leaked invaluable information about the National Security Association's (NSA) surveillance programs. Snowden's whistleblowing, which has landed him in exile in Russia, revealed the NSA's ambition "to collect, monitor and store every telephone and internet communication that takes place inside the US and on earth."[6] The nightmarish images of the Soviet Union and the German Democratic Republic, which brutally repressed dissent and spied on their own people, have come to pass in the United States. This may have appeared as a paranoid or conspiratorial fantasy just a few years ago, but Occupy and the subsequent leaks by Edward Snowden have given us all the proof we need.

Two Post-Encampment Occupy Groups

But the struggle for social and economic justice has not gone away—and it won't. Wherever there is oppression, there is resistance of some kind, and the Occupy movement provided a generation with a new spirit, tactics, and experience in struggle. After the encampments, many Occupy groups have fragmented into various projects, often not under the name "Occupy," which gained a lot of baggage during the movement's public hey-day. The groups and projects formed in the wake of Occupy are literally countless. In New York City in the summer of 2013, it seemed like every activist event I attended began with the announcement that the organizers had met during Occupy and that this was, for them, a continuation of their political involvement with that movement. The movement continues beneath the surface, where it is learning and growing and building connections to people's daily lives outside of the limelight.

One particularly potent set of post-encampment projects that is in clear continuity with the ethos of Occupy is the organized resistance to home foreclosures pursued by Occupy Our Homes and numerous other groups around the country. Operating with the premise that "everyone deserves a roof over their head and a place

---

[6] Greenwald 2013.

to call home," people around the country are banding together to either defend their neighbors from evictions or move evicted people and families back into homes they were forced out of. Groups involved in this project are in New York, Chicago, Minnesota, Missouri, California, Georgia, Colorado, and more.[7] Such actions build solidarity within communities and prefigure the principle that housing is something everyone deserves, not a commodity that banks and corporations should treat as an opportunity for profit.

More than just moving into the homes from which they have been evicted, some groups are also—often more quietly—moving those who have been experiencing homelessness for longer durations into the many vacant homes around the country. Currently, there are more vacant houses than there are homeless people in the United States.[8] This is a travesty that the banks who "own" such houses do not want to see corrected, since their aim is to drive up the prices of homes through creating the perception of scarcity. In response to this, people in cities across the country are organizing to both move homeless folks in to vacant houses and provide community support should they face evictions. Because of the illegality of such actions, those involved usually need to keep a very low profile and operate in secret. Actions like this, centered around building a movement of squatters, have the power to challenge the principle of private property at a fundamental level, asserting a right to housing regardless of what the laws on the books may say.[9]

Another group that has maintained their Occupy name is the Alternative Banking Working Group of Occupy Wall Street, which in 2013 produced a book, *Occupy Finance,* analyzing the financial system as it is and attempting to point a way out of the mess of financial capitalism. Financialization has turned almost every aspect of social and economic life into opportunities for corporate profit off an indebted population, and, according to Occupy Finance:

> When the foundations of our society—education of our children, care for the sick and injured, security for our elderly—are viewed simply as

---

[7] <http://occupyourhomes.org/about>.
[8] Truthdig 2011.
[9] Martinez 2014.

opportunities for the creation of ever more "innovative" financial products and profit centers, we erode the very basis of the communities that keep us all safe. We become prey for the financial predators. (Alternative Banking Working Group 2013)

Their book, available for free online, breaks the financial system down in easy to understand terms. During the process of researching the book, they interviewed various people involved in finance and government regulation, and were surprised to find that "when they spoke to us at meetings of the Alternative Banking Group, they looked to us as the agents of redress and renewal!" Many in positions of power within the financial system as it stands feel equally helpless in shaping it. Occupy Finance points to a number of alternatives that exist right now that offer the capacity to resist financial control. They recommend, among other things, moving your money out of for-profit banks and into credit unions, forming worker-owned cooperatives, and they highlight "land trusts" as a powerful tool for communities taking control over housing and land use. In a community land trust, the community basically forms a non-profit, tax-exempt corporation to steward a property or set of properties for purposes established in its charter, usually to maintain affordable housing, but also for urban farming projects and community spaces.

Both Occupy Our Homes and the Alternative Banking Working Group are just two examples of many that have continued their work in movements for social and economic justice long after the encampments ended. They each took the principles encountered through Occupy and ran with them.

Occupy Sandy

Perhaps the most high-profile post-encampment project of Occupy was the grassroots response to Superstorm Sandy, which ravaged the coast of New York and New Jersey in November of 2012. Occupy Sandy re-mobilized networks of Occupy activists, and allowed them to put the organizational skills and ethos of mutual aid of the encampments to work in efforts of disaster relief.

Superstorm Sandy resulted in over one hundred deaths and massive flooding and damage to coastal communities on the East

Coast. The size, strength, and damage of the storm was unprecedented in the areas affected. While it is notoriously difficult to tie any individual weather event to the effects of global climate change, an increase in such storms is exactly what we should expect from rising ocean temperatures, rising sea levels, and the unusual motions of the jet stream that attended the storm[10]—all of which can be directly linked to climate change caused by the emission of carbon dioxide and other greenhouse gases from various industries.

In the immediate aftermath of the storm, the Federal Emergency Management Agency (FEMA) was unable to reach many of the most devastated areas. Activists from around the region who had been involved in Occupy quickly began organizing emergency relief hubs, collecting and distributing donations of food, blankets, and generators and distributing them on the ground to those in need. Even the *New York Times* had to credit the activists for having accomplished what government agencies and traditional charities could not. Their article, "Where FEMA Fell Short, Occupy Sandy Was There," highlighted the tireless efforts and organizational ingenuity of the former Occupiers in responding to the disaster and providing others with outlets to lend their hand to the relief.[11]

But the Occupy Sandy relief effort—which is still ongoing—is not solely about meeting immediate needs. In some communities, it is also about rebuilding in a manner that is more just and equitable than before. Recognizing that a disaster like Sandy affects the most vulnerable people the most—those who have already been suffering through poverty and racism—the Rockaway Wildfire project has combined disaster relief efforts with community organizing and political education in line with the values Occupy, at its best, articulated:

> Through numerous discussions the needs identified as most pressing to improve in the Rockaways were pre-existing systemic and socio-economic issues that were merely exacerbated by Superstorm Sandy. Out of this systemic critique Rockaway Wildfire was born; a space where we could collectively identify issues and educate ourselves on how to effectively respond to them in a way that would unite and

---

[10] Romm 2013.
[11] Feuer 2012.

empower the Rockaway Community. ("History of Rockaway Wildfire")

Rockaway Wildfire is helping to rebuild with an understanding that climate change will bring such dangerous storms with greater frequency, and that such moments of devastation can be an opportunity—though a tragic one—for rebuilding in re-imagining and more equitable and ecologically sustainable ways.

Influencing Elections

As I've emphasized throughout this book, the prefigurative politics of the Occupy movement were experiments with a kind of politics that was not based on electing representatives—direct democracy. It is to be expected, however, that the energy unleashed around the individual issues that Occupy addressed, would be taken up by progressive politicians. The most prominent example of this is the election of Bill De Blasio to mayor of New York, through a campaign that made a central issue of both inequality and the New York Police Department's racist "stop and frisk" policy targeting men of color throughout the city.

De Blasio's campaign rhetoric spoke of a "Tale of Two Cities"—the mega-rich and the rest. Many of the progressives who were pleased with Occupy's attention to the issue of inequality, but could do without the prefigurative politics, flocked behind De Blasio as a "true progressive" candidate that would address the problems Occupy drew attention to in an effective and practical way. But many Occupy activists had learned the lesson of looking up to people in positions of power to hand down solutions to the structural inequalities of corporate rule. Discussing Occupy activists' views of DeBlasio, Nathan Schneider was interviewed by *New York Magazine*:

> Occupiers "aren't taking much time resting on laurels here," says Schneider. "They tend to see De Blasio, like Obama, as someone who is riding their rhetorical wave without a lot of evidence that he's going to usher in the radical changes that they'd like to see, or anything close." For all of De Blasio's activist cred, Schneider said, "he's an Establishment candidate, backed by a Democratic Party that has always been safely bought off by the one percent." (Coscarelli 2013)

As was common sense in the encampments, both the Democrats and the Republicans are in the pockets of the one percent—though their rhetorical strategies shift with the winds of public opinion, their basic commitments are to the structures that sustain and legitimate corporate power. In an early sign that the hype was overblown about De Blasio being an "Occupy Mayor" or that City Hall was going to be "Occupied," De Blasio appointed Bill Bratton as police commissioner. Bratton, the originator of the Stop and Frisk policy that activists around the city, including Occupiers, had been fighting, claimed that he would not have let Occupy Wall Street stay in Zuccotti Park for even a night:

> Bratton said he is no fan of the Occupy Wall Street movement, which brought back the tent cities he had worked so hard to eradicate from New York and Los Angeles.
> "Many cities made the mistake of embracing them with open arms," he said. "They [created] major problems for themselves. . . . You can't allow people to occupy public space." (Mettle 2012)

It remains to be seen how De Blasio's policies will influence social movements—whether he does succeed, as he promised, in "building spaces" for social justice activists to interface with city officials, or whether he will have simply been one more politician to capitalize on the energies of a grassroots movement.

Perhaps a more promising development in electoral politics is the election of Kshama Sawant, a former software engineer, teacher and activist involved with Occupy, to the Seattle city council. Elected on the Socialist Alternative party ticket, in her election night speech, she said that she is "happy and honored to carry this mantle for the global working class." She also credited Occupy with creating the context for her election:

> We know that times are changing and we know that we have run this campaign at a time when Occupy has completely shifted the dialogue. It has put class back on the agenda. It has put capitalism, the "c" word, that was never used, back on the agenda. And it has put socialism, the "s" word, back on the agenda. (Sawant 2012)

One core piece of Sawant's election platform was to raise the minimum wage to $15 per hour—a number that sounded unthinkably high just a few years ago. And yet, the idea was so popular and her politics so persuasive, that on May 1st 2014 the Mayor of Seattle adopted this policy, outlining a plan of his own to reach $15 per hour in phases over the next several years. The plan is far from perfect, and Sawant herself has reservations about the proposed phasing, which she argues is unnecessary for large corporations like McDonald's that could afford to raise wages immediately. Still, it illustrates how the presence of a radical movement like Occupy can push the dialogue further toward the interests of working people, and how someone like Sawant can, by her very presence in public life, pressure liberal politicians to adopt more progressive policies. At least, that is one way things can go.

A final way that Occupy activists are influencing the way electoral politics works is through a project called The After Party, a new political party that is seeking to rekindle democracy at a local level. According to their website:

> The After Party isn't a traditional political party in any sense. We organize by identifying and meeting a community's needs from beyond the political system, and getting rid of corrupt politicians by getting our own community leaders into local office. We will feed the hungry, educate those who wish to learn, care for the sick, and house those whose homes have been taken. We will break the stranglehold of the broken two-party system by innovating and changing the rules of the game. (After Party 2014a)

The After Party Manifesto states outright that "We are not represented. We have been usurped . . . by millionaires and billionaires and banks and corporations," and proceeds with a list of grievances reminiscent of the *Declaration of the Occupation of Wall Street*, concluding that "we were asleep. But we are waking up."[12]

Again, it remains to be seen how such experiments will pan out. While Occupy eschewed electoral politics, focusing instead on attempting to build direct democratic assemblies, both the election of Kshama Sawant and the After Party signify that many who passed through the experience of Occupy believe it's possible to engage electoral structures not as a replacement for grassroots organizing, but in a way that supports the on-the-ground struggles and more radical organizing of which Occupy was an expression.

---

[12] After Party 2014b.

Strike Debt Against Creditocracy

Perhaps the most exciting single offshoot of the Occupy movement is Strike Debt—an international effort to challenge what they are calling the "creditocracy." In *Creditocracy and the Case for Debt Refusal*, sociologist and Strike Debt activist Andrew Ross argues we live in a creditocracy, a society in which "indebtedness becomes the precondition not just for material improvements in the quality of life, but for the basic requirements of life."[13] Rather than being a way to gain access to luxury goods or to generate capital, creditocracy makes people dependent on debt even the most basic social and material necessities—houses, education, medical care, even food. Ross points out that

> citizens of a creditocracy are not expected, nor are they encouraged, to pay off *all* their debts. After all, we are no longer useful to creditors if we somehow manage to wipe the slate clean. The point is to prolong our debt service until the bitter end, and even beyond the grave, as is the case for loan co-signers. The sober truth is that debts, especially at compound interest, multiply at a much faster rate than the ability to repay. (p. 16)

Debt affects everyone in contemporary society—whether it's student loan debt, medical debt, housing debt, municipal debt which requires cities to slash social services, or sovereign debt which keeps entire nations in chains to international banking institutions like the World Bank. The ultimate aim of Strike Debt is to call into question the very moral principle that debt-servitude relies upon: that a good person always pays their debts. In response, Strike Debt raises the fundamental moral question that goes unasked in that principle: what do we really owe one another?[14]

Formed by Occupy activists in 2012, Strike Debt recognizes that building a movement in which people would, en masse, refuse to pay back loans to the banks, financial institutions, and governments, is a long time in the making. Wisely, they have focused on projects that attempt to de-mystify both the moral power of debt and the process of navigating financial institutions.

---

[13] Ross 2013, p. 11.

[14] This is the basic question raised by David Graeber's 2009 work, *Debt: The First 5,000 Years*.

The first major project they produced, in November of 2012, was called the "Rolling Jubilee," otherwise known as "the Peoples' Bailout." Often, people in debt do not owe the money to the original institution they borrowed from. Financial institutions "package" loans and sell them off to other companies, sometimes for as low as five cents on the dollar. If you're in debt, this means debt collectors may have purchased your debt for a fraction of the price you owe, on the gamble that they may be able to collect the whole sum or at least much more than they paid for it. With the Rolling Jubille, Strike Debt held a telethon and accepted donations to raise money to purchase debt on these cheap debt markets. So far they have raised over seven hundred thousand dollars and used it to buy up over $14.7 million dollars' worth of debt. Rather than collecting all that, they simply forgave it. They abolished it; they made it disappear.[15]

The Rolling Jubilee takes its name from the biblical "jubilee" of old, the fifty-year celebration in which debts were forgiven, property was redistributed, and slaves were freed. In Leviticus, it says, "This fiftieth year is sacred—it is a time of freedom and of celebration when everyone will receive back their original property, and slaves will return home to their families." Various forms of jubilee have been practiced throughout history, but the idea seems outlandish to many today. Strike Debt decided to demonstrate just how realistic it was, and how everyday people themselves could help make it happen. The millions of dollars of debt they forgave was all medical debt—which, in the US, was the number one reason why people defaulted on mortgages and were kicked out of their homes after the housing crisis.[16] Moreover, the medical debt that Strike Debt has forgiven is completely anonymous; donators to the Rolling Jubilee and those who purchase medical debt on the debt-markets have no idea whose debt they are buying or forgiving. This illustrates a kind of mutual aid for the modern world, where everyday people around the country help bail one another out, freeing them from the bonds of debt.

The Rolling Jubilee is an individual project, an experiment, to help lots of people and to illustrate a point: debt is a social relation, and we can change it. While one company who buys your debt

---

[15] See <http://rollingjubilee.org>.
[16] Harris 2010.

might hire ruthless debt-collectors to harass and degrade you, calling you and your family and friends multiple times a day to extract
whatever payments they can, another group of people can buy
your debt and simply make it vanish. Strike Debt's forgiveness of
medical debt not only reveals debt itself is merely one kind of social
relation that could be replaced with a spirit of mutual aid, it also
emphasizes that medical care should be freely available to all, and
that any group or individual that attempts to extract a profit or
extra burden from people in need of medical treatment is exploiting people in their most vulnerable times. Rather than simply
accept that that is the way things are, the Rolling Jubilee cleverly
presents a tool for removing vulnerable people from the clutches
of debt collectors.

Another project of Strike Debt has been series of "debtor's
assemblies" held in cities across the country. The debt assemblies
are an attempt to directly address the shame and isolation that people burdened with debt feel—the sense that they are in this alone,
and that their own personal worth depends upon them repaying.
One of their slogans, written on posters and banners and pamphlets, is "YOU ARE NOT A LOAN," emphasizing that debt is a
collective problem facing most people in the U.S., and not solely
an individual problem that needs to be accepted. As promotional
material for the Oakland debtors' assembly put it,

> Debt keeps us isolated, ashamed, and afraid—of becoming homeless,
> of going hungry, of being crippled or killed by treatable illness, or of
> being trapped in poverty-level jobs. Those facing foreclosure, medical
> debt, student debt, or credit card debt feel alone, hounded by debt
> collectors, and forced into unrewarding work to keep up with
> payments.[17] (Occupy Oakland 2013)

In debtors' assemblies, people share their stories about how they
got into debt, the anxieties that accompany it, and share strategies
for how they are either getting by or managing to evade the collection agencies. Like the General Assemblies in the Occupy
encampments, something magical can happen in debtors' assemblies: they can become sites where people transform their perspectives and come to recognize debt as a system of control, one more

---

[17] Occupy Oakland 2013.

way our future labor, which might be used to create the kind of equitable and ecologically sustainable world we need, has been captured by the powerful.

Another project of Strike Debt is their book, the *Debt Resistor's Operations Manual* (DROM), available for free at www.strikedebt. org. The DROM is a handbook for navigating the various institutions that issue and collect debt of various kinds, with individual chapters on credit card debt, student loans, medical debt, housing debt, and others. The aim of the book is to give us all a thread through the financial maze that has been constructed, awareness of the laws that do protect us, and information about the risks and opportunities for debt resistance.

Debt resistance can mean a number of things, but the ultimate aim of Strike Debt is to build the conditions for a debt strike, a collective refusal to sustain the power of the financial institutions that hold both our present and our future under their control. Although this may seem like a long way off, Strike Debt has pointed out that, in a sense, such a strike is already under way. People around the country are already ignoring calls from debt collectors, throwing out their bills, even changing their names. The problem is that many who are doing this see it as something to be ashamed of, rather than a political act of resistance. To transform our perception of these small acts of refusal, some have declared themselves to be a part of an "Invisible Army" of debt resisters. In 2012, they issued their first communique:

> We are the Invisible Army of Defaulters. We are millions. We are everywhere. We are your neighbors. We are your family. Your friends. We are the 99%. We are going to bring this system to its knees. We can, because we wild the one power that all the armies of the world can never defeat: the power of refusal. This power has destroyed the mightiest empires the world has ever seen. All crumble and dissolve the moment enough people simply withdraw their consent. Not loudly. But quietly, covertly. (Occupy Strategy/Occupy Theory 2013)

The current corporate system feeds on debt, but debt keeps its hold over us through a set of moral beliefs that serve the interests of the powerful. The moment that morality loses its hold and people refuse to pay, the landscape of possibility opens up, and the future currently held in check by debt-servitude becomes our own.

Becoming Commoners

The Occupy movement changed not only how we view the political and economic structures. It also changed how many participants view themselves, encouraging an ethos of direct democracy, a disdain for social relationships of hierarchy, tactics for self-organizing, and a vision of a world based on mutual aid. Occupy successfully opened up a space for experimentation with these principles through reclaiming the commons, rebuilding democratic relationships for managing the conditions of our lives and the products of our labor.

One way that Occupy lives on after the encampments is through "commoning" projects of all kinds, whether that is community gardens, squatting projects, free schools, and forming communes. While some new communes have actually been started by former Occupiers out in the country, there is also an increasing interest in figuring out how to form communes within cities. This can involve collective housing projects, but also can involve finding creative ways to share, to make common, the resources we already have at our disposal, without necessarily dropping out of the lives we are currently living. We can proceed with small steps that build the social skills necessary for commoning more aspects of our lives, with the understanding that in the midst of events that completely shift our sense of possibility— whether they are political interventions like Occupy or disasters like Superstorm Sandy—these skills and networks of relationships can be drawn upon.

In their pamphlet reflecting upon Occupy and other movements of 2011, theorists Michael Hardt and Toni Negri describe these movements as transforming participants in ways that point toward a society that is not currently possible, one that is based on a different set of principles for collective living that are currently held back by the violence of the present order:

> . . . preparing for an unforeseen event may be the best way to understand the work and accomplishments of the cycle of struggles of 2011. The movements are preparing ground for an event they cannot foresee or predict. The principles they promote, including equality, freedom, sustainability, and open access to the common, can form the scaffolding on which, the event of a radical social break, a new society can be built. (Hardt and Negri 2013, p. 103)

Occupy was not the *event,* but preparation for it. But events are coming that challenge the current system to its core, whether they are constructed by those who rebel, brought on by climate change, or from some other source. The point is that we can begin preparing for such events now by practicing the kinds of non-capitalist relations and struggling for justice in solidarity with all who are resisting this system, in order to build the kinds of skills and networks that can create more spaces of freedom, independent from the power of corporations to extract profit, destroy ecosystems, and capture our future with debt.

For Hardt and Negri, this means becoming commoners. Just as bakers bake and dancers dance, commoners *common:* they free resources, whether that is water, food, housing, education, or our time, from the power of corporate and state control. Commoners look for creative ways to collectively manage such resources, following the principle "from each according to their ability, to each according to their needs." Commoners don't need to be activists—though they can be—but are engaged in actions, loudly or quietly, that fundamentally challenge the assumption of private property, creating concrete examples of what it looks like to give one another what we deserve. Commoners answer the basic question of justice, "What is owed, and to whom?", with a principle murmured by the great heretic Thomas Münzer as he was dying from torture: *omnia sunt communis,* "everything for everyone." Commoners attempt to create practices that can live up to this challenging demand. Rather than viewing the world as capital, as potential sources of monetary profit, and attempting to devise ever more clever ways to make money, commoners view the world as fundamentally shared by all, and attempt to devise ever more transparent ways to realize that principle in practice.

The Future Reopened

For many of us, a movement like Occupy was not only unexpected, but appeared impossible. Until it happened. And now, in the years after the encampments were evicted, it seems like once again, the idea of a movement that could capture the attention of the world and transform the lives of people in the heart of capitalism is once again impossible. The world seems so fixed, the power structures seem so entrenched, the authority seems so real. And yet Occupy stands as proof for a generation that our world can erupt with something unexpected, that we can say "enough!" and insist on no longer playing by the rules.

The seas are rising. The bees are dying. The rich are growing richer while the vast majority of people over the world are being pressed into ever more hardships. The states that control us are monitoring our every communication and repressing movements for social justice with as much force as they can get away with, while carefully managing their images. The corporations have seized the globe and are solidifying their power with ever more far-reaching so-called "free trade agreements" like the Trans-Pacific Partnership, currently being pushed by President Obama. Soil, air, and waterways around the world are being polluted by hydraulic fracturing ("fracking") and other extraction processes. It is important that we recognize the magnitude of the challenges facing us all.

Amidst all the complexity of the oppressions and fears created by global capitalism, Occupy revealed a truth that was stunningly simple and powerful. That the whole damn thing relies upon people like us, like you and me. It requires our participation, our labor, our consent. When we withdraw our consent and create cracks with our collective refusal, the edifice of power trembles and reveals the violence that ultimately sustains it. Occupy created spaces in which people could not only withdraw consent, but actively practice a form of organizing based on different principles, principles which are inconsistent with the smooth flow of a world gone mad.

Our only chance at building a world of justice will come from bringing into our own lives the spirit of radical democracy, of collective experimentation, and of refusal to submit to the power of money. The Occupy movement may be long dead, but the organizational principles it practiced and the hope it presented to the world are both hard at work, growing and learning beneath the surface.

Bibliography

Adbusters. 2011. #OccupyWallStreet: A Shift in Revolutionary Tactics. *Adbusters.org*, 7/13/11.
<https://www.adbusters.org/blogs/adbusters-blog/occupywalstreet.html>

The After Party. 2014a. After Party: You Coming? <http://occupywallst.org/article/the-after-party/>

———. 2014b. After Party Manifesto.
<http://www.afterpartyusa.org/manifesto/>

Alexander, Michelle. 2012. *The New Jim Crow: Mass Incarceration in the Age of Colorblindness*. New York: The New Press.

Alternative Banking Working Group. 2013. *Occupy Finance*.
<http://altbanking.net/projects-2/our_book/>

American Civil Liberties Union (ACLU). 2009. ACLU Challenges Defense Department Personnel Police to Regard Lawful Protest as 'Low-Level Terrorism'. <https://www.aclu.org/national-security/aclu-challenges-defense-department-personnel-policy-regard-lawful-protests-"low-le>

Anonymous Pamphlet. 2009. *Unfinished Acts: January Rebellions*. Oakland.

Aragorn!, ed. 2012. *Occupy Everything: Anarchists in the Occupy Movement: 2009–2011*. LBC Books.

Atchu and Jez3Prez. 2011. *Testing Wall Street September 1st*. Video. Novad Collective. <www.youtube.com/watch?v=ayUGOgFaCs8>

Bady, Aaron. 2012. The Oakland Commune. In Lang and Levitsky/Lang 2012.

Barna, Maxwell. 2014 The FBI Is Hiding Details about an Alleged Occupy Houston Assassination Plot. *Vice News*, 3/21/14.
<https://news.vice.com/article/the-fbi-is-hiding-details-about-an-alleged-occupy-houston-assassination-plot>

Bellafante, Ginia. 2011a. Gunning for Wall Street, With Faulty Aim. *New York Times*, 9/23/11.

———. 2011b. Every Action Produces Overreaction. *New York Times*, 9/30/11.

Blumenkranz, Carla, et al., eds. 2011. *Occupy! Scenes from Occupied America*. New York: Verso.

Bray, Mark. *Translating Anarchy: The Anarchism of Occupy Wall Street*. Winchester: Zero Books

Breines, Wini. 1981. *Community and Organization in the New Left, 1962–1968: The Great Refusal*. New Brunswick: Rutgers University Press.

Byrne, Janet, ed. 2012. *The Occupy Handbook*. Back Bay Books.

Caffentzis, George. 2013. The Power of Money: Debt and Enclosure. In *In Letters of Blood and Fire: Work, Machines, and the Crisis of Capitalism*. Brooklyn: Autonomedia.

Cassidy, John. 2012. What Good Is Wall Street? In Byrne 2012.

Castells, Manuel. 2012. *Networks of Outrage and Hope: Social Movements in the Internet Age*. Cambridge: Polity.

Ciccariello-Maher, George. 2012. From Oscar Grant to Occupy: The Long Arc of Rebellion in Oakland. In Khatib et al. 2012.

Coscarelli, Joe. 2013. Occupy Wall Street Is Very Skeptical of Bill de Blasio. *New York Magazine* 11/17/13. <http://nymag.com/daily/ intelligencer/2013/09/bill-de-blasio-occupy-wall-street-candidate.html>

Crawford, Vicki L., et al., eds. 1993. *Women in the Civil Rights Movement: Trailblazers and Torchbearers, 1941–1965*. Bloomington: Indiana University Press.

CrimethInc. Ex-Worker's Collective. 2011. Dear Occupiers: An Open Letter from Anarchists. <http://www.crimethinc.com/blog/2011/10/07/dear-occupiers-a-letter-from-anarchists/>

———. 2012a. The Illegitimacy of Violence, the Violence of Legitimacy. <http://www.crimethinc.com/texts/recentfeatures/violence.php>

———. 2012b. Post-Debate Debrief: Video and Libretto. <http://www.crimethinc.com/blog/2012/09/17/post-debate-debrief-video-and-libretto/>

Cronin, Brenda. 2013. Some 95% of 2009–2012. Income Gains Went to Wealthiest 1% Real Time Economics Blog. *Wall Street Journal*. 9/10/13. <http://blogs.wsj.com/economics/2013/09/10/some-95-of-2009-2012-income-gains-went-to-wealthiest-1/>

De Angelis, Massimo. 2007. *The Beginning of History: Value Struggles and Global Capital*. London: Pluto.

de Cleyre, Voltairine. 1912. Direct Action. Molinari Institute. <http://praxeology.net/VC-DA.htm>

Dewey, John. 1939. Creative Democracy: The Task before Us. In Hickman and Alexander, eds. 1998. *The Essential Dewey, Volume 1*. Bloomington: Indiana University Press.

Dixon, Bruce. 2011. Occupy Where? What's in It for Black and Brown People? In Lang and Lang/Levitsky 2011, pp. 143–46.

Eichert, Benjamin, Rick Rowley, and Staale Sandberg. 1999. *Zapatista*. Big Noise Films.

Epstein, Barbara. 1991. *Political Protest and Cultural Revolution: Nonviolent Direct Action in the 1970s and 1980s*. Berkeley: University of California Press.

Federici, Silvia, George Caffentzis and David Graeber. 2011. Beyond Good and Evil Commons: A Seminar with Silvia Federici, George Caffentzis and David Graeber. Seminar at 16 Beaver Street, New York. <http://www.16beavergroup.org/silvia_george_david/>

Feuer, Alan. 2012. Occupy Sandy: A Movement Moves to Relief. *New York Times*. 11/9/12. <http://www.nytimes.com/2012/11/11/nyregion/where-fema-fell-short-occupy-sandy-was-there.html?pagewanted=all>

Fisher, Mark. 2009. *Capitalist Realism: Is There No Alternative?* Winchester: Zero Books.

Flank, Lenny Jr., ed. 2011. *Voices from the 99 Percent: An Oral History of the Occupy Wall Street Movement*. St. Petersburg: Red and Black.

Frank, Thomas. 2012. To the Precinct Station: How Theory Met Practice . . . and Drove It Absolutely Crazy. *The Baffler* no. 21, 2012. <https://www.thebaffler.com/past/to_the_precinct_station>

Freeman, Jo. 1970. The Tyranny of Structurelessness. <http://www.jofreeman.com/joreen/tyranny.htm>

Fukuyama, Francis. 1989. The End of History? *The National Interest*, Summer.

Geisst, Charles R. 1997. *Wall Street: A History from Its Beginnings to the Fall of Enron*. Oxford: Oxford University Press.

The Global Justice Clinic, et al. 2012. *Suppressing Protest: Human Rights Violations in the U.S. Response to Occupy Wall Street*. <http://chrgj.org/wp-content/uploads/2012/10/suppressing-protest.pdf>

Gottesdiener, Laura. 2013. The Great Eviction: Black America and the Toll of the Foreclosure Crisis. *Mother Jones*, 8/1/2013.

Graeber, David. 2007. On the Very Idea of 'Consumption': Desire, Phantasms, and the Aesthetics of Destruction from Medieval Times to the Present. In *Possibilities: Essays on Hierarchy, Rebellion, and Desire*. Oakland: AK Press.

———. 2009. *Direct Action: An Ethnography*. Oakland: AK Press.

———. 2011a. *Debt: The First 5,000 Years*. Brooklyn: Melville House.

———. 2011b. Occupy and Anarchism's Gift of Democracy. *Guardian*, 11/15/11.

———. 2012. Concerning the Violent Peace Police: An Open Letter to Chris Hedges. *N+1 Magazine Online.* 9/1/12.

———. 2013. *The Democracy Project: A History, a Crisis, a Movement.* New York: Spiegel and Grau.

Greenwald, Glenn. 2013. The Crux of the NSA Story in One Phrase: 'Collect It All'. *Guardian,* 7/15/13. <http://www.theguardian.com/commentisfree/2013/jul/15/crux -nsa-collect-it-all>

Hanson, Russell L. 1989. Democracy. In T. Ball, J. Farr, and R. Hanson, eds., *Political Innovation and Conceptual Change.* Cambridge University Press.

Harcourt, Bernard. 2013. Political Disobedience. In *Occupy: Three Inquiries in Disobedience.* Chicago: University of Chicago Press.

Hardt, Michael, and Antonio Negri. 2012. *Declaration.* Argo-Navis.

Harris, Marlys. 2010. Foreclosure: It's Not Just about the Mortgage. *CBS News.* 1/5/10. <http://www.cbsnews.com/news/foreclosure- its-not-just-about-the-mortgage/>

Harvey, David. 2014. *Seventeen Contradictions and the End of Capitalism.* Oxford: Oxford University Press.

Hayden, Tom. 2012. What the Port Huron Statement Still Has to Say, 50 Years On. *Guardian,* 6/14/12. <http://www.theguardian.com/commentisfree/2012/jun/14/port -huron-statement-50-tom-hayden>

Hedges, Chris. 2010. *Death of the Liberal Class.* New York: Nation Books.

———. 2011. Speech at Occupy Harvard. <http://www.dailykos.com/story/2011/12/02/1041647/-Chris- Hedges-at-Occupy-Harvard-feeding-plutocracy-and-why-the-cops- are-scared>

———. 2014a. America's Kangaroo Justice: Welcome to the post- Constitutional Era. <http://www.occupy.com/article/americas-kan- garoo-justice-welcome-post-constitutional-era>

———. 2014b. Capitalism, Not Government, Is the Problem. *Truthdig,* 5/5/14. <http://www.truth-out.org/opinion/item/23486-chris-hedges- capitalism-not-government-is-the-problem>

Hieronymous. 2012. Oakland's Third Attempt at a General Strike. In Aragorn! 2012.

Holloway, John. 2010. *Crack Capitalism.* London: Pluto.

Jacobs, Ron. 2013. Was That Really an Antiwar Movement? A Look at the Movement Against the U.S. War in Iraq. *Counterpunch* 6/12/13. < http://www.counterpunch.org/2013/07/12/a-look-at-the- movement-against-the-us-war-in-iraq/>

James, Brendan. 2014. Princeton Study: U.S. No Longer an Actual Democracy. *Talking Points Memo.* <http://talkingpointsmemo.com/livewire/princeton-experts-say-us-no-longer-democracy>

Kapur, Sahil. 2014. Scholar Behind Viral 'Oligarchy' Study Tells You What It Means. *Talking Points Memo.* <http://talkingpointsmemo.com/dc/princeton-scholar-demise-of-democracy-america-tpm-interview>

Khatib, Kate, et al. 2012. *We Are Many: Reflections on Movement Strategy from Occupation to Liberation.* Oakland: AK Press.

Kiesbye, Stefan. 2013. *The Occupy Movement.* Greenhaven.

Kim, Tammy. 2011. Race-ing Occupy Wall Street. In Lang and Lang/Levitsky 2011.

King, Martin Luther, Jr., 1963. Letter from Birmingham City Jail. The King Center. <http://www.thekingcenter.org/archive/document/letter-birmingham-city-jail-0>

Klein, Naomi. 2002. Farewell to the End of History: Organization and Vision in Anti-Corporate Movements. *Socialist Register.* London: Merlin.

———. 2007. *The Shock Doctrine: The Rise of Disaster Capitalism.* New York: Picador.

———. 2011. Occupy Wall Street: The Most Important Thing in the World Now. *Nation,* 10/6/11. <http://www.thenation.com/article/163844/occupy-wall-street-most-important-thing-world-now#>

Knafo, Saki. 2013. 1 in 3 Black Males Will Go to Prison in Their Lifetime, Report Warns. *Huffington Post,* 10/4/13.

Knowlton, Brian, and Michael M. Grynbaum. 2008. Greenspan 'Shocked' that Free Markets Are Flawed. *New York Times,* 10/23/08. <http://www.nytimes.com/2008/10/23/business/worldbusiness/23iht-gspan.4.17206624.html?_r=0>

Kraft, Herbert. 1986. *The Lenape: Archaeology, History, and Ethnography.* Newark: New Jersey Historical Society.

Lang, Amy Schrager, and Daniel Lang/Levitsky. 2012. *Dreaming in Public: Building the Occupy Movement.* Oxford: New Internationalist.

Lewis, Penny. 2014. Inequality after Occupy. *OccupyWallStreet.net.* <http://occupywallstreet.net/story/inequality-after-occupy>

Lockwood, Brad. 2011. OWS Evicted: An Unfortunate Minority. *Forbes,* 11/15/2011. <http://www.forbes.com/sites/bradlockwood/2011/11/15/ows-evicted-an-unfortunate-minority/>

Lowenstein, Frank, et al., eds. 2007. *Voices of Protest: Documents of Courage and Dissent.* New York: Black Dog and Leventhal Publishers.

Luhby, Tami. 2012. Worsening Wealth Inequality by Race. CNN Money, 6/21/2012.

Lynd, Staughton, and Andrej Grubacic. 2008. *Wobblies and Zapatistas: Conversations on Anarchism, Marxism, and Radical History.* Oakland: PM Press.

Mackey, Robert and McVeigh, Karen. 2011. Occupy Wall Street: Inquiries Launched as New Pepper-spray Video Emerges. *Guardian,* 9/28/11.

Madison, James. 1787. *The Federalist,* #10. <http://www.gutenberg.org/files/1404/1404-h/1404-h.htm#link2H_4_0010>

Maharawal, Manissa McCleave. So Real It Hurts: Notes on Occupy Wall Street. In Lang/Levitsky 2011.

Mann, Geoff. 2012. *Disassembly Required: A Field Guide to Actually Existing Capitalism.* Oakland: AK Press.

Marcos, Subcomandante. 2002. *Our Word Is Our Weapon: Selected Writings.* Juan Ponce de León, ed. New York: Seven Stories Press.

Martinez, Miguel A. 2014. Squatting for Justice: Bringing Life to the City. *ROAR Magazine.* <http://occupywallstreet.net/story/squatting-justice-bringing-life-city>

McKay, Iain. 2007. *An Anarchist FAQ: Volume 1.* Oakland: AK Press.

Meerkat Media Collective. 2011. *Consensus: Direct Democracy at Occupy Wall Street.* Video. Available at: <https://www.youtube.com/watch?v=6dtD8RnGaRQ>.

Mettle, Heavy. 2012. De Blasio's Commissioner Bratton Would Have Crushed Occupy Movement Immediately. *Daily Kos,* 12/6/13. <http://www.dailykos.com/story/2013/12/06/1260770/-DeBlasio-s-Commissioner-Bratton-Would-Have-Crushed-Occupy-Movement-Immediately#>

Meyers, William. 2000. *Nonviolence and Its Violent Consequences.* Gualala: III Publishing.

Mies, Maria, and Bennholdt-Thomsen. 2000. *The Subsistence Perspective: Beyond the Globalised Economy.* London: Zed.

Milkman, Ruth, et al. 2013. Changing the Subject: A Bottom-up account of Occupy Wall Street in New York City. New York: The Murphy Institute at CUNY.

Mills, Charles W. 1999. *The Racial Contract.* Ithaca: Cornell University Press.

Motavalli, Jim. 1996. Culture Jammin'. *E–The Environmental Magazine* 7(3), 4/30/1996.

Moynihan, Colin. 2014. Officials Cast Wide Net in Monitoring Occupy Protests. *New York Times,* 5/22/14.

<http://www.nytimes.com/2014/05/23/us/officials-cast-wide-net-in-monitoring-occupy-protests.html?_r=0>

Mueller, Carol. 1993. Ella Baker and the Origins of Participatory Democracy. In Crawford et al. 1993.

New York City General Assembly (NYCGA). 2011a. Principles of Solidarity. <http://www.nycga.net/resources/documents/principles-of-solidarity/>

———. 2011b. *Declaration of the Occupation of New York City.* <http://www.nycga.net/resources/documents/declaration/>

Nunberg, Geoff. 2011. Unlike Most Marxist Jargon, 'Class Warfare' Persists. *NPR's Fresh Air* 10/4/11. <http://www.npr.org/2011/10/04/140874613/unlike-most-marxist-jargon-class-warfare-persists>

Occupy Boston Women's Caucus. 2011. Statement. In Lang/Levitsky 2012, p. 128.

Occupy Oakland. 2012a. Move-in Day Flyers. <https://occupyoakland.org/2012/01/move-in-flyers/>

———. 2012b. Move-in Day FAQ. <https://occupyoakland.org/2012/01/move-in-day-faq/>

———. 2013. Debtors' Assembly: You Are Not Alone. You Are Not A Loan! <https://occupyoakland.org/ailec_event/debtors-assembly-alone-loan/?instance_id=>

Occupy Theory/Occupy Strategy. 2012. *Tidal, number 3.* <http://tidalmag.org/issue-3-year-ii/>

Olbermann, Keith. 2011. *Countdown with Keith Olbermann*, 9/21/11. <https://www.youtube.com/watch?v=s4QUePfHFQY>

Olson, Joel. 2012. Whiteness and the 99%. In Khatib et al. 2012.

Palast, Greg. 2003. Resolved to Ruin. *Harper's Magazine* (March); anthologized in Lowenstein et al. 2007.

Potter, Will. 2011. *Green Is the New Red: An Insider Account of a Social Movement Under Siege.* San Francisco: City Lights.

Purdy, Britnae. Remembering the Lenape, the Indigenous People of Manhattan, During UNPFII. *First Peoples Worldwide*: <www.first-peoples.org/remembering-the-lenape-the-indigenous-people-of-manhattan>

Research and Destroy. 2009. Communiqué from an Absent Future: On the Terminus of Student Life. Santa Cruz: Black Powder.

Reynié, Dominique. 2004. Globalized Protest. Demonstrating in the Age of Globalization: The Case of Rallies against the Iraq War in 2003. <https://www.academia.edu/6081355/GLOBALIZED_PROTEST._DEMONSTRATING_IN_THE_AGE_OF_GLOBALIZA-TION_THE_CASE_OF_RALLIES_AGAINST_THE_IRAQ_WAR_IN_2003_1>

Rinehart. 2011. The Occupy Movement Is Made Possible by
    Capitalism. In Kiesbye 2013.
Romm, Joe. 2013 Superstorm Sandy's Link to Climate Change: 'The
    Case Has Strengthened' Says Researcher.
    <http://thinkprogress.org/climate/2013/10/28/2843871/super-
    storm-sandy-climate-change/>
Ross, Andrew. 2013. *Creditocracy and the Case for Debt Refusal.* New
    York: OR Books.
Rossinow, Doug. 2013. "What Happened to Occupy? The Divided Left
    and the Demise of a Movement. *The Christian Century*, 7/1/13.
    <http://www.christiancentury.org/article/2013-06/what-hap-
    pened-occupy>
Roth, Marco. 2011. Letters of Resignation from the American Dream.
    In Blumenkranz et al. 2011.
Roy, Arundati. 2011. Another World Is Not Only Possible, She Is on
    Her Way. *Truthout.org*, 11/16/11.
    <http://www.truth-out.org/progressivepicks/item/23155-arund-
    hati-roy-another-world-is-not-only-possible-she-is-on-her-way>
Ruane, Michael E. 2007. Large Rally Planned Saturday on Mall.
    Washington Post, 1/25/07. <http://www.washingtonpost.com/wp-
    dyn/content/article/2007/01/24/AR2007012401957.html>
Safer Spaces Working Group. 2011. Transforming Harm and Building
    Safety: Confronting Sexual Assault in Occupy Wall Street and
    Beyond. In Lang and Lang/Levitsky 2012.
Sawant, Kshama. 2012. Kshama Sawant at Vote Sawant Election Night
    Party 11/6/2012. Video.
    <https://www.youtube.com/watch?v=O3Ur_4Ur-ss>
Scott, James C. 2012. *Two Cheers for Anarchism: Six Easy Pieces on
    Autonomy, Dignity, and Meaningful Work and Play.* Princeton
    University Press.
Schlesinger, Arthur J. 1945. *The Age of Jackson.* Back Bay Books.
Schmitt, Eli, Astra Taylor, and Mark Greif. 2011. Scenes from an
    Occupation. In Blumekranz et al. 2011.
Schneider, Nathan. 2011. Thank You, Anarchists. *Nation*, 12/19/11.
————. 2012. Occupy, After Occupy. *Nation*, 9/5/12.
————. 2013. *Thank You, Anarchy: Notes from the Occupy Apocalypse.*
    Berkeley: University of California Press.
Schwartz, Matthias. 2011. Pre-Occupied: The Origins and Future of
    Occupy Wall Street. *New Yorker*, 11/28/11.
Sheriden, Kerry. 2013. Iraq Death Toll Reaches 500,000 Since Start of
    U.S.-Led Invasion, New Study Says.
    <http://www.huffingtonpost.com/2013/10/15/iraq-death-
    toll_n_4102855.html>

Singer, Alan. 2012. Wall Street Was a Slave Market Before It Was a Financial Center. *Huffington Post,* 1/17/2012.

Sitrin, Marina. 2006. *Horizontalism: Voices of Popular Power in Argentina.* Oakland: AK Press.

———. 2011. One No, Many Yeses. In Blumenkranz et al. 2011.

Solnit, Rebecca. 2011. Throwing Out the Master's Tools and Building a Better House. In Blumenkranz et al. 2012.

———. 2012. Why the Media Loves the Violence of Protesters and Not of Banks. *TomDispatch.com.* 2/21/12. <http://www.tomdis-patch.com/blog/175506/>

Sorkin, Andrew Ross. 2009. *Too Big to Fail: The Inside Story of How Wall Street and Washington Fought to Save the Financial System— and Themselves.* New York: Penguin.

Stein 2006. In Class Warfare, Guess Which Class Is Winning. *New York Times,* 11/26/2006. <http://www.nytimes.com/2006/11/26/business/your-money/26every.html>

Stelter, Brian, and Al Baker. 2011. Reporters Said Police Denied Access to Protest Site. *New York Times,* 11/15/11. <http://mediadecoder.blogs.nytimes.com/2011/11/15/reporters-say-police-denied-access-to-protest-site/?_php=true&_type=blogs&src=tp&_r=0>

Stiglitz, Joseph E. 2011. Of the 1%, by the 1%, and for the 1%. *Vanity Fair* 5/11.

———. 2012. *The Price of Inequality.* New York: Penguin.

Street, Paul. 2011. Repressing Occupy as Corporate Welfare: On 'The Costs of the Occupy Movement'. ZNet. 11/28/11. <http://zcomm.org/zcommentary/repressing-occupy-as-corporate-welfare-reflections-on-corporate-media-and-the-costs-of-the-occupy-movement-by-paul-street/>

Students for a Democratic Society (SDS). 1962. *The Port Huron Statement of the Students for a Democratic Society.* <http://cours-esa.matrix.msu.edu/~hst306/documents/huron.html>

Sunkara, Bhaskar 2011. Why We Loved the Zapatistas. *Jacobin Magazine,* 1/11.

Taylor, Sunaura. 2012. Scenes from Occupied Oakland. In Blumenkranz et al. 2012.

Tender2be. Testing Occupy Wall Street—September 1st. <https://www.youtube.com/watch?v=ayUGOgFaCs8>

Thomas, Janet. 2000. *The Battle in Seattle: The Story Behind and Beyond the WTO Demonstrations.* Fulcrum.

Thompson, A.K. 2010. *Black Bloc, White Riot: Anti-Globalization and the Genealogy of Dissent.* Oakland: AK Press.

To the Village Square. 2006. Clamshell History.
<http://www.clamshell-tvs.org/clamshell_history/index.html>

Truthdig. 2011. Vacant Houses Outnumber Homeless People in U.S.
<http://www.truthdig.com/eartotheground/item/more_vacant_ho
mes_than_homeless_in_us_20111231>

Newcomb, Steven. 2013. A Dutch Massacre of Our Lenape Ancestors
on Manhattan. *Indian Country Today Media Network*, 8/24/13.

Weinstein, Adam. 2011. 'We Are the 99 Percent' Creators Revealed.
Mother Jones. 10/7/14.

White, Micah. 2009. An Open Letter to Students: We Are Beginning
the Long Struggle to Define Our Future. *Adbusters* Blackspot blog.
11/25/09.
<www.adbusters.org/blogs/blackspot-blog/open-letter-students
.html>

Wild, Nettie. Director. 1998. *A Place Called Chiapas: Inside the World's
First Postmodern Revolution.* Film. British Columbia Arts Council.

Williams, Kristian. 2012. Cops and the 99%. In Khatib et al. 2012.

Williams, Raymond. 1983. *Keywords: A Vocabulary of Culture and
Society.* Revised edition. New York: Oxford University Press.

Wolf, Naomi. 2012. NYPD for Hire: How Uniformed New York Cops
Moonlight for Banks. *Guardian*, 12/17/12.
<http://www.theguardian.com/commentisfree/2012/dec/17/nyp
d-for-hire-cops-moonlighting-banks>

Wolff, Richard, and David Barsamian. 2012. *Occupy the Economy:
Challenging Capitalism.* San Francisco: City Lights Books.

Writers for the 99%. 2011. *Occupying Wall Street: The Inside Story of an
Action that Changed America.* New York: Haymarket Books.

Žižek, Slavoj. 2011. Don't Fall in Love with Yourselves. In
Blumenkranz et al. 2011.

Index

THE TEA PARTY
EXPLAINED
FROM CRISIS TO CRUSADE

YURI MALTSEV AND ROMAN SKASKIW